The Chainsaw Safety System

Surefire Methods for
Cooperative Tree Cutting in Any Situation

Chuck Oslund

The Chainsaw Safety System:
Surefire Methods for Cooperative Tree Cutting in Any Situation

Copyright © 2019 by Chuck Oslund.

Address all inquiries to:
Chuck Oslund
Email: oslundchuck@yahoo.com

ISBN: 978-0-578-51792-6

Library of Congress Control Number: 2019905330

Editor: Tyler R. Tichelaar, Superior Book Productions

Cover Design and Interior Book Layout: Larry Alexander, Superior Book Productions

Every attempt has been made to source properly all quotes.

Printed in the United States of America

First Edition

Contents

Slides

Foreword:
The Plan of Work

CALL ME CRAZY IF YOU want, but I've always involved myself with occupations that placed me on the dangerous end of the "how to" spectrum. I'm not sure how this happened; perhaps it was just my need to make a living, and only jobs that included risky elements were available at the time. It could also be that in some dark corner of my mind, I sought what I perceived as exciting or daring occupations; I never saw myself as someone who could be tied to a desk, and I always pushed that envelope to the limit. Whatever the reason, I have spent most of my working life carrying heavy equipment through miles of densely wooded and brushy terrain, under all types of weather conditions, and trudging up and down mountains through burning timber, often while wielding the world's most dangerous hand-tool. Of course, as indicated by the book's title, you know which tool I'm referring to.

The chainsaw always assured me of my ability to reach my "Get 'er done" goal. Most people with common sense would look at what I was doing as crazy, unsafe behavior, so you're free to do so as well. I guess if we were to contemplate the truth, however, we would agree that *any* person who takes up this tool, brings it into a complex work area, and attempts to impose their will upon that environment would not absolutely need to be crazy, but if they were, it surely would not impede their progress; unless, of course, they happened to sustain an injury in the process.

As I near the end of my experience with the dead and down trees of the world, I feel responsible for passing on to all operators the strategy that delivered me to my current state of health, despite the many possible death traps I encountered. Don't get me wrong; I really enjoy running the saw. I don't think of it as a reckless disregard for my wellbeing to do so, nor do I feel as though I have somehow mastered it; instead, I've grown to revere it, along with the vast complexity of its complimentary subject: the tree. I've found that experience requires accomplishments and creates methodology, a consolidation of thought with action that turned my trepidation into confidence and my stressful work into an enjoyable challenge. Over many years of deliberate personal evaluation and contemplation of my occupation, I forced myself to reason out a logical and methodical antidote for the cavalier and mindless approach I had learned by example from others—to deal with the subconscious fear associated with using a chainsaw to manipulate one of the most complex natural materials on earth. So this is not as much a "How to" book as a "How to think" book, intended to remove most of today's operators from the ranks of the showoffs and the crazy, into the solidarity of the Chainsaw Safety System (CSS).

What eventually occurred to me over my twenty-five years of being trained and paid to operate a chainsaw—what I define as a "professional operator"—was that if I didn't get control of the illogical mental processes driving my work, there was a better-than-average chance I would never make it to that greatest goal of all: retirement. The many near misses, caused mostly by my delusional attitude of my and my saw's total domination over anything made out of wood, soon began to point in the direction of the most probable outcome in my future: an injury that would remove my physical ability to operate the saw, or in the worst-case scenario, maintain a proper blood level to get me out of the woods alive, both of which would nullify my purpose for working in the first place: supporting my family. I convinced myself I had to do something drastic to change my own attitude and behavior, so I consciously began to teach myself as much as I could every time I ran the saw so I could build a method, a set of rules I insisted on performing. The rules were a blending of all my safety training and work experience. Those rules would change my mind from crazy to logical and show dedication to common sense safety, as applicable to my unique situation and psychological attitude. I built this system that I now pass on to you.

I hereby establish a kinship with you because I recognize we are alike in many ways, simply because you are also the kind of person willing to take a chainsaw in hand and attempt to skillfully manage those giant woody objects we call trees toward an intended product. As a fellow chainsaw operator who has lived through the trials and the errors, I know I can lead you through the system, and it will make you a safer operator. If this instruction is taken in the manner intended, it may even form you into an all-round safer person. Through this process, we can join together in an ordered and comprehensive assemblage of facts, principles, and doctrines, in a particular field of knowledge, thought, and action that we will call a system for operating a chainsaw.

I'm not as good with the saw now as I was when I first started building the system; my hand-eye coordination is getting worse as I grow older, and my reflex actions aren't quite as fast. The system, however, just keeps getting younger; more new ideas arise—ways to get the tree where I want it, when I want it to be there—and more refined mental applications are created that build confidence through the mind-altering practice of teaching. That's right; I'm using you right now to strengthen my personal safety system (PSS), forcing myself to become better in order to bring you into the system, despite my increasing physical limitations. I intend, however, to simultaneously show you how to build your own personal safety system so you can use it to teach your children, nieces, nephews, coworkers, or anyone observing you in your common "corporate safety system" (cSS), designated "c" to distinguish it from the CSS. This may not be the best venue for our interaction to take place, however; the ideal place would be at the base of a tree we are sizing up for felling. Since that is not possible, I'll leave it to your obvious ability to identify the next best step, and imagine the earnestness in my eyes and the sureness in my voice as I show you the CSS.

When I retired from the Forest Service in 2013, I immediately started teaching for Bay College in Escanaba, Michigan. When I say "immediately," I mean I officially retired on a Friday, and the next Monday, I interviewed for a job to use my "Class C" chainsaw operator qualifications to teach a chainsaw safety course paid for by the State of Michigan through the Consultation, Education, and Training Grant the college administers for it. I was asked to put together a draft outline of what I was proposing to teach. That was the birth of what you will see herein. I put together the same PowerPoint slides presented here to explain basic chainsaw safety techniques combined with fundamental fire-fighting ideology, which had gotten me through my work life relatively unscathed. I've used that PowerPoint presentation to teach the Chainsaw Safety System (CSS) for the last five years in over a hundred seminars throughout Michigan's Upper and Lower Peninsulas.

What I want to do here is take you on as a student. I will use the PowerPoint slides to convey the same information taught to all my students over the years. I told my students that hearing the lecture makes them a member of the system; I believe the written word has the same power through the memory processes in your brain to simultaneously make you a member of the system; I can't be sure of that since this is my first try at it, and I understand that having a personal teacher makes learning easier. A new problem presented to me here is the diversity of my reader's knowledge, experience, talents, and abilities; different people learn in different ways; in fact, no two are exactly alike. Part of the mental processes taught in the system pertain to building mental pictures, acronyms, stories, and the like, to create an easily recallable mental significance in the brain—a common practice for all who are able to successfully navigate a complex and dangerous activity. It includes brain chemistry, not just memory and neurons, but also the mind's eye, which can predict the future by past and current events and objects. Okay, you're probably thinking, *I thought this was a book about chainsaw safety.* Let's think about it together!

I am absolutely positive, based on my incidental observations of others operating chainsaws, that most people get injured because they were not thinking, or were thinking of the wrong thing when their body made contact with a racing chain or a large and/or fast-moving chunk of wood. Usually, this lack of mental awareness combined with their attitude about the experience allowed them to bypass the most basic and well-established safety concepts developed. What they learned from their dad, grandad, uncle, or wild friend had worked well for them up to the point when they were injured or killed.

I was a psychiatric technician in the military. I don't use that experience to analyze others; I use it to try to figure out what my brain is doing. Through that difficult and lengthy process, I've come to realize chainsaw operators, whether they are the only operator in their backyard, or working with a large cutting crew, can use basic human behavior and intellect to control their own behavior, and thereby teach themselves good habits, along with the cutting crew in general. Many safety experts agree; they call it "behavioral safety." (I just thought of it as "B.S.") Each operator has two basic methods for approaching danger and dealing with stress, which are reciprocal, as in "inversely proportional"; the more you have of one, the less you have of the other. The safety system separates and identifies the two. It shows one as the slimy, smelly mess you stepped into in a cow pasture and the other as something that may save your life through self-control.

Writing this book is a challenge because it must be pertinent to operators of all experience and knowledge levels. In the classroom, a simple verbal survey could ascertain the required instruction parameters to ensure all my students would glean the maximum benefit. Of course, you can understand the different level of complexity that writing a book on the subject presents. Operators with vast experience are very important to the safety system's survival and perpetuation; it is, therefore, imperative that they fully understand its intricacies. Verbalizing and demonstrating their ability to operate a saw safely and productively can become a source of great personal growth when they see the respect they receive for a good teacher who has the students' safety as a final goal, within the system. Operators who are just beginning are the main safety focus for all system members; the system is about laying a sound foundation of safe practices. The experienced and the novice go home with a blended memorable experience.

My primary objective, however, is to reach and teach new and developing operators. To do so, I need the help and example of old guys like me. At one end of the spectrum resides the rookie operator who just purchased a saw at the hardware store in an attempt to save money on heating bills; they felt compelled to read this book because their spouse bought it for them when they purchased the saw. At the other end is the operator who has worked successfully through many years of cutting trees without getting hurt; it's hard to convince that person there is a better example to demonstrate to beginners; it requires humility on the part of an operator who should be proud of their work—a difficult and complex size-up, you might say. The safety system works for both these operators, and for every operator between them, in experience and knowledge. In the system, every operator needs a safety person (SP) to help mitigate obvious risks, so even if you never intend to actually be an operator, if you find yourself constantly giving advice to one, like "I wouldn't do that!", you may become the system's most valuable member to avert injury to your loved one or damage to your property. The system is based just as much on mental aptitude as it is on physical ability, so anyone with a brain and an interest can be a member, either as an operator or as a safety person.

To achieve this task of product delivery without it becoming cumbersome to accomplished operators, I decided to use a gray background paper for beginners. If you are an operator who already has sufficient confidence in your experience and knowledge levels to step into the safety system, adapt to a few simple rules of conduct, and begin teaching the beginners around you, then the text you're reading now with the white background is for you. You can speed-read this book, fit your current system into the CSS, and keep the information handy for your first student to read, which should save you a lot of talking. If, however, you need to formulate or manipulate your current abilities and to garner as much information and persuasion on safe saw operation as quickly as you can, in order to appease the high apprehension you experience when you just look at the saw, rest assured that you should include all the gray background text in your study, or in other words, the entire book. It will lead you through the forest of the safety system beginning with your very first tree. If you are inexperienced with chainsaws *and* safety, you may even find a need to read the whole book two or three times before you find a stress-free understanding of what the system is. Obviously, you've already taken the first step because you're reading it now so you're practically a member of the Chainsaw Safety System already. All you need to do is get your head in the system whenever you read from this book, and each time you put the chain to wood, practice, practice, practice. By practice, I mean the repetition of safe action. By practice, I mean the skill others see in you. And by practice, I mean using the safety system every time you pick up the saw. Hence, I repeat practice three times because it requires three actions.

PART I:
ETHICAL AUTHORITY
YOUR PERSONAL INTEGRITY

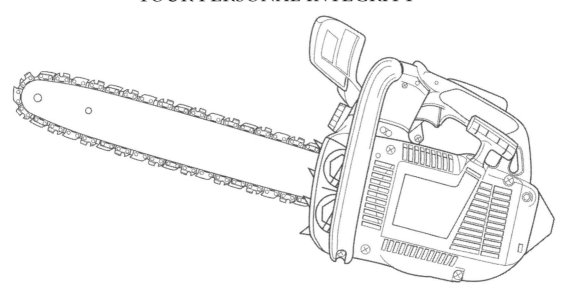

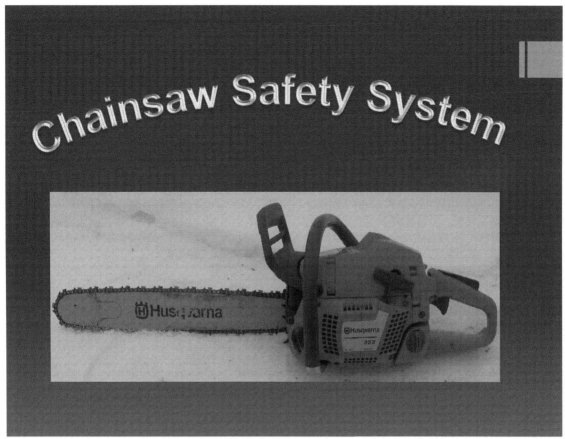

Slide 1: Chainsaw Safety System

SIGNIFICANCE OF "CHAINSAW SAFETY SYSTEM"

THE FIRST SLIDE IN THE PowerPoint presentation shows three words that together make up the name of this system. All these words are important in understanding what is being taught in these pages. The chainsaw is arguably the most dangerous hand-tool known to mankind. What did we use to efficiently cut wood to length before the chainsaw was invented? A long sheet of steel with teeth cut into it, with a handle on each end, dragged across the wood as fast as the available strength of each puller would allow. The forest didn't change with the advent of the chainsaw; only the method humans use to manage it changed. We advanced the power source for running a saw from a "two-man" power source, one man pulling at a time, to an internal combustion engine powered by gasoline explosions, concentrated on each sharp tooth involved in complex, high magnitude forces. The problem here is that some humans have a mindset that the power used to manipulate the wood is still mostly coming from them, and not the saw. If you think you are in charge of the power in the saw because you put the gas in the tank, you started it, and you pulled the trigger, or that you are the kind of person who can "get 'er done" because you are in control, that is wrong thinking that results in more injuries; in other words, you *definitely* need this system! If on the other hand, you are cognizant of the power and its source, and your analytical mind recognizes the apprehension you experience as you foresee all the possible negative outcomes, you also need the system; it will decrease the apprehension as it builds your confidence.

The chainsaw is a very unique tool; it carries heritage. For some operators, cutting firewood represents most of the bonding time they spent with their father or grandfather during their most formative years—incidentally, the same years they developed most of their work ethic. Asking some operators to do something as fundamental as wearing a pair of chaps could be taken as an affront to a deep-seated familial link: "Uncle Joe was great with a saw, and he never wore chaps." Perhaps adopting safety practices not taught to them by their elders presents a sense of abandonment of that person as an honored mentor. Being a father/grandfather/uncle myself, I can truthfully say, "If your mentor was teaching you right now, they would advise learning the method that is defined as 'safe' *today*. Uncle Joe would tell you, 'What I didn't know back then is here before you now, at this point in time; pass *that* on to your son/daughter/student.'" Take your knowledge and experience, blend it with the system to improve it, and teach that to *everyone* as if they were your prodigies.

There is another heritage in the saw: the history recorded in the millions of people injured or killed while running one. The numbers have been added up, the data analyzed, and the statistics calculated. Most of the safety procedures followed in the Chainsaw Safety System (CSS) are the result of formulas or algorithms used to find the safest methods for running the chainsaw; the problem is they aren't numbers alone; each "number" represents one real person in the past who spent time bleeding in the woods, lying in a bed, disabled for life, **or** dead. (Notice the bold print of the word "or"; once one reaches that point, for whatever reason, there is no more "and." You stop building heritage, and become a record yourself, a part of statistics, a calculated probability of a future outcome for those you leave behind. Will the numbers representing your completed heritage be positive or negative?)

Even with the medium-size saw pictured in the slide, the chain is moving more than 50 mph when at full speed; in one second, more than 500 sharp teeth go by a point on the bar. The teeth are designed to cut wood, so what will they do to flesh and bone? Can you see why the first word of the system's name is "Chainsaw"? It is the largest factor of danger in the already daunting task of reducing trees to usable products, which leads us to the middle word of the system's name: Safety.

Safe use of a chainsaw is a minor task when the engine is not running; it is no more dangerous than holding a sharp knife. Start the engine and you enter another level of required awareness; put the saw to work at the task it is intended to do, cut down and process a tree, and you must enter an elevated level of thought and procedure to accomplish the work without undue stress each time you pull the trigger and accelerate the chain. You must manipulate your actions and thought processes to accommodate the various risks associated with the particular wood you are attempting to reduce to smaller pieces.

How you organize those "safe" thoughts and behaviors is defined by the last word of the system's name: System. This is what I intend to give you for your investment: the Chainsaw Safety System (CSS), *all three words*. They reflect proper respect for the saw, proper use of the saw, and a method of obtaining, perfecting, and perpetuating your individual talents and abilities into your operating future by practicing the system in mind and body, with the goal of teaching others all you've learned.

The CSS presented here is a base level system. It covers fundamental, state-of-the-art, safest methods for cutting down a larger diameter tree, limbing it, and bucking it up into manageable pieces. The limbing and bucking practices also make the system applicable for storm damage response and cleanup. If you are currently not at this level of expertise, close adherence to the system, along with deliberate, repetitive practice, will get you there, uninjured, with confidence. If you are dropping trees already, the system will perfect your procedure to a teachable level of excellence—what some call an art or craftsmanship: a creative ability for which you gain respect from others involved, those holding an interest in the product. Since the system is based on behavioral safety, you are in charge of what it encompasses; you control yourself, your thought processes, conceptualization abilities, and thus, your physical talents, endeavoring to perform a complex task without negative effects.

If what you are attempting to do with the saw is too complex to fit into this basic CSS, like bucket work or climbing, just change the first word of the system's name to whatever dangerous activity you are attempting to learn and teach. Get as much information as you can handle on the subject activity; read about it, watch others perform it in person or in videos, practice it repeatedly, put your brain fully into what your body is doing, adhere strictly to the system principles and rules you and your coworkers have thoughtfully formulated, and then add those agreed-upon rules to this basic system. From my experience, if you do this, you will be successful in delivering a safe product, no matter what you are trying to accomplish with any dangerous tool used in conjunction with a chainsaw.

The chainsaw is the dangerous utensil we single-handedly use to dominate trees; safety is the statistically best methods and devices determined by previous users to accomplish the task without negative effects; system is getting the conscious deliberate operation in your brain and brawn into a process of self-instruction: a code that you can *live* by—a predetermined standard with which your particular product is evaluated; a thought process and physical procedure we all recognize, learn and teach, to make running a chainsaw safer, more productive, and even enjoyable.

In this basic system, I will give you five simple rules to follow; they are, in effect, the second part of this book; for this half, I'll just call them the five rules, and give you a hint of what they are. You'll need a complete understanding of the first half of the book to realize the importance of adherence to these rules. The first two rules are applied before the chain touches the wood; they concern wearing personal protective equipment (PPE) and starting a well-maintained saw; the third and fourth involve handling the saw and safe procedures for cutting down a large diameter tree. All these rules are based on state-of-the-art safe practices taught all around this country by professional saw safety instructors. The fifth rule is the system concept I developed over my cutting career by combining safe firefighting ideology with the safe operation of a chainsaw. Many of my past students have told me that learning and using the rules took less effort than adapting their thought process to the ideology and their muscle to the exercise, thus getting the mind and the body to work together in the system. The good news is nobody knows what's going on in your mind unless you tell them, but everybody in sight knows how good you are with the rules by just looking at you; hopefully, that's not the bad news.

Welcome to the Chainsaw Safety System!

> Most parts of the United States are running out of young people willing to pick up a chainsaw and go to work. Most who are willing don't operate the saw safely. As storms and tree diseases take more and more trees down in wooded areas, in the most popular new building zones, and along rural roads, there will be more and more trees to manage before they dry up and burn. Therefore, our society will have to look hard for someone to be a Chainsaw operator who is Safety wise, in a self-taught System.

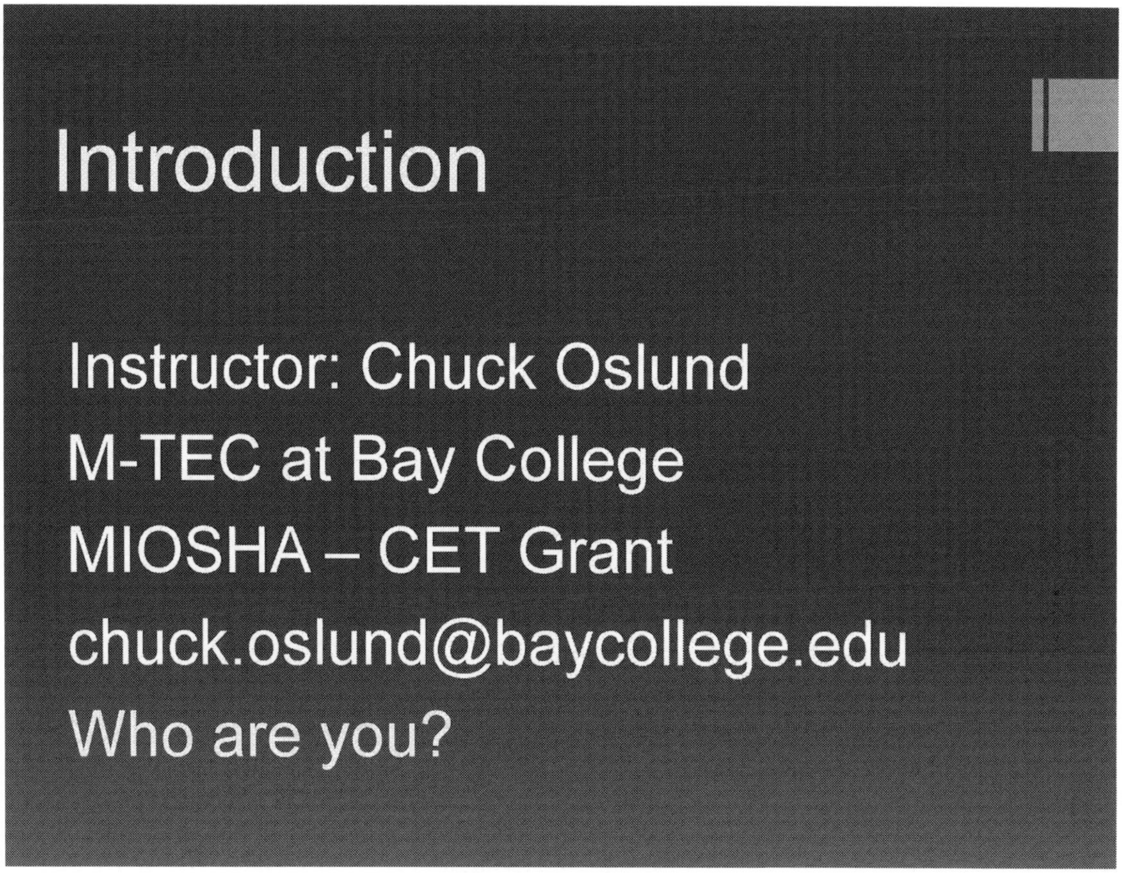

Introduction

Instructor: Chuck Oslund

M-TEC at Bay College

MIOSHA – CET Grant

chuck.oslund@baycollege.edu

Who are you?

Slide 2: Introduction

INTRODUCTION

I USED THIS SLIDE IN my seminars, as it says, to introduce myself. The State of Michigan must think it's pretty important to train its private sector chainsaw operators because it allowed me to teach this class, all paid for by the grant, to anyone who runs a saw along with anyone interested in chainsaw safety. When I started the job, Michigan Technical Education Center asked me to put together a draft lesson plan. When I was finished writing the plan, I realized what I had was a compilation of a system for safe operation of the chainsaw. I had developed this system, through necessity, over the previous twenty-six-plus years; it was the birth certificate of the CSS. It was my "personal safety system" (PSS), laid out in writing before my eyes—the CSS I was about to begin teaching to other operators of various skill levels. To my surprise, over the next five years, I found that teaching this subject matter was the best way to gain a deeper understanding of it myself; my students showed me that the safety system was in itself a simple tool for perfecting safety in any dangerous activity, though, in this case, operating a chainsaw.

~ 7 ~

It turned out that teaching this course was just the next advancement of my PSS; the new knowledge stored in my memory was gleaned from the various safety attitudes of groups of chainsaw operators I was introduced to at various agencies and organizations throughout the state. Up to that point, my experience grew by knowing the person working with me: their work ethic, their habits, and even having an understanding of what they were thinking, which actually made both of us safer in a risky environment. This is why it is important that you know something about me; it's not to brag up my experience, but to let you know what you are joining when we cut together.

I've been running a chainsaw for more than forty years. In my early years cutting firewood, I had that cavalier attitude many young people have; I was full of energy and felt invincible at work. I thought of the saw as just another cool tool that could make me more efficient, give me more than just muscle power, and reduce the amount of manual labor involved in getting the wood where I wanted it: in my stove—like money in the bank! When I began working for the Forest Service at the start of my "second career," I found out quickly the significance of that first word: "Forest"; most of my assignments involved a chainsaw for tree "management." My first chainsaw training covered basic practical operation, with only minor focus on the safe operation of the saw, except for the instructor's insistence that we all abide by the new push to make sure every operator wears chaps while running the saw. That was in the late '80s, and we're still teaching the same thing today to the general public. I worked in "timber", cutting "windows" for mast producers; in fisheries, cutting obstructions and constructing bank stabilization structures in streams; and in surveying, as a technician and crew chief, and later as a forest surveyor, cutting open property lines three feet wide, usually through standing timber. Since your federal government could not afford to hire many workers, and because no operator ever cut fast enough for me, I ran the saw myself most of the time, sometimes using my wife as a volunteer safety person when nobody else was available. During my twenty years of surveying, I cut over 100 miles of such property lines, not to mention the many miles of traverse lines before the advent of GPS.

At the same time during all those years, I was a firefighter chainsaw operator and instructor. Did I have any close calls? You bet I did, on almost a daily basis; my basic survival instincts were just barely enough to get me through a typical workday, which caused an indeterminate amount of stress in my life. (Did someone say hypertension?) I wondered if I would continue to beat the odds against happenstance encounters with danger, so common in my line of work. After one particularly close encounter with a large chunk of tree, I was sitting on a stump, my head down, looking at my hands shaking in response to the fear-filled concoction of adrenaline and cortisol now being diluted by the same blood that could just as likely have been running on the ground if it weren't for one minor evasive movement. It was then that I made a resolute promise to myself, my four small children, and my wife—the people I was there attempting to support; I would not leave them stranded in a life with no support just to maintain my personal pride as a fast, efficient, "get 'er done" saw operator. I didn't know what it was called then, but I can tell you now that was the start of my Personal Safety System, what I fondly call my PSS; a lot of mental contemplation and physical work went into building it. I incorporated safety training ideology from all my occupations and even my pastimes, lessons learned from close calls and accidents, and especially painstaking mental maintenance of my own safety attitude—what I like to call my brain function—to make it come into line with reality as it were; to find a way to learn, remember, and practice safety. It calmed me down and made a "thinking worker" out of me.

I am a member of this CSS—I just happen to be the first member—and I always need to get everyone I cut with up to speed. Am I the go-to teacher for it? Probably not anymore since I have been teaching the system for years. I can only assume there are operators out there who are better system members than I am by now. What I am doing here is my obligation to the system: teaching you what I know about it, and testifying truthfully that the system works. It *will* make you a safer, more productive, and confident chainsaw operator, without it taking years of trial and error, and risk/reward ratios to figure it out; you get it all right here, but you may still find yourself in the same predicament I was in; what you get out of your earnest attempt at running the saw safely will greatly depend on your ability to teach your own brain, with the expectation of teaching what you have learned to students you encounter in your chainsaw future.

You will need to figure out complex mental issues like who you are as an operator, why you want to run the saw, who are you being safe for, what kind of role model you are for others, and how you reach your "best operator" level while remaining unharmed in body and mind. To do these things, you must be able to stand back from yourself, try to take an unbiased look at your thoughts and actions, and make a logical conclusion of what you will require of yourself to improve the future of saw operation for you and those who work with you—a very difficult thing to do. This book will help you accomplish that goal if you read it carefully, and then do what it says. It will help you define who you are now, and develop "who you will be" when you're retired like me, healthy and content that you did your best to keep safe all involved in each project you accomplished.

As I stated in the foreword, I have special information for beginners—those learning the CSS and operation of the chainsaw simultaneously:

The chainsaw safety system is not just about the proficiency of individual operators; it's more about development of a shared personality trait of a group of people; it's about how your idiosyncrasies are self-manipulated to become complaisant with others'; how your brain perceives and supports the single person actually running the chainsaw—the person we all work for. The hardest work will be done in your psyche; in comparison, learning to efficiently operate a chainsaw is simple. The reason people get injured while learning to run a saw has only in part to do with the danger involved in operating it, or even the tendency of the physics in the tree to work against us; it's actually about replacing a collusion with past unsafe practices with scientifically proven beneficial habits; it's about how each operator focuses their mental capacity to keep all involved safe; how the mind prepares the body to respond to risk. Since safety is wisdom from the past, used to control an action in the present, and that blend is used to accurately predict a prosperous future, it really is all about what is in the participating brains, right now. What is the real problem here? What do we need to do to reach that "nirvana," that "best-case scenario" for all of us? We, the characters willing to approach danger with a dangerous tool, must work together; instead of being individuals working competitively, we need to come together, pool our mental capacities, and join our perceptive forces to control this arena of risk where we unite to dominate the dead and down trees around us. The system is what this book is all about, which naturally leads us to the obvious truth: We're all in this together, so no one, as a single operator, has the grave responsibility of figuring it out alone. The possible outcomes of how several layers of high-risk variables interact are too numerous for a single brain to discern the safest path. How dare we hide our heads and send out one person—alone!

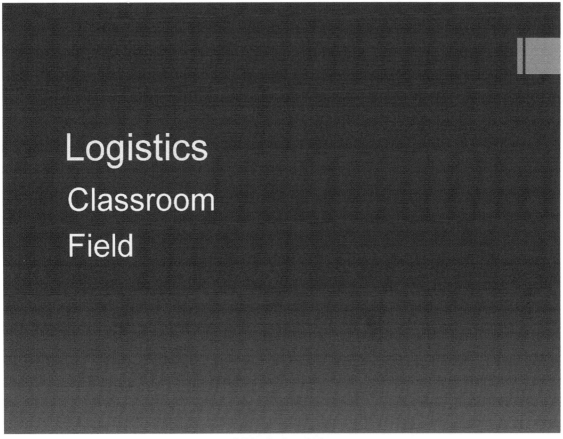

Slide 3: Logistics

LOGISTICS

As you'll see later, "plan the work" is part of the system, so it would be wrong for me to continue without sharing that plan with you. Writing this book is different from any "classroom" I've had before; it's like a classroom outside time and space. The logistics here are much different from the carefully thought-out plans I've formulated with half-awake operators in the breakroom at some county road commission garage. There, success relied on my ability to talk, something I have the DNA for as an Oslund, and keeping everyone awake to hear, usually beginning with the introduction of my assistant, a three-foot-long stick I have close at hand in all my lectures. Of course, Louie or Louise (whatever its name happened to be that day) acted not only as a pointing device, but also as an introduced risk for any student caught falling asleep; a slap on the back of the chair not only wakes them up, but gives a good laugh to everyone else. Obviously, I can't have that kind of fun here, and I'm not as good at composition as I am at talking; I'm not an author—I'm more of a manual-labor, end-of-the-shovel kind of guy. I've never written a book, but believe me, the content is from a long history; it is already logistically formulated inside the system, and is relayed to you here as my best effort.

As I tell all my students, much of what you learn concerning technical or procedural applications of chainsaw operation in this information age is at your fingertips on your cellphone or at your keyboard. There are many good resources on YouTube that I will periodically reference, and probably refer to as your homework, or more accurately, your "brain-work": putting the right pictures in your head of what the best operator looks like, so you have an image to emulate, and methods and practices to teach your brain so it can teach your body, and then you can pass those methods and practices on to your student by word and deed. Unfortunately, much of what you will see on YouTube depicts the exact misconduct the system is attempting to correct. In looking at these videos, your mind will be witnessing many unsafe methods, so before you watch them, assume a very skeptical attitude toward what you are looking at, and use the negative images of blatant unsafe actions as a picture of operators who will sooner or later contribute to the total of chainsaw-related injuries; purposely watch for ways in which the operators do not follow the system's basic safety rules; this safety skepticism can be a good tool to prune the "tree of your plan" for your personal safety system (PSS): what to keep, what to cut off. Be deliberate in your selection of what your future PSS will look like; doing so will help you understand how the system works; in effect, the first student you teach is you; you must be a strict instructor, and allow only statistically proven techniques into your PSS; *never* emulate any operator who breaks a system rule! If you are a beginner, you will be learning new things; if you are an operator with experience, you will be remolding what you already know to fit the system so it can then be taught as a safety system example to logically replace any unsafe practices you see on the internet that may resemble how you currently do it; you must let go of any pride you have in your current abilities; it's the only way to look at them logically enough to know how much they differ from the rules. Look at yourself with the same detachment you use when you recognize an action pictured in a YouTube video as unacceptable in the system.

We may have a problem in our relationship if you are a certain personality type—the same type who haphazardly picks up a saw and goes to work with it, trusting the same instinctive, knee-jerk reactions you have refined and trusted through the years; an operator who merely peruses the book, or becomes disgruntled enough not to read the whole thing. To mitigate this risk, I suggest you start your personal safety system (PSS) immediately, before the next time you cut. Go to Slide 54 and memorize those rules; start using them to the best of your effort, even before you finish the book if you need to run the saw before then.

If, on the other hand, your attitude is one of patience and contemplation, I suggest you not only read and study this information, but garner all the facts you can handle before you begin cutting. Actually, many aspects of the system's rules and mental aspects can be practiced without even starting the saw, as will become intuitively obvious as you learn them.

If you are new to the saw, your field exercises should be done under the guidance of an experienced operator, preferably one in the system, but any experience and knowledge is better than there being none available when you need it; you should start with the simple and work to the complex; start slow and work to fast, and stay deliberate at all times, trying to stick to the rules.

A lot of field work can be observed online, but always remember: Some operators may seem like they really know what they are talking about, but what they *do* might say they *don't*. You need to glean the good stuff that can fit into the CSS, and not dwell on or emulate the non-system behavior, except for educational purposes.

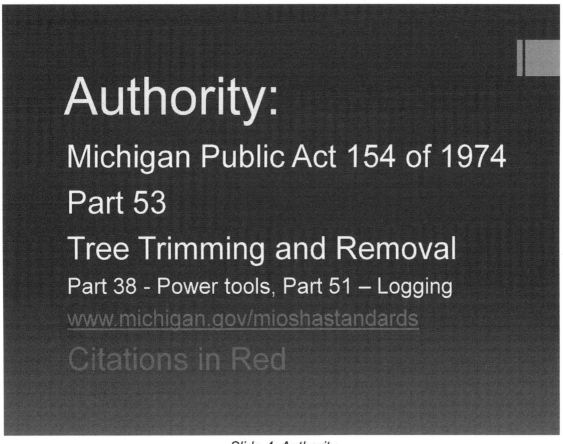

Slide 4: Authority

AUTHORITY

I CAN'T TEACH THE CITIZENS of the state of Michigan about any regulated safety issues without assuring the regulators employed by the state that the information and techniques taught are inclusive of the laws that the citizens of the state have demanded through their legislators. When I submitted my course syllabus to MIOSHA, the information had to be "legally" teachable; this is what its safety "experts" ascertained from my outline before they agreed to pay me state tax dollars to teach the subject to the citizens of their state. The system calls this authority the "legal authority." You can read part 53; just google "Michigan part 53," a short, eight-page official document in which you'll see that the regulations are general; they pertain to various applications of chainsaw operation, but they very deliberately define and detail what is considered acceptable behavior when operating a saw. Wherever the various parts of the regulations were cited on the slides, I highlighted them in red lettering (gray on black and white slides) to indicate that the many elements of risk have been historically recognized. When these regulations were first adopted, of course, everyone involved in their formulation assumed that this action would solve the problem of people in the state getting hurt while involved in tree trimming and removal; it didn't—the numbers of injured kept rising; it worked pretty well with the other tools, so why not with this one? I'm telling you: The chainsaw is a very unique tool!

If your company or agency employs saw operators, the regulations identify your liability or exactly who will pay the cost of recovery from any damages caused by not abiding by the law. If you are in a position of legal authority in your job—in other words, you tell workers what to do, and how to do it—you should be cognizant of your state regulations; they define your "legal liability." If you teach someone the wrong thing, and they get hurt doing it, it is looked on very negatively in a court of law; get my meaning? They will be *looking* for someone or something to blame it on; maybe it would be best to blame it on the system; I'm talking about the legal system from Part 53 to the stump; the ethical-based CSS won't let you teach the wrong thing!

Another kind of authority exists in society upon which the legal kind is based; the CSS is also based on this other kind of authority; it encompasses the legal authority and liability because it is based on ethical responsibility to teach the "right thing" to people involved in a dangerous activity. This other authority originates from the human race's familial structure; the welfare of all is the concern of all; in the system, your "family" includes everyone within reach of your senses in and around the area in which you are teaching by example, learning with respect. A short time spent thinking about this will lead to the conclusion that the law is the least of the responsibilities we have in teaching our children/students. When we show them the best course of action and thought they should employ to achieve a healthy and prosperous survival, that teaching usually has an ethical origin in your brain; it's linked to your DNA and survival instincts, which is completely different, and in many ways, on a higher level than legal authority—what others outside the unit tell you is minimal; it's like an insult to your integrity to imply that the best you would give your own prodigy is what is legally required by law.

This higher level of authority is also exemplified in how people work or fight together to overcome a common enemy. No greater camaraderie is formed from human actions than that born out of a cooperative effort of two or more people to safely challenge and function in a dangerous situation. Any soldier who has seen combat will tell you that they weren't fighting as much for their country as they were for the friend next to them. I've seen this authority displayed on fire crews acting as first responders, including on the saw teams working as part of that crew; a firefighter with a saw in hand is a "double whammy"—the intersection of two danger spectrums. The authority is based on common knowledge; openly identifiable experience levels; and respect for a coworker's talents and abilities, their steadfastness in following the rules, and their uncanny ability to analyze risk of various natures and communicate the risks in a concise rational manner. They always seem to quickly find the best course of action for all involved, but just as readily accept input on how to perfect it; it's like they show up with a memorized "list of things to do," then methodically go down the list adapting it to fit whatever risk presents itself. It is even possible for the respect of an individual worker to evolve into honor for system members who best exemplify the system by actually saving another person from injury or death. These kinds of individuals are not common, but the occurrence of such authentic action is common within the firefighting system, the policing system, the medical system, and now the chainsaw safety system; it's like a separate common sense not defined by the number of people who share it, but by a higher understanding of an extraordinary perception, constantly changing by place and time. All system members are easily recognized by how well they abide by the agreed-upon rules and principles taught to perpetuate the system; so any member, in any given situation, could become a hero, albeit an unsung hero since what they said or did *averted* an accident—a positive result unseen by an untrained eye because it's the negating of a negative to get a positive; only other members of the same system will recognize it. The CSS takes advantage of these human characteristics, and uses them to benefit all in the system with safety; all the hard work of organization has been done by the system before the operator arrives on-site; you know what the other person is thinking when you see them. The system seems to take on an existence of its own; in practice, it does—we call it the ethical authority of the operator!

Of course, many other kinds of authority exist in this complicated life we live, with other people all around. Legal and ethical are the only ones we need to deal with when we run a chainsaw; legal as in CSS, and ethical as in PSS. The CSS does not demonstrate or depend on "moral" authority, even though it could be in your PSS. Moral authority requires all to behave in the same agreed-upon manner while attempting to achieve a common positive goal; the goals in the CSS are defined by each PSS, and by definition, all personal safety systems have different goals, but those goals must conform to the CSS's rules, not vice-versa. A "moral corporate safety system" operating within the CSS could exist and prosper, like a church-based emergency storm response team, for example, but when the saw is started, the CSS's five rules must remain the highest authority.

The CSS is made up of many personal safety systems in groups of two: the operator's PSS and the safety person's PSS; this is the authoritative mechanism to combine the system's effects into one safe action, *based* on ethics; the agreement of behavior between two people, such as parent and child, teacher and student, sergeant and private, etc. etc., all come down to one person working with another individual to achieve one objective; the dynamics change with each combination of two—with each different activity; it's the combination of the PSSs that sets the ultimate moral value of the CSS—an unseen product; pictures are added to the PSS memory bank by doing the CSS—images that tell stories of wellbeing, self-confidence, accomplishment, and peace. You know—the rewards of being ethical!

If your interest in the CSS is to ensure your employees' safety, you will also find in the system a perfect way to exchange your apprehension for confidence, regarding the expectations you have for your operators. Interpersonal relationships are formed at work; that speaks ethical—the CSS allows communication between you and your saw crew, which identifies where more training or better equipment may be needed. The law tells you what you must do to keep your operators trained and safe, and it enforces the consequential liability when you don't. Safety's rewards can never be counted in the asset column since they are an injury that does not occur. The law offers only one remedy for failed communication or excessive expectations; fines or even forfeiture of your business or freedom are explicitly tallied in the deficit column.

The safety system has no finger to point, and it offers nothing for a legal finger to point at. The system is ever present; it exists in the rules and in the talents of the workers, their minds and bodies, operating in the here and now; the rewards of safety are immediate. Since you are reading this, the best-case scenario for your operators is that you are a leader in the system, even if you've never touched a saw or never expect to. You would need to check your state's regulations on training sources, but if it were me, I'd use my best CSS operators to conduct regular chainsaw technique and procedural training on the job as it pertains to my particular application of this dangerous activity; only you can make that happen, by declaring that in your "corporate safety system" (designated "cSS" because it is the CSS in your company), any cutting project is an opportunity to teach and learn; it is "training." There would be regular meetings with my top operators to discuss the risks unique to our application of the system, the growth rate of our PSSs, for the perfection of our "ethical authority," over a cup of coffee. There is no reason for us even to consider the legal; it is encased by our ethical, like hinge wood in the cutting plan.

What? You don't have a tree-cutting company? No cSS? Maybe you do and don't know it yet; for example, you do if your time running the saw includes the wife watching you as the kids stack firewood.

Employer Responsibilities
R408.15311 – Rule 5311

- **Provide training to each new employee**
- **Conduct a job briefing when unusual hazards exist, prior to the starting operations**
- **Do not allow a tool or equipment to be used which is not guarded or is unsafe**
- **Develop rescue procedures**

Slide 5: Employer Responsibilities

EMPLOYER RESPONSIBILITIES

I ADDRESS THIS SLIDE TO the problem: employers who don't naturally fulfill these responsibilities. The legal liabilities legislated by the state obviously came from the legislators, who, in a democratic society, are elected by the people; these are the restrictions we all require of our fellow Americans who employ chainsaw operators. Do we do that to limit your freedom, or to make it hard for you to make a profit? Maybe we do it because we don't appreciate paying high healthcare insurance premiums to compensate for your dereliction of duty, or maybe some of your neighbors don't like to see their family and friends working for you in an arc of danger without proper safety equipment, simply to increase your bottom line. Whatever the case, if you find yourself delinquent in these responsibilities, remember they will, by law, ultimately identify where the liability rests; they will be used to apportion out the blame by the law, and that blame will take on a monetary value at least. I don't want to scare you—well, maybe I do—but I'm talking judges and lawyers, possibly even police officers with handcuffs; the "LLC" part of your business *insurance* plan is what will be deliberated, where losing a lawsuit doesn't just hold the possibility of ending your business; it could also put you in a homeless shelter! A well-implemented CSS will be *assurance* that this will not happen to you; you will instead prosper, while managing your chainsaw activities.

Notice that the slide does not say "Employer Liabilities." Even the legal authority in the regulation recognizes that these are the minimum requirements for an ethical business person; they are your "responsibility." A profit for one person many times represents a loss for another; the CSS is a special agreement between you and your operators that nobody loses. When you are a CSS member, you won't consider the system rules a costly inconvenience. Asking a worker to perform a dangerous task without the proper training and equipment can be thought of this way: gasoline explosions are what run the saw; explosions build up heat; heat increases abrasion; the gas must be mixed with oil to decrease degradation in the cylinder, to prevent the saw from seizing; it is best for the saw and production if you send out your saw team with the proper mix already formulated and clearly marked on the can.

The implementation of safety regulations presents an excellent opportunity for an employer/supervisor to improve worker morale and loyalty. What better compliment can you give your operators than to actively demonstrate to them, through your membership in the CSS, that your primary concern in your work plan is their health and welfare? The system's rewards don't stop there; the accidents that don't happen in a well-supported system, with a smart business mind that is also a wise system leader, keep on adding to the asset column; think about it—every accident/injury/mistake is a costly one by definition. The CSS calls for a "Safety Person" (SP) as an extra set of eyes the operator can depend on to watch parts of the tree that are not visible from the tree's base; a CSS employer is the SP for the entire corporate safety system; even if you never run a saw, you are the first to understand what product is required, and what equipment will be available. The CSS is free, money-saving equipment.

Many employers use the wrong indicator for when their workers need training; they wait until they have new equipment or procedures, or have an accident, to get serious about investing time and money into training; they play catch-up because they are trying to attain several difficult objectives at the same time, deal with the production problems, and develop new plans for safety. The system doesn't wait for things to pile up; it deals with all the minor habits that can add up to big problems as they happen; it allows for safety vigilance. You are not paying your operators to be in the system; that responsibility is included in what you are already paying them to be: functioning workers. The system is under the ethical authority for them, so in order to effectively work in the system, you must also own that ethical authority, in the eyes of your employees. Here's an analogy that will require contemplation: Have the same concern for the operator you pay to cut down a tree on the job as you would when sending your own child into your backyard to operate a saw. You will see how, in the system, these two are the same. You may need to train your mind to think this way. Don't worry; this will not be extra work for you; the system will get you there, and it will return great dividends because you won't be robbed by accidents, harassed by lawyers, or plagued by guilt; the system will increase the probabilities of a positive outcome.

Much of the work in my life has involved supervision and management; I understand the anxiety and stress involved with sending people who depend on your oversight into a dangerous work environment. My early attempts to rationalize the fear away had me telling myself and my workers, "This is a dangerous job; if you can't handle it, find a different job!" That worked to bury the worry somewhere deep in my brain for a while, but it didn't stop the constant accumulation of stress evidenced by my slowly increasing blood pressure during that time; I refused to see past the bark, which does not remove the problem in the wood. I won't even get into how I handled the guilt I felt when one of my workers was injured while following my orders; I'm still in the process of healing in my own psyche; I remain a student in that area. I finally realized in my supervisory role that the teacher/student ethical relationship is the perfection of the employer/employee legal relationship, which, in turn, deals with the stress and the danger; it makes you be all you can be in the caring department, which I believe will allow you to release the guilt; it's almost like blaming it on the system; if there are close calls, the system needs tweaking. If you're not the kind of foreman to deal with ethics on the job, don't worry; when the chainsaws are back in the truck, you are out of the system; you can return to being a "jerk boss" if that's what makes you comfortable; it does work for some supervisor/worker relationships. I've always told my kids, "Your boss's attitude can *make or break* a job." What I wanted them to learn from this common sense statement in part is "make" as in produce, and "break" as in resist the product; in other words, bad attitude produces bad attitude, produces bad product. When it comes to fellow system members in a dangerous activity, my main goal is not production, quality, or profit; I consciously force my mind to be a good teacher who is ready, willing, and able to become a student at any given risk. This is why the amount of respect you earn as an employer/leader in the CSS is so important; you become the most important source for the system's perpetuation and success; the success of your business *will* then follow.

The only working authority in the CSS is the operator's ethical authority. The standard of that authority is established by strict adherence to the rules by your best operators, and their ability to deliver the desired product within the system; they teach your other operators and support personnel throughout each project. If the job doesn't get done to your satisfaction, you may ethically add new rules, provided those rules do not negate any of the system's current established rules, or bring in professional training to increase your CSS's legal authority. You cannot ethically or legally, in any state, order your operators to cut beyond their PSS capabilities, so you should actually watch them cut to understand the liability you are accepting; you need to be able to identify an operator who possesses adequate knowledge and experience to perform the task as opposed to one who may merely be attempting to impress you; the system is self-monitoring in large corporate safety systems. Since the operator is in charge of the cutting area (CA), you could be asked to leave the cutting area when the operator picks up the saw; up until that time, you can supervise, assist, yell, teach, or learn as needed; once a worker has executed the agreed-upon rules without encountering a No-Go, and picks up that saw, you become either a safety person in the cutting area, or you are outside the CA at the operator's discretion.

If you are a firewood cutter in the backyard with your kid watching, all this is up to you; your PSS is your authority; you are self-employed; treat your employee and your safety person well.

If I say that the two types of authority are "legal" and "personal," it is logical that the legal kind deals with laws and regulations, or in other words, liability and compensation. An exchange of money quantifies and "authenticates" the process of sorting out the results of injury, damage, or product loss. This cannot be true in the personal type since it deals with ethical aspects of human behavior like respect and responsibility, which are, as the commercial says, "priceless." With a small stretch of the imagination, it is also possible to associate legal authority with a "conscious state," and personal or ethical authority with a "conscience state." Remission in one costs time and money; remission in the other causes guilt, remorse, and stress. Don't be remiss!

Slide 6: Employee Responsibilities

EMPLOYEE RESPONSIBILITIES

Y OU'VE HEARD THE SAYING, "WHAT goes around, comes around." Here is a perfect example of it: In 1974, the citizens of Michigan said, "Enough is enough; we're tired of seeing people hurt at work, then sent home without pay to recover on the couch with no means of support for themselves or their family." Others said, "We're sick of paying exorbitant amounts of money to hospitals for patching these people up." So they told their elected officials, "There ought to be a law." The lawmakers, of course, studied and debated the problem; that's what they do. They asked the safety and chainsaw professionals to add up all the numbers of those hurt in the past—first to determine if there actually was a problem, then to determine how best to fix it. Once they identified that there were indeed too many workers getting hurt while running the chainsaw, they looked for where to place the blame; as with most regulatory actions, the "fault-line" led to the people paying for the work and making the profit. They decided with the regulation what the employer's communication and expectation would be regarding the mental and physical requirements placed on the employee; in this case, the chainsaw operator. The solution to the problem must end at the source of the problem; it goes full circle; it must. We are not looked at by society as individuals who all happen to be running the same tool; we are considered a "group" of people who require regulation of their activities; what one does, reflects on all; to the general public paying high insurance premiums, it's like all the chainsaw operators are running a single gigantic saw; when it comes to who controls the future "free" use of the chainsaw, we are all one!

In my state, the General Industry Standards are managed by LARA through MIOSHA. LARA stands for "Licensing and Regulatory Affairs." The gentleman who runs the "R" department probably has his office right across the hallway from the lady who runs the "L" affairs. If we, as chainsaw operators, don't start communicating with each other to make this occupation safer, the "L" is going to take over for the "R"; it's the only logical next step. The "R" as in "regulatory" (and "responsibility") will quickly change to the "L," as in "licensing" (and "liability"); this, of course, would focus more public scrutiny on our activity; you won't be able to cut a shrub in your backyard without drawing the attention of your "stressed-out" neighbors.

This country's responsible operators have allowed the idiot producer of *The Texas Chainsaw Massacre* to place a very negative picture of the chainsaw in the minds of his ignorant non-operator viewers; what's worse, we've paid people with "tree service" written on the side of their trucks to do work on our property as quickly and cheaply as possible without insisting on safely and properly; we've let good old cousin George, under the watchful eye of our next-door neighbor, cut that big dead tree that's three feet from the house because he does all the other chores with no problems. The system, on the other hand, ensures that the society's observations will be of professional-looking chainsaw operators providing a safe and productive function of a dangerous but required task—not a bunch of loose cannons in need of restraint.

So what can we do as responsible chainsaw operators to protect the profession, get the job done efficiently, and at the same time, make it safer for all? You're too fast for me; the answer is in your hand, your body, and your brain. You must build a Personal Safety System (a.k.a., your PSS) that will easily encompass these simple responsibilities with safe procedures and practices, statistically proven to work, and placed in effect by your neighbors within the regulations; let's call them "rules." We will make an alliance within the chainsaw community through a personal affirmation to do the best we can with the saw to stay within the rules we have agreed upon; no matter who is watching—the boss, other operators, or our ten-year-old daughter acting as our SP at the woodpile. Commit yourself to this goal; if you find you just can't make yourself conform, you must do the next most ethical thing you can as a positive member of society: Be a safety person or a brush-piler, but please don't pick up that saw. The "personal" in the PSS is simply an indication to *yourself* of your integrity's intensity. It is you demonstrating, one operator to another, what an ethical operator looks like. If you see someone screwing up, you need to say something; you need to teach. If it is you screwing up, you need training and/or practice; you can pay someone to train you, but eventually, it will still come down to you convincing your own brain that what you have learned is the safest and most productive method; with acceptance and practice, you begin to see your own body following the rules; you must first allow your ego to be taught by your common sense, and your common sense to be taught by an uncommon system.

Can you see where this opens a "Pandora's Box" full of all kinds of basic human behaviors? How do you correct someone when you see them doing something against the rules? Do you continue to work when a rule infraction goes unaddressed? How do you teach without sounding condescending? Can you judge other people's actions without bias? Do I have the self-control to recognize and change my unsafe habits? These are all very difficult questions, and there are many more. Finding the answers for these personal questions will be a natural course when you begin working with other CSS members on a cooperative basis; the answers will already be firmly resolved in your mind when you are the operator since they are the same questions you will need to answer for yourself in your PSS; just be as lenient and as demanding on other operators as you are on yourself. Your personal character may leak through the system, but the rest of us are not concerned with that; we are concerned about abiding by the rules that were made to keep *all* of us safe, including someone like me, a stubborn "know-it-all" with anger issues that had to become an attentively listening, soft-spoken teacher around a chainsaw. When I find myself in the position of teaching someone who egregiously breaks a rule, I use the "sandwich method," either on the spot or I think about it for later: I compliment something done well (bread), mention the infraction (meat), and end with, "You are a respected member of the system" (bread). If they correct their behavior to line up with the rule, and keep trying harder, then they are in the system. If they refuse to comply with the rule, they are out of the system; they might still be my SP, but I cannot be theirs; not for my sake, not even for their sake; it's for *your* sake, because in doing so, I show my respect for your PSS, even if the extent of its knowledge and experience is the reading of this book, or the ability to cut a one-inch slice off a log while dressed in full PPE (personal protection equipment), running a new saw a thousand miles away.

Your PSS is your personal rendition of "Behavioral Safety." A revelation popped into my mind once in a lecture for a storm response team when speaking about what "behave" means. It went something like this: You're a kid heading out the door, and you yell to your mom, "I'm going over to Billy's house!" You hear back, "Okay; behave yourself!" What did she mean when she said that? She has taught you from the beginning the right thing to do; she wants you to still have that knowledge when you go away; she wants you to be that person even when you're out of her control, so she's giving you the responsibility to monitor and control your own actions based on your trust in her. You yell back, "I will!" What did you mean by that? You accepted the condition for your release from under her covering; you resolve to respect the advice she gave you, and now you go to prove it; I will *be* what I *have* from you. (I will *behave*.) Your mom in this little scenario is the chainsaw safety system; she defines the rules and helps you learn them; your respect of the system encourages you to follow them; both the mom and the kid are you; both the CSS and the PSS are you if you are pulling the trigger on the saw; it *is* the right hemisphere of your brain working with the left hemisphere of your brain so all the other brains can see how well behaved you are to ensure they are safe! (All you need concern yourself with now is Billy.)

Let's try redefining the familiar word "behave" to teach ourselves a new mental concept: the CSS is the "be" you must "have" in your PSS. When you cut with other operators in a CSS, you are presenting your PSS to them; it's you exemplifying your best; what you have taught your brain and body is how you are behaving yourself; it's your responsibility on display! If others behave differently than you, be it student or teacher, you decide how well they adhere to the rules and what skills they show in the product; they might also be scrutinizing your PSS to decide if you are a student or a teacher. Glean as much knowledge and experience as you can from all whom you work with, especially the one running the saw; if you find nothing new for your PSS, you *are* the teacher, so teach if you see a rules infraction; demonstrate new techniques; learn how to be a better teacher, simply because that is what a responsible CSS operator does. (Teaching yourself to be a better teacher makes you a teacher and a student at the same time, in the same brain.)

Just because you think something, doesn't mean you have to believe it; just because you believe something, doesn't mean it's the truth.

There are only two ways to totally eliminate chainsaw "accidents": stop the chainsaws or stop the accidents! We need the saws and don't want the accidents. Which choice do you believe should get the most attention?

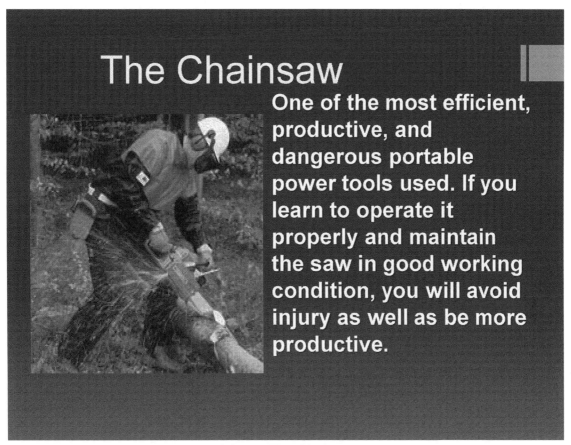

The Chainsaw

One of the most efficient, productive, and dangerous portable power tools used. If you learn to operate it properly and maintain the saw in good working condition, you will avoid injury as well as be more productive.

Slide 7: The Chainsaw

THE CHAINSAW

I FREQUENTLY CALL THE CHAINSAW the "world's most dangerous hand-tool" (WMDH). That any so-called adult can walk into just about any hardware store, put down their money, and walk out with one really freaks me out. The sales clerk might yell as this new-born chainsaw operator is going out the door, "Don't forget to read the manual!" So home goes the new toy/DIY tool, and out comes the manual. "Let's see; the gas goes here; the oil goes here; and you pull on this 'doomaflitchy.'" Now the operator heads out into the back-yard to that tree that fell down in the storm last week; the tree service company wanted $700.00 to clean it up; this brand new power-saw costs a lot less than that; great savings! There's a pat on the back for being such a savvy, able person, as that "baby" is fired up, the trigger pulled to maximum power, and the bar pushed into the branches. Suddenly, faster than the blink of an eye, the tip of the bar on that giant new saw comes flying back and nearly takes a left arm off at the shoulder. "Far-fetched" story you might say; not really! You would be surprised how many times it happens; after all, you have this long, extended bar with a chain going around it; the *common sense* way to cut would be with that small curved part held as far from the body as possible, right?

I submit to you that the reason the chainsaw is the *most* dangerous tool is because in action against a tree, the consequences don't always align with common sense; they require something more! It's not just an understanding of how the saw works; it's about how it works when combined with the unique tree you are cutting, and the individual state of your attitude. This is the reason for this book; the CSS is that "something more" you need to be a safe, productive, and confident operator.

I just had a thought when seeing the acronym WMDH in print for the first time; I'll show you how my PSS thinks: it could also stand for what the saw and I are in our relationship to the tree; we are a "Weapon of Mass Destruction—Here." I guess the tree would agree; do you? It's as if the power hidden in the gas tank of the saw is poised, waiting at my command to deconstruct the potential energy power in the tree into manageable units; it sounds fanciful, but I believe it is actually the truth. Of course, we know that in a responsible operator's mind, the chainsaw cannot be a weapon; it must be a tool because it is used to do work, not destroy an enemy; a gun can be a tool or a weapon, and still remain within the established rules placed by all the users; the chainsaw can only be a tool and still make sense to sane humans. How can the rest of us know what is going on in the mind of a person holding a chainsaw? Does that mind see the saw as a tool, a weapon, or a toy? We can tell by the unspoken word: the dress, the body language, how well they handle the tool, how well they keep the rules on our behalf, the look in their eyes when they teach, and a good stump in the end, with no blood on it.

The chainsaw could be acknowledged as the single most significant accomplishment of the mechanized abilities of humanity when it comes to trees—a focus of amazing power in the hands of one person, living in the forest perhaps; not a weapon meant for conquering other people, but for defense against an encroaching plant; one that man has had a love/hate relationship with since he discovered how to control fire. The tree's mass stores potential energy; we use the saw offensively to obtain the resources the wood contains; a positive product from trees that favor us with it, and fight us for it. The chainsaw was meant to happen; its time had come, and it did its part in the history of man, it is not going away any time soon; its time is just beginning because the trees are not going away; there will always be a necessity for a human to challenge a giant tree in a short amount of time, and be successful. The CSS is the next step in human evolution as it pertains to the chainsaw; we must give this amazing tool the recognition it deserves; we must give its operators the respect they have earned for efficiently managing the trees.

Will the chainsaw become illegal to sell to unqualified people because it's just too dangerous for the average Joe or Jill to operate? I was watching the news about storm recovery the other day—something I seem to be seeing more and more of these days; very strange, violent weather we seem to be having, eh? The reporter said one sentence that caught the attention of my PSS: "Trees kill more people in catastrophic weather events than any other cause." The safety guys down at MIOSHA told me they usually have more people hurt in the clean-up of trees after a storm than are hurt by the storm itself. There are more exotic tree species and diseases being introduced in this country to which our native trees have not evolved the proper immunities; there are die-offs of entire stands in some infected areas. People are into natural things these days, like walking down a worn trail through the beautiful forest; however, trees don't know what trails are; they fall where they stand! More and more people are cutting firewood; it used to be mostly for their sole source of heat; now it's becoming more of a leisure activity around the firepit in the backyard; logs off the back lot still need to be cut up into fifteen-inch lengths. Many folks just can't afford to remove that old dead tree in the yard, so it eventually falls in a storm and hits the house: "What the heck—we've got insurance." Fewer people these days have enough confidence in their physical ability and mental mettle to pick up the chainsaw; they don't want to pay someone to cut down the tree, and drop it on the garage; the insurance company might not cover that.

The question comes to my mind: Where are safe chainsaw operators going to come from if these upward trends continue? All you need to do is take a look when you see a chainsaw being run on television, in the movies, next door, or by your spouse in the backyard to see if the CSS is needed. It's obvious to me by what I see that legal authority is not making things better for decreasing injuries and deaths when trees and chainsaws come together; it is up to each and every chainsaw operator to change the trend from the bottom up with the ethical authority attached to this very unique tool.

If you are an aspiring chainsaw operator, look very closely at the picture in the slide. That, in my mind, is a very good operator. How can I make that assumption with one still photograph? What do you *think*? Now remember that image; it is stored in the PSS memory in your brain; you may need it later.

About the person in the picture in Slide 7: If you are a beginner, and you have no similar picture with you as the operator, put yourself in this one; replace the "he" with "she" as needed. Take a look at the person in the picture; what do you see? I'll tell you what my CSS brain sees as the truth; it's not some preconceived notion of what a *chainsaw* is when applied to a *tree* by a person; it's the method my PSS uses to process and store the information the picture contains.

I see three energy sources: 1) the **chainsaw**; the most powerful is always mentioned first; right? The saw has more power than the potential energy in the wood; 2) the **man** comes in last for power; and 3) the weaker element in the trilogy controls application of the strongest with a brain; by imposing his will through his muscle on the wood—what we call **work**. I see a well-dressed, thinking manipulator of power, about the size of a human being, who respects the power source he holds and thoughtfully directs it. He prepares for the cut; he deliberately delivers the power, his part in a recurring event he calls "making the cut." He mentally processes the interaction of the three participants before he acts; the saw receives the plan of the intended product from the brain; the muscles feel the chain against the wood; the chain goes where the practiced muscles dictate, without an understanding of where the wood ends and the man's body begins; it cannot think, so it cannot make a mistake. The man and the saw work together as one to overcome the resistive power in the tree; they are a power cooperative; the man's conceptual power combined with the saw's obedient explosive power. A lapse in the connection of man and saw gives an advantage to the wood; the energy stored in the wood obeys the law; it seeks a lower level. The force becomes kinetic energy; if the vector hits the man, it hurts. He aims the saw at the wood and pulls the trigger; he and the saw work as one; the teeth are his brain's focal point; the bar is an extension of his body to place the work. The saw or the wood can overpower muscle but not brain; his body, the wood, and the saw are simultaneously controlled; knowledge and experience from past cuts are remembered with the aim to arrive at the safest probable outcome. His protective equipment speaks anticipation and understanding of the physics, the blur of the chain, the snap of a wooden plant, and the risks he pre-mitigated. His stance and movement are a choreographed dance where he leads his partner on a wooden floor, not intrusively or rudely, but respectfully guiding; held close; firm grip; always watching; careful not to slip. Think; anticipate; act; evaluate; expect a force reaction, a sudden release of energy in a pre-planned direction. He lets the saw work; he analyzes how and directs where the force should be applied to methodically persuade the energy from the tree with the power in his hands as directed by his understanding. When the stop-switch on the saw is flipped, he experiences his new knowledge with a pat on the back; it's a picture of a unique job done well; he sharpens the chain, pours in more fuel and lubricant, fires it up, and is ready to power the work again. One is doing the work for three; he is a "chainsaw operator."

I know, these pictures are not pretty, but they are images of actual events. I'm sure these operators didn't get up that day and say to themselves, "I think I'll go out in the woods today and cut myself with my chainsaw, or maybe drop a tree on my new truck." There was nothing "planned" about it! The results you see in the pictures and the numbers you see in the text are proof that the operators' plans were inadequate, or they had no plan at all. You might ask yourself, "How could anyone be so idiotic as to pick up a chainsaw and attempt to control a tree without a plan, without thinking it over first?" Obviously, they must have had some sort of plan or they would not have found the tree; so they had a plan, but it was a *bad plan* they were unwilling or unable to change while attempting to work out the problem. They assumed that because past application of the same bad plan resulted in firewood in the furnace, this one would too. That same assumption is made in most cutting mishaps; bad plans accumulate into a large number of people getting hurt while running a chainsaw; each operator hurt or causing damage becomes a statistic that can be analyzed to predict the most probable

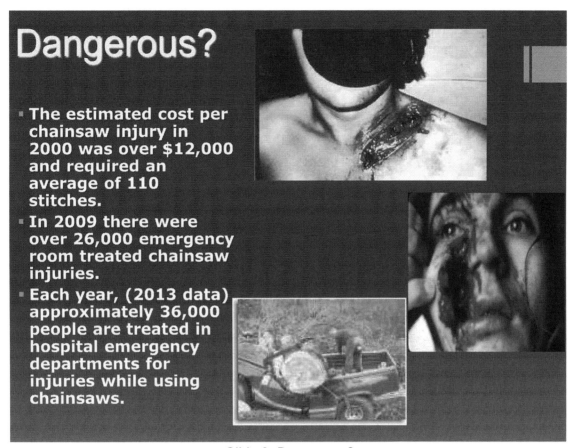

Slide 8: Dangerous?

outcome for failure. In the pictures, the failure is obvious, but numbers can be dismissed as "someone who's not as good an operator as I am; I've got this."

So how do we change the trend? How can we be confident we will not be a witness to or be part of the count of such statistics—the sum of the injured, painful, time-consuming, costly, embarrassing, and sometimes deadly mishaps, each representing a significant event in the life of at least one chainsaw operator?

We humans figured it out! We call it *safety*! We added up the numbers, developed statistical trends, and identified the work habits that caused the most injuries; then we invented barriers to the risks that we call safety *equipment*, rules that help us abide in safe action, which we call safe *procedures*, and tried and true actions and thought processes that we call *training*. What a person does when they pick up a saw and work it with a bad plan, or allow another to do so, is to thumb their nose at all their predecessors in chainsaw operation history upon whom safety was built; they disregard the example of error in a poorly planned trial by limiting their mental and physical abilities with the same poor plan; they keep making the same "stupid" mistakes. If the wounded operators in the pictures were standing in front of these careless operators, they would ask, "Why are you discounting my life-changing contribution to the truth; why aren't you passing on the only positive element of my injury to those who watch you operate your saw?" Would any thinking, empathetic person answer, "Look, I've been doing it this way all my life, and I still have my health; I'm going to keep doing it my way. To hell with your safety suggestion"? No, only an insane, fearful, self-centered person would say that; a person whom a "normal" operator would refuse to cut with unless they put down the pride they use to neutralize their fear, changed themselves into a good role model, and put the damn chaps on, not only out of regard for all the limping operators, but for the scar-less legs of an observing student!

Today, everybody knows what PTSD stands for; its occurrence in the United States is higher than in most of the rest of the world. I first heard the acronym during the Vietnam War when I was working in a medical evacuation ward for battlefield wounded. My buddies and I were a bunch of psych techs assigned the grunt work of changing dressings and taking vitals; we wanted to help more, so we started talking to many of our very transient patients in an attempt to define this new term for shell-shock. We found that like everything else in life, the symptoms were demonstrated in broad spectrums of behavioral differences and severity levels. We found that the soldiers least depressed about their injuries were those who showed remorse for leaving their friends behind, and to our surprise, many expressed a desire to get back into the fight. How they seemed to be handling their trauma-related stress was by concentrating on helping others avoid similar trauma.

When I started working as a first responder years later, I got another glimpse of this strange human behavior of moving toward possible trauma to save another person from it. I thought it must be the same brain function used to produce a similar behavior, but first responders don't need to experience a traumatic injury to respond to it effectively, so where does the knowledge of the trauma come from? How can they know what they are getting into? I answered that question only when I first had to deal with PTSD. I was successful in changing the D into an O for "Order" with the thought processes and behavioral changes taught in the CSS.

No clinical trials have been done to support my belief; that's all it is, a belief, but it is one I have held since my youth—one that is part of the reason the CSS was formed in my brain in the first place. I don't really know how to say this; it's more of an emotion than a thought; some people are predisposed by the size of certain parts of their brains to have empathy and do all they can to avoid pain, trauma, and fear for everyone they are near. There's no spectrum here; in any potentially traumatic situation, each individual will either attempt to unite with everyone else to alleviate the trauma, or remain an individual entity that moves away from the potential stress for personal interests. In the CSS, we bring our "Personal Safety for All System" into an agreement on how we train ourselves to help each other avoid the trauma as the first response.

Slide 9: Safety Management System

SAFETY MANAGEMENT SYSTEM

I'M REALLY BIG ON DEFINITIONS. I've learned over my years of work (and marriage) that most conflicts, arguments, delays, and mishaps occur because of bad communication between coworkers. One of the most significant elements in poor communication is the definition of terms; for example, when two people use the same word, but each holds a different definition of what it means in their brains. This issue is what occupies most of the communication time in the CSS; you not only need to say what you think, but you must know if the people listening correctly received the information you intended to transfer to them; this knowledge is particularly important if the other person is your safety person—your extra set of eyes. Common definitions can only happen when you both use the same words to describe an action or item; it can be any word, or even a hand signal, but you must have a common definition of what it means, and use the same word or signal for that action *all* the time; in the CSS, it's like "chainsaw talk." The word "talk" here is very inclusive; it includes, but is not limited to, words, signals, body language, how you work the saw, the condition of your safety equipment, how many times you get the saw pinched in the wood, and how well you adhere to the rules. These are all examples of speaking in chainsaw talk; having a common definition within the system allows the operator, safety person, and all involved to speak and mime the language.

When I started putting these slides together, I needed a firm definition in my mind of what I would teach: safety. I went to an online dictionary and cut and pasted the above definition into the slide. I was reading about Safety Management Systems, which were a big push for the state safety specialists at the time. As I compared the various meanings of safety, I noticed the word "contrivance," so I decided to look up the definition of contrive. Definition #2 caught my eye because it used words like "plan," "scheme," and "manage." *That sounds like a system*, I thought, and sure enough, when I looked up the word "system," I had one of those "Oh, yeah!" moments. A system is a contrivance, and contriving is a big part of being safe! The safe operation of the chainsaw didn't just come with use of the safety equipment alone; the equipment and the work requirements that forced me to wear it were just a part of the grand scheme I had developed over the years—a scheme that I decided was a "system," just like the ones they set up in a factory or on a construction site after an employee gets hurt on the job. They analyze the problem, make some rules, and train the best action to the worker. I thought that if an operator of a dangerous tool or machine in a factory gets their own safety system set up for them by the state, why shouldn't each chainsaw operator have their own personal safety system too? (We pay our taxes!) Why shouldn't operators of the WMDH get a state-supplied contrivance? You do! Here it is, invented for you over twenty-five years of trial, error, training, and success, while enjoying the work, with nobody getting killed.

Here's how my "crazy" system brain remembers complicated aspects of CSS's definition:

A simple premise of logic is: If A = B, and B = C, then A = C. If one has an average grasp of mental reasoning, and they prove to themselves with confidence that A does equal B, and B does indeed equal C, they can skip the proof that B = C every time they see a B, and go confidently from A to C when they see an A they know is the same as a B. B = C is like a logical value judgment that circumvents a pre-programmed instinct or impulse, and creates, through self-determination, a new automatic response. That response is like building a logical bridge between A and C; wait a second, it even looks like a bridge (=): A = C.

Safety offers no certain assurance of wellbeing until it is mentally processed through a personal contrivance; that contrivance must be proven to prevent injury through trial and error; repetition of action combined with reaction force predictability. When the contrivance is tested and proven to avert danger through behavior learned during the trial, and a change in that behavior is enforced to correct the error, it is possible for all involved in a dangerous activity to agree: If you reason together that A = C, you have yourselves a safety system. From the definition of safety: If safety (A) is a contrivance (B), and a contrivance is a system (C), then your chainsaw will be made a safe tool by the concepts and practices in the system; those concepts and practices are a universally proven contrivance, refined through decades of trial and error by millions of operators; it is pre-determined and agreed upon that B = C. Each time you use the system, you are teaching others how to make the leap to A = C; to more productive and enjoyable saw time. If there is a B that does not equal C, the system's response is the return to the "instinctive reaction"; the system watches, and is watched; it has a prime objective to make all Bs = C before continuing. The stress and time involved in perfecting your B so it is equal to A is alleviated by the confidence the CSS gives in the fact that your $\underline{C}$ already equates to your $\underline{A}$ through your $\underline{B}$ehavior. This leads me to another basic statement of logic: If A = C, then C = A. If your PSS = CSS, then…. You get it!

(You $\underline{C}$over Your $\underline{A}$ss through your $\underline{b}$ehavior so well that you direct everybody else in the system on how to cover theirs.)

Slide 10: Three Levels of Complexity

THREE LEVELS OF COMPLEXITY

THE THREE IMAGES IN THIS slide represent the three basic levels of complexity or variation involved in running a chainsaw in the CSS: the operator, the human brain, and the wood. There are more, but focusing on these first will develop in your behavior a routine to help you recognize when other levels of complexity introduce themselves into a particular cutting scenario. Why do we need to understand concepts like levels of complexity anyway? If you think about it, your entire existence, your very survival on this earth, is highly dependent on how proficient you are at learning from your past to affect the present to predict your individual future; this instinctual and common sense interpretation of our surroundings is what we call living—surviving in the present. The variables can be thought of as each being in a "spectrum," as in light, sound, speed; the list goes on to nearly every aspect of life; each resultant set of variables represents the consequences of different intersections of the broad spectrums of possibilities and probabilities (most probable outcomes), for each individual involved in each particular saw operation. The brain subconsciously finds stored information in the brain's neurons that is similar to the present reality, and indicates its pertinence to the conscious state by means of chemical reactions in the brain's synapse, prompting confidence or apprehension. You can see how what you perceive as reality in the present is greatly swayed by what you have accepted as truth in the past. Confusion or panic may ensue if some threat never before encountered is realized, which, in turn, can lead to increased stress, sudden fear, and mistakes.

These particular spectrums are most applicable in your chainsaw life when you are approaching a tree you intend to cut down or a branch you intend to cut off of it, but they are always in your memory combined as one event, recorded there simply by the fact that you own a saw. The brainwork of sorting out interconnected variables can be practiced with non-complex spectrums presented to you in everyday life, in places that don't present risk. The human brain is constantly attempting to predict the future on its own spectrum of pictures from the best success of survival to fear of the worst failure. A person can teach their brain to picture the best-case scenario (BCS) through training and rational, logical thought. The brain willingly stores positive data with rewarding pleasure chemicals—what we sometimes call daydreaming. The same brain, however, will reshape the truth to avoid nightmare scenarios; for example, here are two possible outcomes: 1) After the work is done, proceeding to a meticulously controlled set of variables we call home, or 2) An outcome where we have zero control, a hospital emergency room; two very different outcomes, with two very different futures, one calm and expected, one stressful and uncertain; both related to our ability to identify the next outcome in the complex mix of real variables before us. Why is this so complicated? Does the inherent danger in operating a chainsaw demand this much brain work? Yes, it does, but like everything else you practice, it will get easier as you proceed with the development of your unique method of dealing with mental issues involved in controlling your own behavior in your personal safety system.

Take the variables presented by the first image of the operator with a saw: How many different makes, models, and horsepower saws are there? How many different size bars and chains? How many states of condition are they in? How many different operators are there? Or, you could ask: How many people are running saws that are different from all others on earth? Now take each available operator and place each different saw in their hands, and you will see how some complement each other, and others, not so much. The saw and the operator must be a good match; they must have the capability to deliver the desired product. If they work against each other, productivity in the saw, or even worse, the operator's health, can be diminished.

Now, let's look at the second image: "The Thinker"—what is he thinking about? He's probably not contemplating the best way to show off more muscle; he's more likely thinking, "How could I have been so stupid as to go skinny dipping and leave my clothes and my friends on the same beach?" He's trying to figure out how his brain works—why it chose an action that led to such an enormous error in judgment: "How could I be so stupid?" If you've never said that to yourself, the CSS will be an enigma to you, and developing your PSS will be a challenge. Mixing the two will be very difficult for you until you admit to yourself that you are also human. We learn to trust our brain because of all the things it does for us instinctually, or subconsciously; we believe it; we don't have a choice in whether to trust it or not, unless questioning it is part of our original thought. Not questioning it is fine when you're involved in activities that present low risk, like sitting in your favorite chair watching an action movie, but in dangerous situations where you are part of the action with others' wellbeing involved, the brain must be trained to respond consciously, right now, with only pertinent information considered. The focus point of your senses is naturally very narrow; it needs to be that way for your brain to function within its normal capacities, but it can be trained to widen its perspective. A good example is how our brain is tricked into focusing on only one small item mixed in a flood of information; watch the video on YouTube, "The Invisible Gorilla." The title tips you off to where this is going, but you can still preview it, and then show it to your unsuspecting friends or family. You will be amazed when people look at you and say, "What gorilla?" You will also be impressed with yourself when once you have seen the clip and know what to look for, you will easily be able to count the basketball passes and be aware of the man in the gorilla suit. Your brain can be taught, by you, to focus on the most pertinent input without losing focus on everything else. If you are still skeptical, YouTube has many other great videos that will prove to you that your brain may not be aware of something right in front of you; that it cannot be trusted! (I'm not much for the whole internet thing, but I really like sites like YouTube that give mostly usable information!)

Now, let's consider the third image. How can a beautiful forest be full of variables? After all, it looks like the same trees repeated over and over; isn't that the definition of a forest? Far from it! Every tree in the forest is as much an individual in physical makeup as you are an individual in the human race. They are different in age, species, mass, height, diameter, shape, levels of decay and defects, location in relation to other trees, location in relation to the topography, etc. Their differences are much more numerous than their similarities, but we momentarily choose to regard them as one risk, when, in fact, every tree you cut in your lifetime, if you cut all day, every day, can never be *exactly* the same as any other. Even if you should happen on two that are very similar, *you* have changed since you cut the first one, and cutting a tree down is much different from just looking at it; cutting it down involves the whole tree, down to the fibers in the wood—something impossible to see with the naked eye, let alone something we normally consider when thinking of variations.

One certainty I have found in my cutting life is that trees do what nature has determined they must do; they don't suddenly change their habits and decide to lay down for a nap, then get up and go back to producing oxygen; they stand there doing what they are made to do until some disease or calamity in the environment brings them down, and they seldom get up again. The chainsaw comes in many colors and sizes, but its shape stays pretty much the same because of the job it has to do; it has an engine of some type to produce the power, and some kind of fast-moving cutting component supposedly able to penetrate wood; even operators themselves are fairly predictable; I've never seen a lazy, beer-drinking jokester suddenly transform into a healthy, efficient, and productive operator as they pick up the saw.

One deceiver exists in the three elements pictured, however: the human brain. It doesn't do things the way you *think* it should, or even the way it has in the past; it's all over the place, completely unpredictable, especially in a suddenly dangerous situation. The most difficult variable to isolate and evaluate is one that literally keeps changing right before your eyes—like the difference between a lateral and a Hail Mary, a tin can and a grouse, a putt through ten feet of fringe and one on the carpet. Your brain, without a practiced system, believes it can do something until a sudden extraneous challenge presents itself; then it stops to think about it at just the wrong time. The brain must be systematically trained to respond quickly and correctly without getting its bare ass kicked; the Thinker's biggest muscle for carrying it around will, by reflex, instantly produce the maximum it has been trained to produce by the brain's will; it's really the brain that is causing its own injury, and it knows it's coming, in the subconscious; we call it stress, apprehension, and fear!

Note: Something just popped out of my subconscious; there could be *four* "sources of forces" represented in the three levels of complexity: operator, safety person, saw, and cutting area. Think about it; ponder it; make a story about it in your head; store that picture in a special place; you know the name of the place, right? The "P" part of your PSS! Your single brain must always be like two—the operator and the safety person (SP) in the same brain. You really only give part of the safety watch responsibilities to your SP; the P part you hold on to when you run the saw.

The world around each individual is complete chaos until another person of valor influences it with order.

Merriam-Webster defines valor as: strength of mind or spirit that enables a person to encounter danger with firmness: personal bravery.

Slide 11: History of a Safety System

HISTORY OF A SAFETY SYSTEM

I MUST GIVE CREDIT WHERE credit is due; here I will discuss the history of the first four rules of the safety system; how I managed to mentally and physically find confident safe passage through the maze of variables in my cutting career. Maybe someday you will teach a course like this, and your corresponding slide will have my name on it, but only give me credit for Rule 5; I was a student of the other rules before I taught them. They were freely passed on to me, so it cannot be advantageous for me to pass them on to you because that is not ethical.

Way back in the 1970s, Soren Eriksson came to the United States from Sweden and started teaching chainsaw cutting and safety techniques, many of which are still resisted today. The trees and chainsaws in Sweden are no different than they are here, but for some reason, Americans are hard to teach; maybe some believe that accepting methods developed in foreign countries is somehow betraying our heritage as timbermen. I might have easily agreed with this concept since my paternal great-grandfather was forced to leave Sweden to find prosperity. If the procedures Mr. Eriksson taught weren't safer and more productive, if I hadn't gained respect for his effort to teach a logical system for chainsaw operation, and if I hadn't moved off safe ground to a new promise for the sake of my own family, it's possible my heretic pride could have cost me the very future my ancestors have provided for me.

Tim Ard worked as an instructor for Eriksson, and later, he started teaching the same concepts. He put on a seminar for the Forest Service (FS) in Kentucky in the early '90s that I attended. I learned many new techniques from Ard, and several other instructors employed with the FS, that followed the same basic rules for safe saw operation; they became the foundation of my infant safety system, and helped mature me into a different kind of operator through training, practice, self-control, and determination. I accepted the principles these gentlemen taught because I had respect for them as safe and efficient operators, and at the same time, excellent teachers who looked me in the eye, told me the truth, and then showed me how to make the truth real through demonstration.

I found that learning in a classroom, or even through a book like you are doing, only amounted to half of the brain work that needed to be done. I had to receive the teaching by learning to trust the practices, and that only came through their continuous repetition. The government is very good at providing information in the form of safety training, so my biggest challenge was keeping my experience at the same level as my knowledge. The job also supplied me vast opportunity to operate the saw, but I found that the experience only kept pace with the knowledge when I purposely imposed a change in my attitude. Today, every operator has an endless source of essentially free training on their phone or laptop; if I was starting my system today, and looking for a way to keep my experience equal to my knowledge, I would look into volunteering for a conservation district, trail club, storm response team, or forest reserve; these organizations are always looking for saw operators, and many have told me that proficient and available operators are becoming harder and harder to find. I suppose most saw operators today can be found cutting firewood in the backyard, or cleaning up storm damage on their property or in the neighborhood; the firewood cutting presents a good test for sticking to the system even when it gets to be repetitive and plain hard work, and the storm damage response in your yard is, hopefully, rare. If you enjoy the challenge of running a saw in the CSS as much as I do, look around your area; there are organizations that really need your skills. You'll find opportunities to practice and maybe even teach until you're at least sixty-eight years old. You were helped by other operators; in return, please help out the next generation of operators.

The training was at Land Between the Lakes National Forest Reserve in Kentucky in the spring when there was still snow in Michigan, so I really enjoyed the weeklong visit down south, all paid for by your federal tax dollars; thank you very much! I was there attempting to test up to a C-faller. In the FS, operators are split up into A-fallers for beginners, B-fallers for intermediate, and C-fallers for advanced, with assigned tasks in each level defined by a set of field-tested skills. I had been a B-faller for a couple of years, and I wanted to be able to go out cutting on my own with a couple of Bs when on fire details; it was always more fun for me without the crew boss looking over my shoulder. Tim explained what was required in the test: "I want you to cut at least two large diameter trees with me acting as your safety person; with the first, verbalize everything you're thinking to me, which must include hazards, lean, escape route, hinge and cutting plan as a minimum. If you miss any, you fail. Use all the proper handling techniques; if you miss any three times, you fail. And, of course, have all of your personal protective equipment and your saw in good working condition."

I spent the evening before the test in my little cabin preparing my saw and equipment, practicing the saw-handling techniques, and trying to memorize all the elements of the steps Tim had listed. I was nervous when I took the test, but I found it strange that the stress was different from what I usually felt when cutting a complex tree on my normal job; the apprehension I felt was caused mostly by a lack of confidence in my ability to communicate all my intentions rather than actually perform the task while cutting the tree. I had much more confidence, with virtually no stress; the first tree fell exactly where I said it would. For the second tree, Tim explained that I didn't need to verbalize what I was thinking; he would attempt to read my actions as I went through the process to determine if I had missed any of the required elements of the felling procedure; I was impressed with myself when the second tree hit the target because of the confidence I experienced mostly from my success with the first one. No stress whatsoever; it was actually fun, kind of like showing my teacher my talent and ability within the system.

The most valuable thing I took away from that training, along with my C-faller rating, was that this method would be a good way to teach my B-fallers: Use it all the time! What I mentally developed from what I learned in the experience, which you helped pay for, was a methodology for an operator and a safety person to work as if in the same frame of mind, independent of who was the tester and who was the tested. It was a way for both to know what the other is thinking; I transformed that testing procedure into a "standard operating procedure" in everyday practice during the following years while testing and working with my Bs; we never even had a significant close call after that, through many complex tree drops; it became *us*: you, me, and the saw, against the tree! (You helped pay for all that through your federal income tax; you helped keep me safe; I am here, paying it forward by verbalizing it to you.)

Einstein said, "The only source of knowledge is experience." That begs a question: "Ah, excuse me, Mr. Einstein; is understanding what is fact and what is fiction included in that formula?" Did I have an ear to *hear* the truth when I learned the facts? Did I have an eye to *see* the result of experience? The only usable information you will get from this book must be experienced by you through practice; only then will it become knowledge equal to your ability to experience it. The CSS attempts to provide a teacher who helps you balance your knowledge and experience through the operator/safety person interaction. Knowledge and experience (K&E) are best when in balance; I would not choose to cut with an operator who had a PhD in chainsaw operation (probably not Albert) but absolutely no hands-on experience; nor would I gladly work with an operator who had thirty years of cutting experience but insisted on injury over advice on how to do it safely. Try to keep your knowledge about the chainsaw and the tree on a similar level with your experience; turn all new information into recallable knowledge by *doing* it. If that's what Einstein meant by the quote, then I would have to agree with the man many have called the smartest who ever lived. I need clarification of the information through demonstration before education; that's just the way Swedes are, especially when they're part French.

See if you can wrap your brain around this; all history can be reduced to "communication" and "expectation" in word and in deed; all history is based on keeping the people who communicate the best, "safest." We spend our time in this life talking about how to get what we need, then testing those communications with whatever or whoever is talking to us based on how much we expect the interaction to get us what we want. What we want the most is for all the people around us to be truthful, to aid us in getting what we need. The brain remembers and records that information based on how much the communication met our expectation and satisfied a need. Satisfying a want gives a higher level to the communication because it more than meets expectations; there is a caveat here in that the communication may take on a new significance when needs and wants are considered the same; the brain may rewrite history—embellish the communication. (So maybe all history is based on each individual's definition of needs and wants.)

Foundational Principles

- No rank in the system
- Operator controls cutting area
- All teach and learn
- Verbalize and demonstrate
- Go – No-Go option
- Five rules rule

Slide 12: Foundational Principles

THE FUNDAMENTALS

THE SLIDE ABOVE DOES NOT contain an exhaustive list of the CSS's principles. Instead, it describes the basic system; that's why the principles are called foundational; some of the concepts the CSS is based on are like the root system in a large oak; it holds up the trunk foundation, but you don't see it, even though it has to be the strongest force in the structure, or the entire tree will topple. The principles are the ground support of the systematic methods for proper use of a chainsaw when using it to fell a larger diameter tree about the same diameter width as the length of the available bar on the saw, including cutting the limbs off the tree, and cutting the bowl of the tree up into a manageable size to fit the product. The principles in your PSS might be more complex if you are required by the saw work to cut more complex trees; if that is the case, you may need to develop, along with the operators and safety people in your CSS, other foundational principles to suit your unique situation; that would most efficiently be accomplished by adding a rule to your corporate safety system.

These principles are not rules; at some level, they are higher than rules; they are the basic logic for following the rules, and they are too complex a safety issue to deal with in this book; you just need to trust me that they are vital until I can explain why in my next book, *The Fifth Rule*. These are the instinctual or common sense approaches to a dangerous activity that status- and objective-driven humans chose to leave out of our safety programs; these are the "extra effort" ethical responsibilities we intentionally add to our work to keep our coworkers safe, to properly teach beginners, and to show proper caution when dealing with the WMDH as applied to giant woody plants.

Let's now look at each principle in more detail.

No Rank in the System

A problem with rank exists in the CSS that you don't have in your PSS. If you are teaching a beginner at home, you will be teaching the same student for a long time, usually a close relative or friend. Don't forget to be a student once in a while yourself, and when your student becomes the operator, you are the best choice to be their SP. Do what you're told according to the CSS: Give control to the operator. Some experienced operators may also have a problem dealing with the fact that there is also no gender in the CSS; there's no father/son or aunt/niece; as soon as the saw is started, there can only be one relationship in the cutting area: operator and safety person. The only time you look past the chaps of a fellow CSS member, or the face shield on their hard hat, is when you are looking for apprehension/confidence in body language or in their eyes; that can be hard to see behind the screen, or when they're working at the base of the tree. In that case, your student's body language will indicate to the experienced teacher fear or faith in the system. Try not to evaluate any activity, whether done by another operator or by yourself, based on anything except how well the rules are followed, observational skills, and the product's quality and timeliness.

I learned the principles through observation of my personal safety attitude and the behavior I saw in others similarly trained for firefighting with a chainsaw in hand. Is there rank in a fire-suppression agency? Yes, in fact, the entire system, the Incident Command System, used to manage fires is developed by the federal government, and its foundational principle *is* rank. A type 2 firefighter (FT2), basically one step up from a volunteer in rank, could possibly have three or four supervisors on a twenty-person crew. I noticed almost immediately as a new employee how the chainsaw crew, usually members of the same squad, with three or four people in it, was treated differently by the crew boss, more as peers than grunts. When they walked into the cutting area—a giant half sphere, its center at the middle of the stump, with a radius twice the height of the tree—it was like the saw crew had entered a zone with no bosses at all. When we decided who would actually cut the tree, that person was called the operator, feller, or sawyer, depending on what part of the country was burning. After that decision was made, that person became the ultimate control for the area; the operator got a higher level of respect than a line-chinking crew member when the crew boss or division supervisor was giving orders. No one near the cutting area dared do anything except what the operator ordered, unless it was to stop everything long enough to point out how situationally aware they were by identifying an overlooked risk; they couldn't overextend their privilege to command, though, or they would be handed the saw and be asked to demonstrate. Once all involved decided there was a qualified and willing operator in their midst, who was willing to stand in the most dangerous spot possible in the cutting area while a nasty old burning tree was being sent to a hillside covered in a deep layer of ash, everybody in earshot of the safety person always seemed to become very cooperative and helpful without the need to prove any legal authority; it was more like "Watch and learn, please, so I don't need to do all the work tomorrow."

Operator Controls Cutting Area

Since a chainsaw is not "automatic," the person who controls the saw is the only logical choice for who controls the cutting area. That person legally accepted the liability and ethically accepted the responsibility when they started the saw, or when they dressed for the part, or maybe when they established assurance in their own mind that they had the ability to cut the tree safely based on their knowledge and experience: their PSS. Once a supposedly normal person starts the WMDH, holds it to their hip, and moves toward a nasty-looking tree, everyone else in range of that tree should definitely do what that person says if they are operating the tool within the system rules. (If it looks like an operator and acts like an operator, it's an operator, or at least the best you've got.) We already learned from watching videos on YouTube that the brain cannot be trusted to see what the eyes are looking at, so how can an operator who is looking down at a cut in the trunk of the tree possibly be in charge of the area up above, where all the heavy, rotten branches are? The answer is they can't!

The best person to be in charge of safety in the cutting area is the operator, but the limitations presented by human perception don't allow it, so the next best choice would be an extra set of trusted eyes. The communication between the brains controlling the two sets of eyes is the ultimate benefit of the foundational principle. If any operator ever tells you they don't want you to be their SP, remove any responsibility you have for a mishap by leaving the cutting area. If you prefer to cut by yourself, please check your attitude, maybe mix in a little humility or reality into your behavioral safety, and hold your demonstration of your ability until you have found a person willing to keep you safe; you will gather valuable information on how you can teach them, or establish that you will be the student in the cutting area.

If you cut alone, the statistical probability that you will eventually get some kind of injury while running your saw is much higher than an operator who has employed an extra set of eyes for watching what you can't physically see; unless you have eyes in the back of your head. If there is only an operator in the cutting area, that is undefined in the CSS! I know for a fact, without even being there, that there are risks present that cannot be mitigated by one brain or a single set of eyes and ears. You need another person; in the CSS, that person is called a Safety Person (SP). The presence of two PSSs in the cutting area is what holds up the system; to be in the CSS, you will need to find another person willing to enter your cutting area to also CYA (cover your ass) or mitigate risks. That person will be your safety person, and they could be just about anybody with acute senses, except your dog.

If you want to find a good SP, look among the "swampers"—these are people in the area who have an interest in you using the WMDH on a tree; they will deal with the many small pieces of wood you are making. Make sure your swampers are already members of the CSS, or they are willing to join the system with you, which immediately puts you both in the CSS; start teaching and learning. What the body looks like that holds that extra set of eyes, and how that brain works to interpret what those eyes see, becomes a part of your ability to adequately control your cutting area; it's your perspective combined with another person's perspective that allows for 3D vision. Just like your chain needs to be sharpened, your safety person needs to be taught. At a minimum, the SP must be taught what you are planning to attempt, and where to stand to get out of the way if you can't get a good read on the tree, or if it contains hidden risks, like rot, defects, and other things you didn't see. Having a good SP is your acceptance of the CSS because by finding that other person, you mitigated the added risk of not having them at all. Welcome, both of you, to the CSS. Now go find a cutting area (CA).

The size of the cutting area is contingent upon the work being done, and the length of stems being felled; it could range from a minimum of three times the saw length for something like cutting firewood, to a maximum of 2.5 times the tree length for felling. The extent of the cutting area you are taking charge of should be apparent to your SP since they will be defending its boundary and keeping the area safe while you are concentrating on the cut. They aren't there solely as a brush piler or to watch you cut; they are to watch the area for safety issues; thus the name "safety" person. A brief discussion would seem appropriate; tell them where best to stand, what to look for, signals to use for communicating with you while the saw is running, and what kinds of actions to take based on the concerns you've assessed in your size-up for that particular cutting project. Think of the cutting area as a "dome of danger" that follows the saw through the trees; the better the operator at following the safety rules, and the better their observational skills, the better the chances that all concerned will remain safe without undue stress. A good SP can only be born of a good operator, unless the roles are purposely switched and the teacher becomes the SP for the sake of observing the student in action in the CSS. (Two PSSs: one is learning, one is learning how well the other learns; ya get it?)

All Teach...

Would a father worth his weight in firewood ever tell his son or daughter to do something of high risk without showing them what to watch out for? Of course not; after all, the heat from the wood, and the money saved by cutting it are ultimately to warm and nurture that same person. It would, however, take an exceptional father to learn a system for safe running of the saw, bring the son/daughter through the maze of variables with logic passing between them, and in the process, create an everlasting bond between the two as operator and SP, working together to calculate and mitigate the risks they recognize together. You may get less wood cut teaching the CSS to your future woodcutter, but you will definitely have a lot more to talk about in front of the fire. When I am operating the saw, I have two basic foundational goals: 1) to remain inquisitive as to whether I can use this operation to practice what I have learned, and 2) to establish whether there is valuable information here that I can teach to my SP or to other operators.

If you have been successfully operating the saw for much of your life, you use your know-how (your PSS), you have the many years of knowledge garnered with the saw, you relearn your experiences to line up with the system, and you start practicing the first four rules to the letter, you have a very fortunate prodigy. If you are that kind of operator, then I'll tell you what will happen next: You'll develop a desire to teach your PSS to somebody else's kid, or maybe your twenty-something cousin with the dirty hat and old Homelite that is less able with the saw than your twelve-year-old kid. Try to remember that no matter who is watching you, one of your own, or some neighborhood kid looking out a window, you are teaching every observer, every time you run the saw! You'll get to a point where you won't be able to tolerate anyone doing something outside the rules, in *any* cutting area; that's when you'll know you are an ethical teacher; that and the fact that you can safely and efficiently demonstrate what you teach verbally.

...and Learn

I learned most of what I know about running a chainsaw from other operators, and from many different trees. Experience is, indeed, the best teacher. The only thing that really makes a person a student is to receive information from another entity that answers a question and provides an opportunity to *affirm* the *confirmation* of knowledge by experiencing it, validating the truth in it, and building a successful picture in their minds. I suppose it would follow that to be a good student, one must keep asking questions, and keep trying to improve. Being a good student is easy for those surrounded by operators with higher levels of K&E who have been in the CSS forever, but it is difficult to be a student when surrounded by newbies; unless you are trying to learn the best way to teach a particular student, the intersection of the spectrums of K and E are much too complex to easily negotiate. How do you effect your SP? How do you effect the cutting crew? Do you know the cutting abilities of each person you cut with? Do you add cohesion to the crew? Can you correct someone without sounding condescending? Can you take an order from someone with less experience just because they happen to be operating the saw? Can you bring another to a place where their K = E? Can you swallow your pride enough to allow your student to discover the answer themselves by actually operating the saw?

If you cut in the woods around your property with your spouse or other family member as your SP, you may find it difficult to integrate the CSS teacher, with your PSS as a student; you must be both the teacher and the student first, and a relative second; emotional ties within your PSS can introduce risk into your CSS. Fear mechanisms in the brain are more pronounced when we are dealing with coworkers we are close to, and anger issues many times are quick to surface; anger chemicals in the brain released over time equal stress. You might find yourself talking to yourself with harsh words; you need to find a mental "trick" to help you "tone it down" when communicating with your student in this situation; try to make your brain act rationally and subjectively. This is a difficult mind game that is looked upon as strange by some because it involves "talking to yourself" in a voice you will remember, preferably under your breath, then immediately flipping to a quiet calm voice for your loved one. You can't let them hear the apprehension you may be feeling; that just spreads stress. Talking to yourself is normal; we all do it. The secret to using it as a progressive teaching/learning aid is never to lie to yourself or another PSS; the best way to ensure that is to use the established and accepted truth in the thought processes and rules of the CSS when you speak in that whispering voice of student to student, with the CSS as your common teacher. You must force yourself to "do it right," be a *nice* member of the CSS; be on your best behavior. My wife has worked with me on many occasions; she even volunteered for the Forest Service as my SP and swamper; I've found through experience and adaptation of my PSS, and now pass it to you as K&E that the husband/wife interpersonal relationship does not fit well in the CSS; if you tend to yell at yourself when you find you're not setting the brake, you can't teach your SP with the same enthusiasm; you need to let your SP teach themselves also. The husband and wife must become the operator and the safety person when in the cutting area—two professionals, two coworkers in the CSS; no worries, no stress; stop and smell the roses once in a while; you'll like it!

Verbalize and Demonstrate

The best way to teach a lower K&E operator is first to be efficient with the CSS yourself; then show them by example. This example will imprint positive images in their brain, and give you a chance to show off your natural talent. Start with simple tasks like cutting one-inch wafers off the end of a well-supported log, or doing simple limbing on a standing tree and then a down tree; they should be activities that help build experience in small increments. Be sure to teach the rules that apply to the activity before beginning. Comment truthfully about your students' abilities, and stop the learner in a safe pre-planned manner if you notice practices that do not follow the rules. Try that sandwich method: 1) Tell them something they are doing well for the top piece of bread; 2) Point out the error, and if it is a flagrant rule violation, do another verbalize and demonstrate (V&D) for the meat of the teaching; and 3) Finish with the bottom piece of bread, a slap on the back and a compliment on someday being able to cut for the entire family. Of course, if you are in the back forty and your SP doesn't run the saw, you are going to have to learn how to compliment and correct yourself in a similar manner so it sticks in your brain—that's not an easy thing to do for some people, but you'll get used to it if you're a beginner yourself.

When I first started training my mind and body to follow the rules, I thought of building an ass-kicking machine for when I caught myself going against the rules, since my old man, who filled the role naturally, isn't around anymore, but I found that yelling at myself out loud with his voice works well for remembering my mistakes; plus, it's not as painful, and doesn't look quite as bad as pulling a string connected to a boot. Is it crazy to talk to yourself out loud? Yes, but only when you're telling yourself to do something insane. The point is: Make it a big issue to yourself or to your student. Don't let either a mistake or a job well-done go away without the recognition needed to make it something that will be remembered next time. You must mentally convince your brain to ignore the chemical reactions of fear and stress brought on by your common sense and instinct in order to purposely do something dangerous. In the CSS, we turn that brain function around; that chemical reaction is associated with a particular set of neurons firing in the brain, imprinted in our instantly recallable action; we call it a habit. The system only makes good habits that are to our benefit; we force our brain to collect the most pertinent information to condition our muscles, to memorize the safest method by any means available. Even if you have to shut off the saw, put it down, and start over when you catch yourself starting it outside the rule, you have to make a BIG deal out of it!

Go/No-Go Option

Every operator must have and exercise the right to stop cutting whenever they feel they are not comfortable with what they see coming. Without this fundamental principle, behavioral safety and, therefore, the PSS will not be effective for making the operator safer; the operator will never get better unless they learn to identify all work processes through which they cannot foresee a safe path. Whenever a No-Go is encountered, the reason for halting the work should be clearly stated, and all members in the cutting area should discuss the best course forward; this may involve helping the current operator resolve their concerns, changing operators to a more experienced member, or even going outside the cutting area for help. Most of the time, resolving a situation that stops the operator from continuing in the direction originally planned is simple; it just requires some thought and slight variations in the plan. The evaluation and subsequent change in the plan should be verbalized to other members before proceeding; this is a good teaching experience because everybody must be a teacher and a student. This is where a good SP is very valuable to an operator; usually when the SP needs to stop the operator while actually cutting, it's because the SP saw a No-Go that the operator missed; a No-Go for the SP is automatically a No-Go for the operator, or the SP loses their definition.

Every No-Go requires either contemplation in the operator's mind, communication with the SP to determine the best way to change the plan, or halting the cutting—what the system calls Mid-Action Mitigation. Most of these communications are made with simple gestures or body language, like a spousal SP waving her arms and jumping up and down; then you've got yourself a No-Go! Here's a piece of advice to husbands, based on personal experience. In this situation, she is your SP, not your wife; you are the operator, not her husband; talk to her respectfully as a coworker in the system, or next time she may just let you go! When the words "This is going to be a 'No-Go' for me" come out of your mouth, they are not a sign of weakness or inability; they are proof of an intelligence-based PSS working within the CSS; your concern is not just for you, but for others and the CSS.

What about the tree and the chainsaw—do they have Go, No-Go options? You bet they do, as determined by their physical characteristics and the level of understanding you have of them. If you are expecting the tree to do something that must defy the laws of physics, or you are asking the saw to do things it is not intended by its design to do, no matter how detailed a plan you may have in mind, actually working through the plan is an attempt to do the impossible: the ultimate No-Go.

The Five Rules Rule

Since the CSS is based on behavioral safety, it must have rules to define what the desired behavior is. "Rules" here is a plural noun indicating there are many possible behaviors to control. "Rule" can also be a verb, indicating that the behavior, selected as the desired safest action, is governed by how much ethical authority each saw operator expresses by their obedience. The rules define the statistically safest actions to take while attempting to accommodate the many changing variables involved in manipulating a large woody plant with a chainsaw; they set a nearly unattainable goal of optimum performance; they form a picture in a thinking mind of what perfect looks like, but only the operator's voluntary compliance with the rules offers any chance of delivering the best-case scenario for continued wellbeing in a dangerous situation.

Each operator must use the rules for self-governance; each has to make themselves adhere to them; each has to carefully observe every other operator to compare their current locations on the broad spectrum of safe operating. It's more than team work; it's more like a reverence we all hold for the agreement we made before we walked together into the cutting area. It's knowing what each other is thinking about, and having an understanding that each has the other's best interests in mind, because we behave ourselves by adherence to the same pre-established rules; we demonstrate our allegiance to the safety of all by that behavior.

It's no secret that jobs in this country are rapidly being impacted and even eliminated by technological automation and artificial intelligence. Many jobs are disappearing forever, replaced by computer software programs and the robots that use them—one application removing many people. I wonder how long it will be before a robot can take a digital assignment to go along the edge of a forest road and remove all the hazard trees without itself becoming a hazard. I believe the chainsaw as it exists today is around to stay, despite the number of people who get injured operating it. After all, how much will it cost me to have a tree-cutting robot delivered to my house to have a tree removed from my driveway? I think a "CSS member" entry on a resume will become more and more valuable if things continue to trend as they are. The intelligence in the CSS cannot be artificial; it must be a mix of a PSS with the CSS. The PSS is a human personality; the CSS is self-manipulated intelligence.

Picture the Facts

- Safety is a frame of mind around a picture of practice
- Procedural regiment applied to practical application (System)
- Aim for Perfect; then adjust
- Personal Safety Attitude
- Know and Extend Limitations

Slide 13: Picture the Facts

PICTURE THE FACTS

THIS SLIDE ESSENTIALLY CAPTURES MY Personal Safety System (PSS). There are other elements to it, and as I understand what's happening in my head, there are new ones being developed all the time, but these are the highlights. My PSS is a mental tool with the main purpose of getting my head right; it's not an easy mental task to remember broad concepts so they are available for immediate recall. Memorization techniques developed by people a lot smarter than me have been the single subject matter of some pretty thick books. I know that my brain, like yours, works with pictures, stories, anecdotes, and the like, so I borrow concepts from other parts of my life that are, for whatever reason, important to me, and build CSS concepts into them while I practice my PSS. The PSS is never complete; since every project is unique, it offers new learning experiences.

My brain can't download data like a computer; I actually need to watch myself succeed at an activity over and over to etch that data in a rapid recall area of my brain, a.k.a.:

gray matter. I know my brain functions not only with the electrical firing of neurons like the 1s and 0s in a hard-drive, but also by the chemical reactions in the synapses—almost like little pieces of software programmed by a repeated practice. The PSS is my overt attempt to utilize this simple memorization method for application to complex and dangerous procedures; when used properly, you will find that you can train your brain to confidently approach and analyze your way through a high-risk activity by just collecting the data into your program. The CSS provides the parameters for the collection of good data. (Like the data collector I use while surveying!)

Let's look now at each of the concepts on the slide that makes up my PSS.

Safety Is a Frame of Mind Around a Picture of Practice

I was lying in bed one night somewhere between sleep and awake when a picture popped into my brain: a picture of a picture hanging on a wall. It's a framed picture of me running the chainsaw. The four sides of the square frame are the first four rules of the CSS. It is made of fine wood: mahogany or teak; it is intricately carved, inlaid with turquoise and mother-of-pearl. I'm very reluctant to change it, and I would be very upset if you insisted on taking your knife and carving on it; I like it the way it is. I have learned to trust the frame to draw attention to the picture it holds. I might be willing to change it—perhaps carve in a new detail you have taught me, a new rule that makes the dangerous activity even safer, drill a small hole, and push in your pearl of wisdom. Before I do that, though, I would take the pearl to have it appraised so I could tell others of its value. The backing on the picture, perhaps even the wall the picture hangs on, is the fifth rule: a wall in my PSS room for anyone in the CSS house to see, holding the picture up at eye level; it's the authority on which it hangs while it stimulates conversation about the picture's meaning. Danger, fear, apprehension, and confusion are outside the house, but it's quite comfortable inside.

The picture in the frame is of me, the last time I cut with the saw, or worked as a safety person for someone else; look, I have all my functional personal protective equipment (PPE) on, all the rules have been properly followed, there's a smile behind that face shield, and I'm proud of my product, so I display the picture in a prominent place for all to see; I pat myself on the back for a safe job well done. If, however, the last time I ran the saw, I caught myself breaking some of the rules for the sake of expediency, or from an unwillingness to step out and defend my PSS, the tree didn't fall where I expected, or maybe it sat back on the saw, a bad picture is now in the frame for all in the CSS to see; now I've got to find another cutting project so I can make a new and better picture worthy of that beautiful frame.

If you are a new operator, recall the picture of the operator I asked you to stare at a few slides back. Put yourself in that PPE with a good stance while holding the saw properly, and use that picture of yourself operating the saw as a goal for your PSS. This can also be a good mental tool for operators who have gained all their experience and knowledge outside the CSS, and their current PSS needs to be touched up to make it look like the guy in the slide—maybe buy some new chaps and a hard hat to improve your image.

Procedural Regiment Applied to Practical Application (a System)

The mental picture I use with this system concept is a line of soldiers standing, "toe the line," at attention. They are all dressed in the same desert-camo uniform; they all have the same gear, in the same location on their body; they have all had the same training, and they understand how their unique role complements the mission and adds to its success; they are a regiment. If something works, they try to do it the exact same way every time; they blend in with the troop. If the enemy should infiltrate the ranks, he would be immediately recognized and eliminated. Once the planned mission has been accepted, each soldier is an important ingredient for success, or they would not be there; they know each other from past missions, so much in fact that they often communicate without sound; a hand gesture or a particular look holds meaning for the entire patrol. If you were to ask one of these brave men and women in service to their country why they do it, they would tell you they do it for patriotism; they keep the soldier next to them safe by overcoming the enemy; they have a system they all agree on.

Aim for Perfect; Then Adjust

I got this picture story from a statistics class lecture on random and systematic error. The instructor told us that all measurement contains error because clumsy humans can't consistently reach perfection because of the system we function in: earth. He was explaining the difference between accuracy and precision and used a picture to demonstrate the point. (Actually, this is where I started using the mental picture method as a memorization technique back in school; the picture subsequently became part of my PSS.) He said, "You're at the shooting range, sighting in your 30-06 for deer season; you put a target up 100 yards downrange with a bullseye and eccentric rings. Where do you put the cross-hairs in the scope? The center of the bullseye! You fire three carefully held shots, and they all land in a tight group low and to the right; the gun is precise, but not accurate; you adjust the screws on the scope up and left, and fire three more shots; they all land in the center. How did you know how much to adjust the scope? You wouldn't know if you hadn't first aimed for the center of the bull."

How do I use this jewel of wisdom while running the chainsaw? When a tree is faced in the direction of the fall, a notch is cut out of the side of the tree with two cuts that *must* meet; if I want to visualize what the completed cut will look like, I say to myself, "Aim for Perfect." I make the cut, then see how much one cut missed the ending point of the other, and create an adjustment in my action to make them meet; I might always aim a little high! When I drop a large diameter tree, I want it to hit the ground in a controlled location at a controlled time; where do I aim the tree? I aim at the *exact* spot and time; I might even imagine a target at the spot where I want the center of the crown to land; then I squeeze the trigger.

Let the control for systematic error do its work. The chainsaw is the rifle, you are the scope and the trigger, and your product is the hole in the target at the center of the bulls-eye. These are the parts of a system to make sure you make a killing shot on the buck, or see a falling tree hit the mark before it happens.

Personal Safety Attitude

My dad was a master sergeant in the National Guard. When I was twelve, my younger brother and I thought he had this really impressive uniform. My younger brother and I had some rudimentary job in the backyard that my mother had assigned us while dad was on a detail; of course, we did a fair amount of complaining about working while the other kids were free. We were standing there holding up our shovels when Dad suddenly appeared at the sand pile in his fancy uniform; of course, he had been given a thorough debriefing from Mom about our stubbornness in performing the work. I looked up to see his stern face as he said, "Boy, you better change your attitude." He went on to elaborate for several tense minutes before turning and walking away. I found myself very confused; was that man my dad, or was he a drill sergeant? Do I have to take orders from the military now? Then it occurred to me that it did not matter which role he was in; my attitude was always the problem when it came to complaining and lack of performance; I *never* once heard him say, "Boy, I need to change my attitude to cover for your screwups" when I ignored his authority. His uniform was legal authority to me; his being my dad was ethical authority; either way, I was subject to both if I wanted to live in his house, so it was my attitude that needed to change if I were to get the work done and go play.

Today, when a teacher calls me back to the system with correction, I see my dad in that uniform; that picture is the CSS in the flesh, and I adjust my attitude to accommodate it. I put the damn chaps on; my fancy uniform as the authority of the system insists on it without question. When I was twelve, I behaved myself to demonstrate my respect for the family as the oldest son. Did all these thought processes actually take place in my mind at the time? Maybe, maybe not; the point is I use this "picture show" to trick my brain into thinking this is very important to me, and it always believes me! When I see that picture of my dad in that uniform, it changes my attitude into one I can live with in the CSS.

The PSS acronym is a "picture the facts" element using letters. When you live in a place most of your life that is referred to as the U.P. (Upper Peninsula of Michigan), you learn to talk in acronyms; they become a valuable tool for recalling large amounts of information along with the simplest mental picture—a written word, a set of letters in particular order, capital or small. A PSS is a very important part of the CSS; they are the blocks in the foundation that come in twos: an operator PSS and a SP PSS. But they cannot be a foundational principle since the true definition of a PSS must include the entire personal safety attitude back to the early childhood of the individual to be an effective tool for monitoring the true level of behavioral safety. They must be something that grows into the CSS by a free will, ethical response to other people in the cutting area. They are the *individual's* foundational principles, checked against the system principles by the other PSSs in the CSS for validity, inclusion, and education.

Know and Extend Limitations

One of the primary reasons for chainsaw accidents of all types is the tendency of operators of all knowledge and experience levels to take on more than they are able to safely negotiate—that could be a definition of an accident. This picture is Dirty Harry saying, "Man's got to know his limitations," as he's watching the consequences of a bad cop operating outside the system. When I'm standing next to my saw with my eyes skyward, sizing up a very complex drop, I will sometimes actually hear those words spoken in my mind. Just because I have knowledge of an action does not mean I can do it safely; just because I have successfully executed an action in the past does not mean I know what I'm doing this time. Repeating an action, like a system rule or a particular cut with increased complexity by small segments of difficulty and obtaining a safe outcome each time, adds clarity to a mental picture, just like adding more pixels makes HD TV clearer. Carefully planned practice within the rules is the best way to extend limitations. Never stop practicing toward better. Even if you've been running a saw for thirty years, don't think you have a better way than the system to get to a place you've never been; keep practicing toward a safer, more productive outcome for the CSS, while watching out for your unique No-Go. Whenever the saw is in your hands, look at that action as extending your limitations; after all, if you are operating within the CSS, you are Dirty Harry, not the bad cop. Was Harry speaking about his boss's limitations, or was he reassuring himself that he would set the timer again for the good of the profession? (YouTube: "Dirty Harry A Man's Got to Know His Limitations")

As I said, all these elements are a part of my mental PSS; they address particular problems in my cutting career that I foresaw as a source of potential accidents; I had a problem at times with losing sight of the big picture; I would work with production as a goal rather than safety; then I saw a problem for me supporting my family from a hospital bed, so I had to change that picture into a productive and safe worker, saw in hand. When I started surveying, I was supplied with lots of equipment, and a truck. I found that having "a place for everything, and everything in its place" in the back of the truck saved lots of time. I realized the redundancy and data checks incorporated into survey methodology not only worked to make me a more meticulous measurer of the land, but they could be applied to safer chainsaw work when the same principles and ethics were applied to that part of the job. I always had the tendency to work too fast in an attempt to set a new production record; then I would get sloppy, and I discovered that it was at those times that I would have more close calls—ones where I sometimes had to sit and settle myself for a while, or cut my saw out of a log with the other saw from the truck a mile away; any increase in production was lost.

I found it more efficient and safer to concentrate on precision as I always demanded of myself in the surveying system. Sometimes in firefighting applications, I had stress-building situations with my personal safety attitude. I would allow some "jerk" crew boss to use his legal authority to command ethical authority over me while running the saw. When he would order me to do something dangerous, I found that pointing out the difference in the fire-fighting system and my CSS was usually adequate for me to convince him to allow me to operate within my PSS limitations, get someone else to cut the tree, or chink line around it. Most of the time while cutting survey lines, I was the only operator; to get the line cut on schedule as stipulated by my boss, I often extended my limitations to a point just this side of injury. I had to think about those limitations every time I cut, so I made it an issue in my PSS.

Of course, you can use these elements in your PSS if you want; by buying this book, you bought them. But try to build your own stories and pictures that are near and dear to you as you progress with your training; how you use the peculiar mental processes of the human brain in your favor is completely between you and your PSS; you are the only one who knows and owns them; that is, of course, until you start teaching a safety person, or working with other operators; that's when you will share your unique PSS, your distinctive talent, and your support for the CSS; your simple mental pictures will contain hours of teachable material; the right picture says more than a thousand words.

> You know what a quantum leap is, right? A quantum leap is when you mention quantum leaps in a book about chainsaw safety. If you think about it, and you grasped what was in the text above, you'll realize you saw this topic coming—the reasoning behind the concept, the messages between the images. Our entire existence is based on leaps of perception; for example, the first "moving pictures" were a series of pictures on a stack of cards; when you thumb and fan the deck, it puts motion to the picture, especially when there are lots of cards, and each picture differs only slightly from the previous one. Now, take that visual picture, and add sound, taste, touch, and smell; each one is a moving projection in its own sense, and they must all complement each other to make sense—to maintain a plot for the movie. This is your PSS, you behaving. It happens without making it happen; if we have all our faculties, the pictures are completely based on how we interpret what we are seeing, and we control that with attention to our attitude details. Helen Keller couldn't see or hear, but she learned to communicate; she saw pictures and "drew" them on her teacher's hand. A chainsaw operator usually has all their faculties available to tell the story (movie) of a tree falling to others who have no such picture available to recall; that's the bad news, actually; the good news is that each individual has the mental capacity to manipulate their own brain into thinking, *This is the best movie ever*, while leaping from still picture to still picture; all recalled in proper order. (Stories just like the one I just put in your brain that you will recall in the future; when quantum leap is mentioned, all this information will instantly jump into your consciousness as a moving picture with no leaps. (Whaaaat? Hey, I just write this stuff; it's up to you to understand it.)

Train Your Brain

- Situational Awareness
- Analysis of Complexity
- Risk Analysis and Mitigation
- Plan the Work – Work the Plan
- Logic and Common Sense?

Slide 14: Train Your Brain

TRAIN YOUR BRAIN

A REQUIREMENT FOR ALL FIREFIGHTERS in the FS is to attend a full day "annual refresher." To keep the subject matter focused on safety, a major theme is selected for the instructors of the various topics to base their presentations on. The first four bullets in this slide are from those training sessions over several years. The basic courses S130 and S190 taught the procedures, concepts, and best practices for all beginning firefighters, but when it came to highlighting safety in later years, these kinds of subjects were chosen as the most important in the refreshers, and they all had to do with how a person uses their brain. Knowing how a dangerous activity can safely be conducted, or even safely conducting the activity, will not make future attempts safer unless the brain successfully negotiates the various challenges encountered; if the questions born from the scares and near misses are not adequately answered during each encounter with danger as it happens, the result must be diminished confidence, increased apprehension, and thus, less safety. Sugarcoating it, refusing to think about it, or dismissing it as a one-time thing will not work if the endeavor is to use the WMDH the rest of your healthy life.

The only remedy for a lack of mental preparation is: You have to see the danger coming! You have to "train your brain" on what to look for, how to figure it out, and how to deal with it, in the present situation, your current here and now, whatever "it" is, such as an app for your brain pertaining to each particular element of danger or concern. This is not something you can just read about, or try once in a while; it must become your new best pastime, in all aspects of your life, in all activities, whether they involve danger or not. Practice vigilance; trust me, it will make your life much more enjoyable; you must take your eyes and ears off the screens and give attention to what is around you. You will know when you are properly educating yourself about your world because the word "bored" will be removed forever from your vocabulary; you will find yourself watching out for the wellbeing of everyone who happens to be fortunate enough to be under your watchful eye, whether in your cutting area, under your dome, or in your venue. When you have become good at this, and have learned how it is best applied in dangerous situations and activities, chainsaw operation (and life in general for a very smart few) will become a welcome challenge that you have fun with! You will become the truest form of a "first responder."

During one of my seminars, I noticed how many times I was repeating the first three bullets. I decided there were too many words to say to bring my students back to the subject; then this acronym suddenly jumped into my mind: SAACRAM (I immediately decided it would be pronounced sack'-rum.) If you look at the elements, you'll see how I came up with it; I was just trying to have a little fun, and it stuck; it became part of my PSS, and since I'm the teacher, also the CSS. SAACRAM stands for:

Situational
Awareness,
Analysis of
Complexity, and
Risk
Analysis and
Mitigation

SAACRAM is simply knowledge and experience brain development tools or "programs" in your PSS; they are what you educate yourself with on your own time; they are what you bring as your unique talent and ability to the CSS. Your ability to accurately evaluate the small parts of the big picture will get better each time you practice it; each time you "play the game," where the screen is everything around you, your score is your SAACRAM! The chainsaw is to the operator what SAACRAM is to your brain. SAACRAM is to your PSS what the chainsaw is to the CSS. Stay with me here; this gets better! You have a scoreboard in this; a brain game with a progress report; it's the fourth bullet: Plan the Work, Work the Plan (PWWP). How much your "Work the Plan" is like your

"Plan the Work" is a truthful and reliable evaluation of how good your SAACRAM is. Your PWWP paints a picture of you exercising your SAACRAM; you already know what to do with that picture, right? (Frame it in the rules, and hang it on your PSS wall.)

Now let's turn to looking at the various elements of SAACRAM in detail.

Situational Awareness (SAACRAM)

SA is exactly what the words say it is; it is the mental information consciously collected by the brain to accurately interpret and negotiate the elements of the current surroundings. Since every item in the present contains information, the brain's different lobes must learn how to prioritize memorized information, compare it to present information, and then use that new deduced and evaluated data to identify the significance of each object based on its influence to aid or alter the desired path through the environment presented as reality. Perfecting this ability is an ongoing life process that can be practiced in safe, controlled locations; it can be practiced on items or actions of very low risk first, then confidently and naturally applied to higher risk situations; it becomes part of *your* common sense, instinct, reflex action, and ability to instantly select the best first response. In a healthy and safe person's life with good SAACRAM, no matter how benign or how dangerous a situation is, the ability to "see all" (identify the significance of the various elements of the surroundings, and evaluate the risks they present in reality) becomes second nature; it becomes ordinary work from which many would run away screaming.

I first witnessed some of these super-humans on the fire-line; on one particular occasion, two crews were starting a burnout; a guy on the Type 1 crew came on the radio and calmly said, "We got some fifty-foot flame lengths here in the burn, just south of the rock outcrop about fifty yards out; they look like they're trying to curl over on top and come back in the canopy. You might want to have those people in that area follow us up the line for a spell." No exclamation mark! His brain obviously has a more refined method of dealing with adrenaline than mine, or maybe adrenaline was not being produced in his brain at all! I said to myself, "How do I get where he is?" His reaction had nothing to do with advanced education or experience as a smoke jumper; it was all about *understanding* what he was looking at—an understanding gained by paying close attention to what was being recorded in his brain and why, at all times. We can't always control the brain's chemical reactions, but if we learn to recognize them for what they really are, we can learn to think calmly and rationally in any situation, even in one where an inexperienced brain sees a great threat. "Always practice SAACRAM." It is the best method for building confidence in the understanding that your PSS is built on; it provides your brain instant access to a practiced behavior that decreases stress when you enter the cutting area.

Now that you are determined to play, try this SAACRAM mind game for yourself: What's the best way to apply it to chainsaw operation? Once I became a firefighter, I thought like a firefighter, even when I was not assigned to a fire; when I became a surveyor, I became a professional, not just at work, but all the time. A question always on my mind was: What information is there in what I am currently doing that would be useful in future survey or fireline work? I would trick my brain by telling it that some minor discovery of how a fire burned up the side of a leaf pile was a great and powerful revelation of fire behavior, or perhaps play a little with the flames—attempt to predict the outcome of various scenarios for mountain topography, like a kid would do; in doing that, I was training my brain for dangerous activity, in a controlled low-danger "playtime." I wanted to be a good surveyor, so I never walked past a boundary marker or failed to carefully examine every map or plat I happened to run across; it became second nature to explore all information in search of the most pertinent.

Of course, we all want to be the best chainsaw operator we can be in the CSS, so you will find yourself looking at that gnarly old tree, that storm-damaged, tangled mess of trees on your forty, or that pulp cord of firewood in the backyard as a place to just walk around practicing your SA, perhaps without even having a chainsaw in the picture. My game has turned into always looking as far as I can see in all directions, even far beyond what would be the cutting area, and then bringing my attention in to where I'm standing while trying to recognize each individual object in between; any one thing that is unusual will be instinctively highlighted by your memorized brain data as you proceed 360 degrees, then up and down. (If you've ever still-hunted for deer, and snuck up on a buck while doing it, you know how to do this already.) I give myself a test by asking myself hypothetical questions like: How would I cut down that giant ugly tree? What is beneath the bark at waist height? Which side of the tree has the most big branches? Which branches add the most cantilever effect? Which way would the tree fall if it just suddenly fell over by itself? Would it reach that fence if it fell that way? What is that discoloration on the bark? Why is it dead only on the top? How would I look at this cutting area if I had a D25 dozer to work with? How about if I had ropes and a come-along? How about if I had just a saw and a helper? I may have done all that "chainsaw brain" exercising in just a few minutes while staring at a tree outside my wife's doctor's office; I also gathered lots of SA about the parking lot and the area around the building; all that useful information when I could have been sitting in the car playing a kid's game on my phone, deceiving my brain into thinking it is invincible, and when I "die," I just push "new game."

When you get good at this, the size of your cutting area is very flexible; it can be as small as the area around the saw, so when you actually do pick up the saw, it will become a single unit in your tree-size cutting area—a single tool made up of many properly working parts, each of which you will have information on already stored in your memory, because you examined each individual part when you inspected it and cleaned it, then took the smallest and fastest moving part of it and sharpened it like a razor. (You'll know what each tooth of the chain looks like. Naming each one may be going a little too far; they should look pretty much all alike, but marking one with a flat file as the "first one" may be useful; maybe name just that one, and extend the same SAACRAM respect to all!)

Analysis of Complexity (SA**AC**RAM)

This is not "analysis paralysis"; it's "analysis stimulus." Information about how something works can only make you freeze if you don't have it, or you see it and don't understand it. Many people say there are only two reactions to fear: fight or flight; that is not true; there is also freeze, faith, and figure it out.

AC has a lot to do with prowess (defined as exceptional valor, bravery, or ability, especially in combat or battle) in the CSS. The only way you can confidently take on a dangerous endeavor while considering the wellbeing of all present is if you have an experience and knowledge base in physics, chemistry, engineering, and electrical concepts. Does this mean you need a college education to safely operate a chainsaw? Obviously not, because accidents happen just as much with educated people, who are more likely to overestimate their powers of observation. College teaches the origins, principles, mathematics, and definitions needed to communicate the complicated concepts of what is right in front of you when you pick up the saw; fortunately, while running the saw, you only need to communicate these natural abilities from one part of your brain to another, as if one side of your brain were debating the other. Even if you had an app for that, it would only be as useful as your level of prowess, which can only be achieved from repeated successful executions of an activity that consistently removes or negates the risk.

It's all in the do, done, and did! You need to be able to see things in your present situation for the forces they contain *right now*—what they can realistically do to you, your saw, and the tree—not only on what they have done to you in the past or by their current orientation; this tree is different, if only because it is the current *do*. You need to understand, for example, that a motionless dead branch stuck in a tree has weight and speed waiting in it to be released; it contains potential energy as indicated by your observation of its condition, location, and understanding of gravity; you need to understand that the tree is doing work by holding that massive branch up; that if you make the tree stop its work and drop the branch, that F = ma [force (F) acting on an object is equal to the mass (m) of an object times its acceleration (a)]. In other words, the longer it drops, the more energy you get when that energy becomes kinetic energy, which will have the capability to *do* work on your head. You need to see the forces in your cutting area for what they are—not a formula necessarily, but as with all brain issues, a picture can definitely help make the complexity simpler and recallable when it counts, in your instinctual analysis of the dangers, risks, hazards, and concerns. A good picture to have is how it did the work last time a similar event took place, but that will not make you progressively safer if you did not understand the physics involved the first time. It will become instinct when it is part of your everyday thought processes; it will become instantly recallable by the pictures of success you have formed in your brain.

It's only with repetitive mental practice that reliable physical ability comes; every time your finger pulls the trigger must be considered practice at predicting. Estimate the reaction in your mini-size up; make the cut while watching the kerf (the void the chain creates in the wood); watch the reaction of the wood to see how well you saw it coming; and store that information in your special picture story called SAACRAM. Prowess operating on false information is a lie; it's insanity; it leads to failure and injury; prowess operating on understanding can look crazy to an untrained eye, but that doesn't make the action any less effective at promoting safety because the whole thing is a brain game—what some call intelligence.

As you look around the situation you are in, your awareness should include "how things work." Young or inexperienced people should not attempt complex cutting because the source of the answers to How?, Why?, How much?, and How fast? don't have enough established successful safe history to formulate the best response to what their senses perceive; in other words, they lack "common sense"; it's why you need to watch your young'uns so they don't walk out into the street. They don't have a recallable set of data in their brain that allows them to understand the forces they are dealing with. If you are a beginning operator, you may have the same problem with the saw and the tree; if you are an experienced, healthy operator who does not look at things based on AC, all I can say is either you've been lucky, or there is someone or something stopping you from proceeding with what you want to do. It could also be that you have learned to live with stress, a.k.a., bad saacram (small letters = no savvy/prowess, inevitable bad picture coming) while cutting.

The chainsaw is rather complex mechanically, so maybe we should include a maintenance course in the complexity; trees are made of wood, a very complex natural material for which I have a degree of understanding, so maybe I should write a book titled *Wood Engineering for Chainsaw Operators*, but none of that is needed; you have better options; you can ask your teacher in the CSS, or you can go on the internet to learn all the college-type information you will ever need, as you need it. If you don't have internet at home, go to a library and ask the help desk how to find information on "how things work"; take a look at some YouTube videos; search for "Chainsaw Fails," which are usually best for showing you what *can* go wrong, but, of course, can only teach how *not* to do it.

Practice AC as part of your SAACRAM; don't walk by a construction site without figuring out what they are doing; whenever you get the chance, watch others cut when you are not involved, and try to anticipate the result before it happens. The problem with this game is that as a CSS member, you may be forced to step in and start teaching when you see a fail is inevitable. Beginners can practice handling techniques without the saw running and realize what complexity is addressed by the various handling rules; be sure to put your personal protective equipment on; maybe go where you won't be seen, like when you're practicing your dance moves. Experienced operators may have a harder time with these types of concepts regarding the brain function, particularly if they have remained safe during the garnering of that experience; remember the close calls, and try to keep yourself within the rules by considering which close calls in your history would not have happened if you had been better at seeing forceful surprises before they happened. Your brain has the ability to understand complex issues even if you don't know how to communicate them to others; it's in your DNA. The problem is that waiting until you are actually cutting to gain understanding does little to make you safer. You must train your brain before you attempt a complex action at your level of K&E.

The videos you watch on chainsaw safety, the books you read on chainsaw safety systems, and even the teacher you watch cut over and over will only increase your knowledge. Your experience can't suddenly catch up with your knowledge level by starting with a complex cut; K&E must be balanced in increments, one safe step at a time; it takes more time for your muscles to "memorize" an action than it does for your brain. Your physical ability is the subject of the picture; your brain only captures an image of it. Don't make the cut until you have a "picture of success" so you can confidently predict what the reaction of the cut will be. (So if you bought this book to help you figure out how to safely cut down that big ugly tree in your backyard and save the $1,500 that the tree service wants, that tree will have to wait until you build your PSS through practice, in simple steps of increasing complexity; perhaps begin with some smaller jobs around it.)

Risk Analysis and Mitigation (SAAC<u>RAM</u>)

RAM is a fun one; over the years, it has become one of my favorite brain games. If you think about what life on this planet really is, you will agree that everything contains risk; in this existence, there is no such thing as zero risk, nor is there such a thing as 100 percent risk, except when a risk actually meets the subject that it threatens—what we call an accident! So think of risk as ranging from 1 to 99 percent in any single object in your environment; risk exists in moving things, things making loud noises, maybe a foul smell; they give a warning sign of some kind that draws your attention; your instinct kicks in, and your common sense dictates a response based on your knowledge and experience pertaining to that object or those similar to it; many different people can observe the same object, and it can present a different level of risk to each. Risks can be high level and static; they can give no warning of their existence; they can be moving with a highly probable trajectory to raise or lower the level; they can be mistakenly identified, or disregarded as low risk because they don't command the usual reflex or compensatory action. This is why RAM must be part of your SAACRAM. You see the item; you understand the complexity of the risk as it pertains to your individual, unique brain and body; only then can you find the best way to stop the risk from negatively affecting you or others around you.

If risks were simple to see and mentally process, their mitigation would not require a system with rules; they are very complex since they come in groups of varying degrees of severity; they can come several at once—a higher percentage risk that carries no warning can be overlooked by lower risk with sudden impactful warnings, or a lack of noticeable risks can lull one into a sense of secure action; how can they possibly be dealt with using my "common sense"? Many risks in cutting a tree are *under the bark*, invisible to the eye, but relatable to similar indications of their presence in past experience. The good news is that risks can be anticipated, their increase averted, or a prebuilt barrier placed on their line of trajectory. (Did someone say safety equipment?) You can train your brain to be good at dealing with risk by never leaving even the simplest risk unmitigated in your everyday life; if your SAACRAM identifies a quick solution to negate a risk, don't walk past it; if you see a small round rock on a sidewalk and it pops into your mind that someone could step on it and roll their ankle, tell yourself in a strict voice, "Move it!" How many examples are there? I don't know; look around. Can you find them where you are right now? Take a SAACRAM walk through your here and now; keep your head on a swivel of casual observation for hidden information; find the highest and least risk item in your sight; try to identify hidden risks in the objects you see; combine two things of low risk to see if they could together form a high level risk. Life is all about analysis and mitigation of risk; the ones that hurt you physically are always found in the present; if you train your brain to identify risks and your body to mitigate them, you will already have the ability to thoughtfully do so when you enter the dangerous activity of running a chainsaw. Put down your cellphone for a while; take your eyes off the screen, and enter the environment around you with your brain training session; you will find it much more fun than playing some kid's video game. Try it for a while; you'll like it, and it will make your life much more interesting; when you get good at mitigation of risk, you will find that people start coming to you asking where something is they can't find, or how to approach particular problems because you always seem to come up with good solutions; that is the brain function you must bring out of your cutting area, as you confidently look for another. The ultimate PPE is in my brain; it's my SAACRAM. I know I'm not going to get hurt while running a chainsaw; I wear the chaps and the hard hat for you!

Plan the Work, Work the Plan (PWWP)

PWWP is like the grading system for the student in you from the teacher in you; it is the evidence of how good your SAACRAM actually is; it is the education of your PSS. Most of the time, nobody knows how good you are at making sense of reality except you or someone you have cut with. The rules in the CSS, in practice, are a list of mandatory elements that must be included every time your plan of work involves touching the saw's chain to wood; remember, the ethical encompasses the legal. They become the common sense starting point for the thought process in your plan; working the plan will yield good results to the extent determined by the blending of your knowledge and experience levels at any particular task you plan to do. If you are an operator who only runs your saw once or twice a year after a windstorm, you can't wait until there's a tree over your driveway at 6:00 a.m. to learn how to plan your work; you need to be proficient at making plans and executing them before you need to run the saw. People who do this don't end up a statistic in the chainsaw injury studies; they train their brains at it until it becomes common practice, which elevates their common sense to an uncommon level.

Beginning now, start making PWs. Carry out the task; then evaluate how well you executed the WPs. Start with very simple activities that present a very small level of risk, and tell your brain that it is very important to get this right; like going to check the mail or take out the trash; then work your way up to more complex jobs, like changing a kitchen faucet, or changing the oil in your motorcycle. Start by developing a simple plan; then expand the plan and change it as you go, based on the information in the objects around you. You will be exercising your SA. Try to anticipate what forces are at work in what you see, your AC. What risks will be hidden in the complexity of the work, your RAM? Find the most significant risk in this task as you walk through it. When you are done with the activity, evaluate how well you planned the work, how well you worked the plan, and what happened that was different from what you foresaw. What did you miss, and how did it force you to change or reformulate your plan? Did you run into a No-Go, and why? I know what you're thinking, *All this to run a chainsaw?* To that I say, "No, all this to train your brain to a level where you have the ethical authority to exhibit to others what good SAACRAM looks like, no matter what you are doing, but especially while running a chainsaw." The work you are doing may be running the chainsaw, or simply carrying the equipment from the truck. It doesn't matter what the work is; you will be the teacher of how to get it done without anyone being hurt; you will be the ethical authority because SAACRAM will become "common" in your brain's left hemisphere.

Logic and Common Sense

I didn't always have this bullet on this slide; I added it because of a comment I got from one of my students, who said, "I already have a safety system; it's called 'common sense.'" I told him, "That comment is the exact reason why the safety system is needed, and why it helps only those who are willing to lay down their pride for the benefit of beginner saw operators; that line of thinking may be valid for an ordinary tool, but it is not for the most dangerous tool because it is also 'common' to be injured when operating one; two 'commons' mean that, statistically, you will eventually be injured if you don't start using your head for something besides telling everyone around you how 'good' you are with this 'manly' tool. Logical thought must be ever-changing to remain pertinent, based on facts you personally learned during practice. Your willpower to make rational positive changes to your behavior is very uncommon in the chainsaw world—it's uncommon to positively change what is common sense into confident PSS logical sense, your contribution to the CSS, your SAACRAM planning the work, and your practice of the rules working the plan. The CSS is based on common sense, but when you and your personal safety attitude are added to the picture, that makes it uncommon; I would even venture to say that makes it absolutely unique to you as a person holding the WMDH."

P.S. Here's an acronym definition that popped into my mind while thinking about SAACRAM:

SA = **SA**y something to yourself about what you're sensing.

AC = Understand the **AC**tion of the forces around you.

RAM = Investigate the **RAMifications** of your unique perception in the CSS perspective.

("Say 'Action Ramifications'" whenever you are conscious! Look at everything without concentrating on any one thing, until one thing draws special attention; just don't be freaked out if your brain likes this so much that it starts doing it while you are subconscious, i.e. dreaming; it's mentally calming.)

SA (Situational Awareness): I walk into a room, staring at my phone; somehow I automatically find a spot to put my butt. I have more SA of a place other than the one I'm in, through the cell tower, like down the rabbit hole. It may be very relevant to my here and now, but I really don't know if it is or not; I haven't even looked at the place I'm in. I just expect it to remain what I saw at first glance.

In SAACRAM, SAA (Situational Awareness Analysis): I walk into a room, staring at my phone, then slip it into my pocket. I make a general 360 scan of the room; if I'm the only one there, and I have some time, I look the room over. I look for any obvious risks; if there are none apparent, I proceed with my inspection of every single thing in the room. As I look, I go around the room observing each individual thing for the information it contains. I ask myself questions like: What is that? What's it there for? How did it get there? Why is it that color? Is there a story in it? Does it contain any risk? If my appointment is late, I look at how the building is put together; how old it is; how it is built; and where are the doors, fire extinguishers, or anything I can use to mitigate possible risks. By this time, only a few minutes have passed, and I find myself reading things on the walls: safety rules, work shifts, regulations, maybe a list of employees with their photos. I may be able to say some guy's name when he walks in the room, even though we've never met. All these questions (pictures) and the data they link together are loaded in the left hemisphere (LH) of my brain with very little effort; if practiced all the time, they become reflex, instinct, and even common in the PSS. If I'm in the system, I'm just trying to do the best I can, with my SAACRAM in the here and now, with the best-case scenario and wellbeing of all present my foremost objective. SAACRAM is like a basic program I have pictured in my brain; it runs by itself, all the time. I see what's in front of me, and then keep my head on a swivel whenever I can make my RH (brain's right hemisphere) look away from a screen.

Slide 15: Personal and Corporate Safety

PERSONAL AND CORPORATE SAFETY

THIS SLIDE IS MY ATTEMPT to teach the differences between the PSS and the cSS; mental processes are different when the CSS includes more than one operator. If you only run the saw in your backyard, your PSS and the PSS of your SP will look pretty much the same; they will have a combined affect to define your CSS, but if you are a "professional operator," you get paid to run a chainsaw; if you occasionally run the saw at work, on a volunteer saw crew, or with a bunch of your friends or relatives, the rules alone are what constitute a cSS. The corporate safety system is usually determined and mandated by whoever is paying for the work or has requested your talents and abilities to accomplish the work—e.g., the landowner, or the trail crew leader—the legal authority to run the saw and cut down the trees. The legal (corporate) authority may exercise its right to select who the operator will be, what the equipment will be and how it will be used, what risks will be accepted in the cutting area, who will be on the crew, and other factors that will affect how you apply your PSS.

Depending on the existing hierarchy, you may find yourself in the midst of a bunch of amateurs, or at the other end of the spectrum, surrounded by professional operators who actually produce a good product and have the rules down to an art. Regardless of your stature in the cutting area (CA), you still carry the same legal authority under the cSS, and ethical authority under the CSS; nobody can order you to do something you see as self-disparaging; it is illegal. You have an inalienable right to protect yourself, and nobody can expect you to work contrary to your conscience; that is morally indecent and usually translates into you ignoring the legal authority; the choice of what gets done when the saw is in your hands is purely up to you. The picture of acceptable practice in the minds of beginners and newbies usually is colored "green" with a symbol that looks like $, and it is about keeping the job and satisfying the boss. Your ability to contribute to the CSS will be determined by your willingness to be both student and teacher at the same time; however, in the cSS, it may be changed to employee and boss—the same thing you were when it was just you and your SP working under your backyard CSS to save money by cutting firewood. Asking questions and testing the SAACRAM of the authority is often the best path to understanding and mitigating the risk variables in a cutting scenario. If you are the most advanced operator on site, you show your willingness to learn from your employees by verbalizing and demonstrating the CSS. If you are the least experienced on site, your questions and concerns should be a primary consideration in a good teacher's PSS; is the operator asking your opinion? If you see a rule being ignored by the boss in the corporate system, or by the authority itself, that should be a No-Go for even the most inexperienced member of the crew; if it has become an accepted oversight for the people who have been there previously, you may be the only one capable of identifying it; you would need to be dedicated enough to the CSS to speak up; you become a boss when handed the saw to at least verbalize the proper way to function within the rules; the cSS has a lowercase "c" for a reason; your loyalty must remain with the place where your PSS was born: the CSS. (The C stays capitalized because your P must be capitalized.)

Although it would be very unusual, if the corporate system refuses to yield to what you see as a blatant, unrelenting infraction of a basic rule, you must be willing to leave the cutting area. Ask to be assigned to other work or even to go home rather than jeopardize the integrity of your PSS by also breaking the rule. I don't like thinking in negatives, but when you are a "professional" operator, and that's what you are in a corporate situation when you're getting paid to run the saw, the question has to be asked, "How much of my integrity am I willing to give up for fame and fortune?" If you don't say anything, and someone does get hurt or even killed because you didn't, how much guilt will be loaded on your PSS? When you do speak up, all the CSS members who knew the infraction existed, but didn't have enough confidence in their own PSS to speak up, will build respect for your PSS; from what I have learned about how the human brain works and reacts to danger, I guarantee you that if a person is a CSS member, even if they do not show it outwardly, your actions will become a picture in their PSS, to be emulated by them when next involved in this dangerous occupation. That presents another way to leave the cutting area (CA) without quitting—hand this book to the authority and ask them to read it; then you become a "corporate teacher" of the CSS.

The PSS and cSS are two sides of a crotch in the same tree. You keep the learned experiences and knowledge of your PSS in your head, or maybe in a log or ledger if you have a particularly advanced personal safety attitude; there's no such thing as a bad PSS, except one created by someone with a bad memory or taught by bad teachers; the memory of the cSS needs to be recorded too; it's the pSS (small p because it must be contained in the PSS) of the company/agency/organization; that authority brings the CSS together; the "c" is not capitalized because the ethical authority of the CSS supersedes the legal authority of the cSS in the cutting area; one encompasses the other like a legal bubble inside an ethical bubble.

The Forest Service uses the JHA - MAM- AAR (Job Hazard Analysis, Mid-Action Mitigation, After Action Review) to teach the pSS. Here's how it breaks down:

- **JHA (Job Hazard Analysis)** is usually a form that lists the dangerous job in a table format using Windows Word with three matched columns; the first column is a procedure in the job; the second is a list of hazards, risks, or concerns associated with that procedure; and the third column contains the actions previously learned to be adequate for mitigating those risks. It represents a general PW for all the operators, SPs, and swampers who work for the cSS. Good examples of the JHA can be found by searching "Forest Service, chainsaw, JHA." These examples are valuable for even the simplest corporate systems, and they should definitely be employed for complex saw operations; they can be used at tailgate safety meetings on the job site to cover general safety concerns before the specific concerns about the project right in front of you are discussed.

- **MAM (Mid-Action Mitigation)** is a documentation of concerns or hazards encountered on the project that were not listed on the JHA; they are usually project-specific methods employed to mitigate various risks; how they were "engineered" by the crew is very valuable information that should be documented by work leaders and safety officers, possibly with key word search formats so future crews can have access to their predecessors' accomplishments.

- **AAR (After Action Review)** can also be an electronic or written document, or it can be as simple as a bitch session, where after the project is completed, all involved get to credit or condemn what took place. If the meeting is documented, it must be agreed upon from the start that names or any information that identifies who contributed the information will not be recorded with the information offered, for obvious reasons.

These are very valuable elements of the CSS. Particularly in the cSS, they stop the same mistakes from resurfacing because of the loss of K&E pertinent to the specific cSS because people quit or move on to another cSS, or they take their PSS and go home.

Your PSS and the Corporate SS you work in are very similar when it comes to learning and teaching; there should be a sense of dedication to the CSS for the sake of beginner and intermediate operators. Don't be a "saw hog." Let the less-experienced operators do some cutting too; they can do the limbing and bucking for you, clear out escape routes, and even cut smaller trees in your lay; it's still your tree, though, so don't stop watching and teaching. I like sitting on the stump and watching them cut, then encouraging them to stick with the system rules, and work on their SAACRAM in the most appropriate applications; the one right in front of them. The corporate saw team is an extension of the best qualities of the combined personal safety systems of each worker and saw operator; the rules and each individual operator and safety person's SAACRAM will yield a safe productive work crew if each member considers themselves a teacher and a student at the same time, just as you did when you first taught yourself with your own PSS.

Something I found very helpful in taking much of the effort out of building my PSS was to think constantly about what I saw myself doing as what I would be teaching my son or daughter some day; it made me more aware of my current attitude about the job. That was a good frame of mind for me to work in since I found in later years that the basic premise of the entire CSS is doing it properly so you can teach it properly; there is only understanding attached to failure if you did the best you could. This is why you need to be a little harsh with yourself occasionally; make it a memorable occasion when you find yourself breaking a rule to cut corners. Remind yourself who the safety is for: the beginners—all the beginners, even other people's sons and daughters—your prodigies in the CSS.

Set a high goal for yourself, such as: "Your PSS will someday teach young operators to respond in emergency situations all around the country." Given what is being said about plant diseases spread by global warming, increasing occurrence and severity of forest fires, and of storms, such a goal is not an idle pipe dream; we will never lose our need in this nation for qualified first responders to move the hazard trees and open the streets; it's your patriotic duty in a big storm; it's your family heritage in a small one. What will the cSS with your PSS leading it look like? So, am I saying that you will become an excellent operator only when you reach that goal? No! You don't reach understanding when you obtain the goal; it was accumulated over time by the understanding you were wise to in each small cut along the way. The only fulfillment in reaching a goal is in realizing the confidence in your new goal—to verbalize and demonstrate it to the CSS that got you there. Can you see how any goal works? If it's your first cut, or you're chosen as the best operator to cut down the national Christmas tree, it's your PSS in a cSS! You may want to have all new PPE, in case it makes the news, not to make you look smart, but to give credit where it is due—to the cSS that got you there in one piece because it was born in the CSS.

Part One Notes:

PART II:
LEGAL AUTHORITY
THE EVER-ELUSIVE RULES

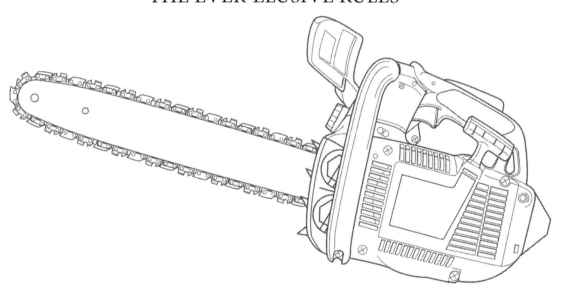

THE FIVE RULES

Rule 1: Personal Protective Equipment

Rule 2: Proper starting procedure

Rule 3: Proper handling techniques

Rule 4: The felling size-up

Rule 5: Stumps don't lie

THE RULES ARE THE SECOND half of the system; they are the visible consensus of "pre-mitigation"; they are a picture of you exercising your chainsaw SAACRAM; they are you, safely demonstrating your ability/talent and knowledge/experience levels, by how well you adhere to them, and what you expect others to emulate. Each rule requires adherence to all the other rules to best serve safety and be valid. The first four rules are well known in the chainsaw safety community; the fifth rule is to encourage all chainsaw operators to abide by the other four rules; in other words, to get with the program, or demonstrate your allegiance to ethical responsibility by what you safely produce as indicated in your product.

The internet, particularly YouTube, is loaded with great teaching videos on proper chainsaw use; search "How to Fell a Tree With a Chainsaw." Then look for the Husqvarna-sponsored one; you will know you have the right one because it begins with the back of a pickup truck pulling into the frame. This forty-five minute video shows, step-by-step, the field exercise I used in my seminars to demonstrate the safest method for felling a large diameter tree: the "open face, bore cut, with a strap" (OBS) method. Did the guy in the video and I go to Michigan State and take "Chainsaw 101" together? No, this stuff has been around for many years! So why isn't everyone doing it like in the video? Because they didn't have the fifth rule—*you*—holding them accountable by your example! Many good videos show the right way to fell, and some, as in "chainsaw fails," show what can go wrong when the rules are ignored. Watch each video and try to determine if the rules are followed, and if not, how they are broken. These are great mental pictures that will help you build a strong PSS. The CSS is not intended to make you follow rules; it assumes you will do all in your power to follow them without debate or consternation; the CSS is designed to build a new "uncommon sense" chainsaw thought process in your brain that will not allow you to cut with operators who refuse to follow the rules based on a poor, outdated "personal safety attitude."

The first four rules are the state-of-the-art safest methods established by the legal authorities, bean counters, insurance companies, safety experts, and the rest of the smart people who work mostly with their brains, but they made their deductions and formulated these basic rules out of the numbers of operators injured and killed while running a saw. What the CSS is trying to do is bring the brain/logic into chainsaw operation for everyday chainsaw operators; and for everyday corporate systems, good SAACRAM cannot exist if the statistically proven safest methods are ignored. We can no longer go on thumbing our noses at our ancestors who bled and died to provide a number for the statistics. The foundation of my PSS is to affect the statistics by making every operator and safety person safer; if following the rules as closely as you can is your PSS too, we have ourselves a CSS!

Rule 1 is about dressing yourself for the job. Rule 2 is about dressing your saw before you pull the starter cord. Rules 3 and 4 are about running the saw in the safest possible manner without detracting from production. Rule 5 is the truth of what you did. An operator can be dressed in the most expensive equipment, hold the best saw on the market, and handle the saw exactly according to the rules, and still not be able to produce the stump they planned on; that's acceptable, if it is done within the entire CSS; it's called practice—not just practicing safety, but practicing the rules while processing the tree! The CSS allows everyone in the cutting area, after the tree is down, to read the stump and learn from the entire experience; eventually your stumps will all look alike and become a normal result; maybe someday you will start practicing and teaching some other abilities with your additional rules that you assigned yourself in your improved PSS.

A concern I have about this book is that it will become too wordy for most chainsaw operators; a lot of us are not the reading type; we are usually the kind of people who do something first, and read the directions only after we first fail. There is a whole book in the explanation of the rules, and since my plan of work here is the addition of the fifth rule, defining it is how I work the plan. For this reason, I will leave it to you to consult your teacher, or go online to gather whatever further information you may need on Rules 1 through 4 beyond what is in these pages. If I tried to teach you all the details of my many chainsaw training sessions on the rules of running a saw, this book could add up to a thousand pages. Much of the first four rules is "chainsaw common sense"; it's the fifth rule that makes it common to you and your safety person. The fifth rule combines the CSS and the SAACRAM to chainsaw operation, so most of what I write in the upcoming pages is to demonstrate to you how the SAACRAM is applied to the rules. At my age, I must consider time as a critical factor if I am to live long enough to write my next book: *The Fifth Rule.* That is not to say that the first four rules are less important than the fifth; all the rules must exist together to define the CSS, but information on the first four is ubiquitous and probably taught by much better teachers than me. However, I will try to point out what I see as key elements of understanding the first four—enough to get you started on a practice that will guide the rest of your chainsaw operation career toward perfect, and make you a very informed teacher.

(Yield your will to the rules and use them as a legally authorized tool to exemplify your dedication to the CSS.)

This book is like me felling a complex tree; I find a very ambivalent picture in my brain when I contemplate its meaning. In teaching you about the Fifth Rule, the subject matter is both the product and the stump. The dilemma is: Am I making a stump, or procuring wood to use? In order to make sense of the PW, and properly WP, I need to think of the reader as a stump or a sapling—a stump of a tree that had to be removed for the benefit of the stand, the message in its stump telegraphed to the stem of the tree or a sapling given open sky to afford maximum straight grain growth, all the improved and new PSSs being born as the wood in all the healthy trees, not firewood, but high value wood, like the wood in my "rule picture frame." You are my stump when you read the book; you are the high value lumber when you understand the book by doing what it asks of you. Practice, practice, practice toward being a perfect stump and beautiful wood on the walls of your mansion—a PSS you can be proud of without being arrogant because it is evaluated with respect, and all are welcome in it. (I know; hard to understand—it's my PSS, always ahead of me!)

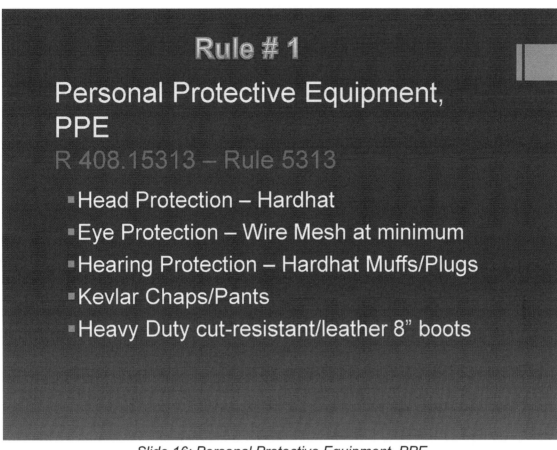

Slide 16: Personal Protective Equipment, PPE

RULE #1 – PERSONAL PROTECTIVE EQUIPMENT

I CALL THE FIRST RULE PPE; simple, right? This is the "uniform" required by legal author-ity, at least in the State of Michigan for anyone getting paid to run a chainsaw. It is also the same dress required by the CSS's ethical authority if you are a tax-paying, law-abiding citizen of the state; you abide somewhere near the center of the common sense curve; you're not a rebel, or self-destructive, and you have no special quantum force field around you to protect you and your SP. Even if you have an especially high level of luck protecting you, what you are wearing is the first thing others in the cutting area use to determine how your behavioral safety appearance is going to impact their lives. There's no harm in believing you are lucky, as long as your chaps and hard hat say to your SP that you have prepared for the rare contingency where, according to accident statistics, and the defini-tion of luck, the luck is not going to be there when you need it; then, the only magic shield between a leg and speeding saw teeth will be Rule 1.

With regular clothes, it is said, "The clothes define the man." In the CSS, the opposite is also true, since all the clothes are a rule: "The man defines the clothes." The initial indication to other members of the CSS is that the operator who is equipped, even minimally according to the rule, is a cooperating member of the system. The attire's purpose is more to indicate the operator's concern for the safety of all involved than it is armor for the wearer. Because it is regimented, it indicates joining the cause.

A hard hat, earplugs, and safety glasses are a very inexpensive compliance for the first three items. If that is all you can afford right now, that's good; you are still giving the same message in the CSS, and chaps are kind of "one size fits all," so they can be easily borrowed without infringing on your germ-fighting system. The chaps are the Kevlar barrier for your leg; the CSS is the Kevlar barrier for your confidence; they allow you to comfortably hold the saw in the "home" position. Be careful where you buy your chaps; some products called "chainsaw chaps" do not meet the standards for stopping a chain; if you buy yours at the same store that sold you your saw, they will only sell approved chaps. (The same thing is true of your confidence; watch out for counterfeiters!) The 8" leather boot element is to ensure that the chaps overlap the top of the boot so there is not a gap of unprotected leg; so don't show up with a pair of jogging shoes on; but then, you wouldn't—it would ruin your image. Many safety experts suggest steel toe boots; they are a very good idea when working with heavy log segments, but usually your feet are not a high risk factor if you are good with Rule 3: Know where your feet are before you make the cut. The "wire mesh at a minimum" statement is something I put in this slide to prompt discussion of when one safety item—in this case, safety glasses—embellishes another—here, wire mesh screen. They provide a barrier for different-size flying objects, but if you are like me, working in hot weather and a profuse sweater, you'll spend more time wiping your glasses than cutting wood. The solution is SAACRAM; if the cutting I'm doing presents a risk that can only be mitigated by safety glasses, and my hard hat has an attached wire mesh shield, I use both.

In the CSS, the PPE is not to force you to think or act a certain way; it's to make your "look" and your actions project what you think. You see what's in front of you; you understand the complexity of it and why it is a concern; you identify the risks involved, and how to work around or through them while others watch you. I know what some of you "old timers" are thinking: *I've been doing this all my life, and I'm still alive.* If you are a healthy, old operator without PPE, you understand above all others why the PPE is needed—because the PPE is really not for you; your ability to avoid the accident is in your K&E; the PPE is so you give the right picture to the people watching you; you have always considered them in your size-up; and you want to give them the right impression of what is being sized-up. If you currently run a saw without this basic PPE, your safety system is probably based on a history of "trial and error," where the trial was the fact that you lived through your close calls, or that you got back on the horse, and the error is a bad memory that you fear will happen again; this image is what the CSS is asking you to help take out of the picture for the new operator, by wearing the equipment; trust me, you'll learn to like it; it will turn your fear into confidence in what you are teaching by example!

Remember the story about my dad dressed in his National Guard sergeant's uniform? The uniform is the outward appearance of your PSS; since one person can have many different personal safety systems in their life, especially if they enjoy doing dangerous sports or other high-risk work activities, the uniform helps the operator's brain get with the program; it puts your mental processes in the right gear; it helps the memory access the proper data for the interpretation of risk; it is a picture to your senses that tells a thousand reasons for its existence in less time than it takes to put it on. There are many other benefits to it, and very few minor negatives; at the end of all the debate over the uniform, it keeps you safer. Not putting it on does the same thing in the other direction on all counts.

> In order for your PSS to work in the CSS, you need to go "P" behind the tree; your (P)SS hides behind the (C)SS; if it stands out where it can be seen, you are out of the system; you have exposed yourself in front of your peers. The CSS provides an easy way out of this embarrassing situation, however: Just start asking questions. You just became a student; all good teachers (observers) must respond as such or *they* are out of the system; you refocus on the CSS so your PSS can get behind it better.

This next slide lists the elements I added to the legal authority demands from the previous slide; they are part of my PSS—issues of risk I have found to be common to most cutting areas. I try to include these all the time, but they are mitigations to risks that can be manipulated depending on the particular risks presented. If I'm doing a lot of brush handling, working around briars and pickers or sharpening the chain, I like to have a pair of good leather gloves; cowhide gloves are what I prefer, not canvas gloves or some fancy lambskin driving gloves. In that same type of cutting area with a lot of brush and branches, or when cutting storm-damaged trees, I like to wear a long-sleeved shirt or jacket to protect against scratches that can easily become infected. My 8" leather boots have non-skid soles on them for when I'm working on wet and uneven ground or walking among limbs and brush. Do I put them on if I'm cutting a limb up in my mother-in-law's backyard? Probably not, unless I'm trying to impress her with my professionalism in order to extract a higher compensation. The risk the PPE item is meant to mitigate is not always present; these are rules in my PSS that I added to the CSS legal authority, so *I* decide if it's required.

I like to know where the closest Band-Aid is in case I get a small cut. As with scratches, I've had production halted by the sight of a minor amount of blood, especially when it's mine. I also want to know where the closest first-aid kit is, not necessarily for myself, but for other people on the jobsite; my concern for their welfare is part of my confidence that I will never need to use the items in the kit on myself; my PSS will protect me, but other operators and SPs represent hidden risks. I have a small backpack I bought for fifty

PPE – Also:

- Leather/Kevlar gloves
- Arm protection – Jacket or long sleeves
- Non-skid soles
- First Aid Kit
- Communication Device
- Safety person/Swamper

Slide 17: PPE - Also

cents at a rummage sale that I keep with my saw and always take along; it contains extra wedges, gloves, starter cord, a pre-stretched chain, a sparkplug, files, an extra scrench (screwdriver/wrench), and a small first-aid kit. In the kit is a large triangular bandage; a couple of packs of 4x4 sterile gauzes, and a tube of antibacterial cream. My plan of work is: If someone cuts themselves with the saw, put the whole tube of cream on the wound; cover it with the gauzes, and wrap it tightly with the bandage until the bleeding stops; then get the person to the ER, ASAP.

I insist, for myself (behavioral safety), that I have some sort of communication with the outside world when running the saw; i.e., NEVER CUT ALONE! Of course each one of those words in caps has a range of definitions; ask me no questions, I'll tell you no lies. The PSS is very temperamental; if you lie to it once, it may take three difficult truths, what might be called "close calls," to bring the rule back to a trustworthy state in your own mind; the main hope is that one of those truths does not involve a doctor bill. If you are in the backyard cutting firewood, make sure someone is around within earshot to hear you yelling at the top of your lungs!

This brings me to the issue of my Safety Person—what we called a swamper in the FS—someone who functions as a helper in the CSS, and a part of my PPE, in my PSS. Some safety trainers teach not to have anybody in the cutting area when you are dropping a tree; for me, that increases the risks; a thick canopy could make the top of a tree invisible to the eyes I'm depending on to see what I can't; I place my "extra set of eyes" like I place my other PPE—strategically. I like to have a SP/swamper who is also a member of the CSS; they know what I'm thinking and I know what they are thinking; we communicate on a higher level of communication and expectation than I would with a casual observer. At one point, I used my eight-year-old daughter as my SP while cutting firewood in the backyard; the cutting area was small and well controlled, but I'm sure the experience not only increased her self-confidence but also mine for my PSS. My instructions to her to "Go get Mom" if something went wrong had to be followed with an explanation of what *could* go wrong; it made the firewood job a little more time-consuming, but I always liked getting a "3-fer": her self-esteem, my PSS, and cheap heat for the house. Once again the definition of this PPE element depends on the risks presented and the tree's complexity; if I am cutting a tree with a definite lean in my favor, a good forward lean, I have no problem placing my SP in my safety zone with instructions on what to look for and expect; if, on the other hand, I am cutting a very unpredictable, rotted tree or a tree with lots of back-lean, I usually send my SP to a spot on the outer edges of the cutting area where they can see the top of the tree, and I make sure to give the warning that "This tree could go anywhere."

Sometimes a "plan of work" for a day of cutting may involve using a relative, friend, or neighbor as your SP. Someone who understands your ability enough to request your help can also be brought into the CSS. I keep a hard hat, an extra pair of safety glasses, and some earplugs with the rest of my PPE. Your SP needs to be prepared as if the person is part of your PPE; just like you prepare your saw, you need to properly dress your SP, verbalize and demonstrate your intentions, and be willing to accept a No-Go from them if they don't have enough faith in your size-up to trust their house to it. You are in charge of the cutting area; any infrastructure in it may be covered by insurance for trees falling in a storm, but it is most likely not covered for trees being felled under the assurance in your plan; the property owner must know and agree with your strategy or it constitutes a higher level of risk for both of you.

I always want an extra set of eyes in my cutting area attached to a brain that knows beforehand what we will be doing, what part they will play in the plan, and what to do in the event that things don't go as planned. If your SP does not have the proper K&E to fully understand their assignment, they should not be in the cutting area when a tree is felled; you must accept the dual role of operator and watcher because you'll need to watch yourself and them. That's not added risk; that's multiplied risk. If you think you have all the risks mitigated, and do not run into a No-Go from you or your watcher, extend your limitations.

We used the word swamper in the Forest Service to be synonymous with SP; since then, I've learned to think of a swamper as a helper who is doing things in the cutting area other than standing in one spot watching me cut down a tree; a swamper is someone who piles brush, hauls logs, and watches the cutting area; there may be one, or many; you, as the operator, get to pick which swamper is going to be your SP, depending on what you want to teach or what you want to learn. Remember, when you put down the saw, you are in essence just another swamper until it is determined by all in the cutting area that you have the best K&E to be the operator in a particular saw application, or a SP for a particular operator. This situation works much better if all in the cutting area are compliant with Rule 1 from the get-go; then you just hand off the saw!

In chainsaw operation, there are so many different types of applications and cuts that can be made that it is nearly impossible for an average operator to safely continue a steady rapid pace to the work without a mental error or physical mishap occurring. When a particular cut is perfected and regimented into the work (practice only makes perfect when perfect is what is practiced), it can be methodically processed in the brain, and then many similar actions rapidly repeated. Having a high level of K&E, repetition, for each individual cut produces "muscle memory" of the best possible outcome for the cumulative event; you'll be working methodically, processing each cut with a mini-size-up, but others in the cutting area will think you're working rapidly. Many information-gathering processes in your brain work at the speed of electricity (neurons); you don't need to think about an action once it becomes engrained in your brain as the best response through the wonders of chemistry (synapses). A tranquil reality is created when your conscious mind convinces your subconscious control mechanisms, through enough successfully performed iterations, that risks can be successfully mitigated or removed by an average brain—what we call confidence. This is what the CSS does if you have a PSS that strictly practices the rules at all times and uses SAACRAM to train the brain about all the fears (concerns, hazards) in the cutting area; it provides a place to practice safely under the watchful brain of a teacher. The CSS does not have any average operators, however, because it uses the best in each PSS. There really is no such thing as muscle memory; the closest thing to it is your PSS; it's all in your head until you physically (muscle) remove a risk through your mental (brain) processes. Your PSS becomes added safety equipment for the CSS, and it could be the most valuable piece of safety equipment in the CA. Something above and beyond the legal authority dictates is needed to stay safe. If you are the SP, or even a swamper, the response the operator gives your inquiry may even turn out to be a lesson for their own PSS.

In this slide, the picture on the left shows the result of taking a good pair of chaps, wrapping them around a fence post, running the mid-sized Stihl to full rev, and dropping it on the chaps. In the right photo, the side cover was taken off the saw to show how the

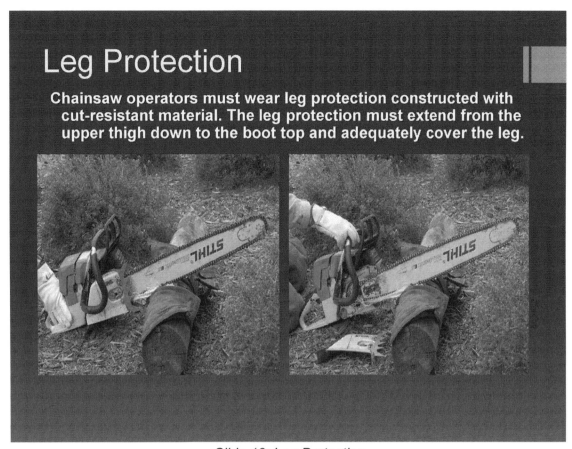

Slide 18: Leg Protection

Kevlar in the chaps gets pulled out in strands, wrapping around the chain drive sprocket binding it up, and stopping the chain. Notice that the Kevlar, which is stronger than, steel in tensile strength by weight, pulls out a distance that would include about 8-10 teeth; so, if that many teeth went by the cut spot before the chain came to a stop, you've got to wonder: Would you still get cut? I suppose you would at least have a scratch or bruise, so what good are the chaps if you still get injured? I'm glad you asked, or perhaps you already have reasoned that the chaps remove a part of the risk; the Kevlar removed a segment of force from the chain before it got to your leg; if it actually makes it to the leg at any particular speed, the injury would be less than if the chap were not there. It removes a segment of risk, but from what?

Your instinctual brain knows what a speeding chain can do; if in the past you have attempted to rationalize a truth in your brain that it can't get you because you hold the saw out away from your legs, that would work for diminishing the apprehension, but you are still not handling the saw the way it is designed to be handled. If you can find contentment with handling the WMDH incorrectly, you have been lying to yourself! The chainsaw is designed to be held close to the body; the right hand and arm are used as "anchor points" on the side of the body, holding the inside edge of the rear handle in the area on the top of your right hip pocket with the right elbow feeling like it is wrapped around your back; it's what I call "the home position"; I bring the saw home as often as I can while cutting; sure, sometimes it goes out to the bar, but it always returns home. If you are not wearing chaps, it is a home where there will be no piece with your instincts; you will subconsciously keep the bar out there where forces in the saw have a much better chance of having a small center of rotation in a "kickback," and, therefore, a much better chance of hitting you. Hitting you where? In a place where there wouldn't be chaps even if you had them on. The chainsaw cannot be run or handled properly without the chaps on! If you are not wearing chaps, you introduce more risk; you are not in the system.

When you put your chaps on, your brain will automatically mitigate the subconscious fear of holding the saw close; you are using the CSS rules to eliminate a percentage of the risk; you are altering your behavior to give your brain a new picture that replaces caution with confidence. Of course, if you follow the other rules in the CSS, you will never be in a situation where a wide-open chain would hit your leg!

This brings me to the next good reason to wear the chaps (and all PPE); if the use of safety equipment talks to your brain so effectively, the sight of you wearing it also speaks volumes to anybody who is watching you. If you don't have the basic equipment on, no one in the CSS will be able to work with you; you become an unmitigated risk for your SP and others: a No-Go! In effect, Rule 1 is your admission into the cutting area, especially if you intend to run the saw. It is the indication to other PSSs that you are assuming legal and ethical authority and, therefore, responsibility; it shows that the safety of all involved is your primary concern, that you put safety first, and to prove it, you literally wear it on your body. It's like a policeman's uniform and badge; the PPE is your uniform, and the CSS is your badge; they declare your right to operate the saw; they are the best evidence of your PSS intent.

Remember that youngster looking through the curtain, or your young safety person closely watching your every move? To them, you are like a real-life superhero; you are there to conquer that tree that was a main source of stress in their family; they will remember that picture of you removing the threat with professionalism, and recall it automatically the first time they pick up a chainsaw. What a great picture for a future chainsaw operator to have permanently recorded in their young brain—exactly what the safest, most productive chainsaw operator looks like. If you are an excellent CSS operator, the PPE will be automatic, stored right next to your saw, used as much for the other members of the CSS as it is for you; wearing it actually removes a percentage of risk in *their* size-up.

All safety equipment only removes a percentage of injury possibilities; the equipment must be affordable; it must be effective for low-force reactions; it must be comfortable, not in the easy-chair sense, but in the sense that you can wear it for extended periods of work without it adding unusual fatigue or causing an injury itself; most of all, it must be available for use. If all those conditions are met, the equipment will remove certain risks: the glasses for small rapidly moving particles; the face shield for branches flying, poking, and slapping; the handkerchief for stopping sweat from running into your eyes; and the gloves with Velcro fasteners so they don't slip on your hand if you get a kick—they are all kinds of little things that add up to coverage. Coverage from what? I don't know; you tell me, and I'll set up a little test like the one above to show you why the safety equipment is better to use than not. Only you know what your PSS needs to build confidence with the methods and equipment you use. If you have lots of money available, you might even use the fanciest, very best equipment "personal image" as part of your PSS; I guess it comes down to how much you're trying to impress the observers! Now, I'm not exactly poor, but I would be asking myself, "Why do I want to impress them—for the benefit of my PSS or for the prosperity of the CSS?"

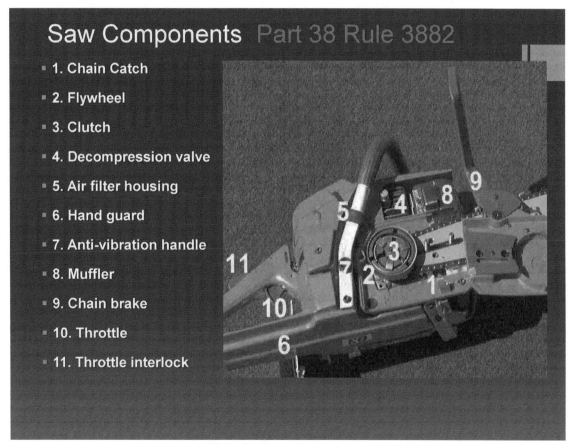

Slide 19: Saw Components

"Analysis of Complexity" requires that you understand your saw's various components—what they do, and how they work. See where it says "Part 38 Rule 3882" at the top? Those numbers mean the legal authority agrees that these things are required. These components are mostly the saw's PPE; they are how the saw is "dressed." If your saw doesn't have some of these safety features, it probably means you are using an old saw. If that is you, your new goal must be to get a new saw that has all the risk-mitigating ability that is standard in a modern saw. If you can't afford a new saw, tell each person you cut for that a contribution to your PSS is required before you cut; you must be working toward following the rule to be in the system. YouTube has many videos on saw maintenance. The best way to learn how your saw works is to keep it well maintained; take it apart and put it back together if you have that ability. SA each part of the AC to determine how it helps RAM; figure out how it works mechanically for promoting safe operation.

Now let's look at each of the individual parts as labeled in the slide.

1. **The chain catch:** The chain catch is a part that even advanced operators sometimes miss, or should I say "don't miss," when it is broken off; it's made out of soft alloys because its function is to catch the chain if it is thrown off the bar; it can easily be broken off during normal saw use, but it is very important to have in place, especially when cutting small diameter brush or the chain loosens up. Without the catch, the chain can keep rotating as it comes off the bar and slaps back toward your right hand and arm. If you ever have a chain thrown off the bar, let off on the trigger and hold the saw still until the engine idles down.

2 & 3. **The flywheel and clutch:** This entire assembly is the drive system for the chain.

4. **The decompression valve:** It opens an airway to the compression chamber; it comes in handy for big saw/small person combinations or cold saw starts.

5. **Air filter housing:** Make sure the air filter is clean; when having any trouble with the saw running improperly, check this first.

6. **Hand guard:** The hand guard is the wide base on the rear handle. Its purpose is to protect the hand in the event of a thrown chain or from small items thrown back toward the right hand and arm.

7. **Anti-vibration handles:** Springs are attached to the ends of the handles to dampen vibrations; they work well until the bolt holding them down falls out; then it introduces more risk because the bar is more difficult to hold freely in the kerf; make sure the bolts are tight.

8. **The muffler:** Keep an eye on the condition of the metal, especially when cutting in hot/dry areas; it muffles the sound of the saw, but not to a decibel level safe for human ears. I've heard that most of the damaging frequencies being emitted from the saw are above what the human ear can hear. (You don't hear most of the sound that injures your hearing, just like you don't see the widow maker; with the latter, however, you can train to be more efficient; with the former, you cannot; it will require a physical barrier to stop the ears from going there.)

9. Chain brake: As labeled on the slide, the chain brake is better thought of as a parking brake handle, connected to the chain brake, which is a band of steel wrapped around the fly wheel; the braking mechanism in the saw is actually an inertia brake; it's the sudden jerk of the saw in a kickback that sets the brake. Take a look at it; you'll see how it flips back and forth over the top of a spring. I told you that so I can tell you this; your left hand can be anywhere on the front handle, and the brake will still work if the saw kicks and the kick provides enough kinetic energy; you don't need to keep your left hand behind that guard.

10 and 11. Throttle & throttle interlock: These go together; the interlock stops what I call the trigger from being pulled until the hand is wrapped around the handle; they are close together, aren't they? There is a risk that they could both be depressed if the saw was set down or it got tangled in brush or branches. This is where the "parking brake" comes in handy; it can be set before you put the saw down or hold it in one hand.

Rule 2 also includes handling a saw that is running properly and has a chain sharp enough to make the required cuts. Risks are sometimes dynamic; they increase over time. You begin the job with a saw that's running well; later, the saw begins to run poorly; you find yourself revving the engine to keep it running between cuts; you're pushing down on the saw to make it cut fast enough; the saw keeps stalling, and you keep starting it. To adhere to Rule 2—to mitigate the risks presented by a progressively poorer running saw—you must stop and maintain the saw to use it in the CSS; if you can't bring it back to standard, and you don't have another saw available, that's a No-Go!

I have never been interested in saw maintenance; if an operator knows how the various parts of the saw work, and the physics behind them, that's good enough for me; when advanced maintenance requires more K&E than I have in my PSS, I take the saw to the place I bought it and pay a chainsaw mechanic to fix them; that's what government workers are told to do.

Is it all these items on a saw that make the "power saw" safer to handle, or is it the collective power of the human brains that created them? Perhaps it's the perception of your brain that understands what they do, and why they are there that makes application of the power safer.

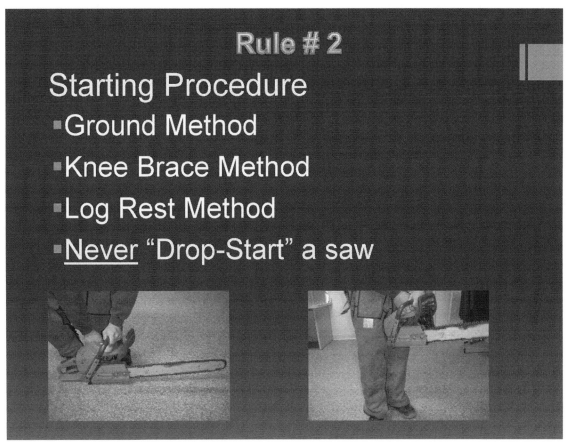

Slide 20: Starting Procedure

RULE #2 – STARTING PROCEDURE

DID I MENTION THAT YOU can tell if an operator is in the CSS from a thousand feet away? The drop start is the most noticeable reason—you can see it a long way off, and it says to all knowledgeable observers: "That operator is not in the system; they are not starting the saw the way it is intended to be started," which, by the way, is also the safest way. Who knew? Do I mean to tell you that a little thing like that can kick you out of the CSS? Yes! Unless when you catch yourself drop-starting the saw, you shut it off, set it down, pick it up while calling yourself a couple of memorable names, and start it again with an acceptable CSS starting method; make a big deal out of it in your mind. Why all that? The problem is not the risk inherent to the saw; an injury happens when your brain is willing to let you go past the risk without mitigating it. The injury happens when you become willing to accept something in your own thought processes that is less-than the safest method: regimentation!

The rule says you must have two points of contact on the saw when starting it. Why? When you pull on the starter rope, you are introducing rotational forces on the saw because there is a radius between your left hand and the hole where the rope disappears under the cowling. Chainsaw operators who understand SAACRAM have a natural, common sense aversion to things that move in a circular motion. "Every action has an equal and opposite reaction"—who said that? It means there is a reactive force vector 180° from the original, and it is just as strong when the original force is suddenly stopped; when the force is on a circular path, the reactant vector is on a tangent of the circle, which also adds centrifugal force—an additional force vector on tangent to a circle, moving in one of many different directions. The circle is replaced by a line when you use two points of contact resulting in a simpler reaction. Is this too much for you? "Too much thinking," you say? If it is, you need to work harder on your AC; there are no formulas, only thinking about how you nearly got hurt in the past. The thinking only needs to be done once if it is followed by learning a new action intended to be habitual; only when you find yourself circumventing the rule of the action will you hear the thought process being recalculated loudly in your mind; it may even force you to say "No" to continuing, make you shut the saw off, put it down, and start over, damn it!

The problem with the drop-start isn't the first start of the day; it's the last start at the end of your cutting when injuries are most probable. Then you're tired, pissed-off at the limbs on the tree, the boss is yelling at you, and it's starting to rain; the damn saw won't run right, so you pull out the choke and push it back in, ignore the brake, and try once more to drop-start it; the bar drops down as the saw starts a half rev and hits the end of a limb you just cut off the log a few inches back from the end of the bar. Suddenly, with the same downward force you pushed into gravity, multiplied by the added force of the chain movement, the saw pops up off the log with an equal and opposite force. Because you are holding the saw away from the contact point, you introduce a man-eating rotating radius; it's a saw bar covered with sharp teeth. Your single hand on the handle becomes a turning point, a point of least resistance upon which the saw will rotate—the center of a circle in which your body is standing. I know what you are probably thinking right now, *I've been drop-starting the saw all my life and that never happened to me.* So, has that scenario ever happened in real life? Yes, it has happened many times; I've seen it several times, so the risk is there. When you teach yourself to stop drop-starting the saw, you will need to know the starting method designed into the saw; it's mechanically the best, the safest, and the easiest on your body because it doesn't introduce a torque in the lower back; it's easier on the starter cord, has two points of contact, and puts you in the CSS. How many positive reasons do I need to list to convince you to start working on your PSS?

I mentioned the *mechanically best* way to start the saw. Let me tell you a story about that. I was working security in a fire camp in Northern California. My job was camp patrol. The job is kind of like being a deputy sheriff in a gold mining tent city; I walked around talking to people all day exercising my SAACRAM. A contracted chainsaw mechanic in camp had a heavy duty red truck and trailer with "Stihl Chainsaws" in big letters on the side. I'm a chainsaw operator; I live chainsaws, so it follows that I stopped and talked to that gentleman on nearly every one of my rounds. We got around to talking about the best way to start the saw, and this is what he told me: "There is only one correct way to start a saw: the knee-brace method. The saw is designed to be started that way; you set the brake, hold the saw with your left hand on the front handle by the curve just left of the brake so the plane of the bar is angled away from your body, set the choke, grab the starter cord handle, then step over the rear handle and grab it with your legs just above the knees; straighten your left arm, and with short quick pulls, as fast as you can repeat them, keep jerking that rope until the saw "fires"; push the choke in, and pull once or twice more; grab the back handle with your right hand; hit the trigger to idle it down; bring the saw to your hip, and release the brake; physically, it's the best method, but that's not why it's the best method." The reason it's the best method in the mind of a chainsaw mechanic is because the carburetor on a saw is designed to be started this way; the carburetor's jets aerate the gas into tiny droplets; the longer those droplets linger, the larger they get, and the larger they get, the more heat required from the spark to ignite them; the drop-start lengthens the time between pulls on the cord, allowing the gas to coagulate, making it more likely to flood out.

So you see, you learned how to start the saw from someone who was doing it wrong! I did the same thing for years, but then one day I asked a question of an operator I would call an expert; he gave me a lecture on his AC; I tried it out to see if he was right; I can't remember ever having a flooded saw since I started using this method; it's safer, more productive, and easier on me and the saw; it uses the saw as it is design to be used; I like it, and it became part of my PSS; I shared it in the CSS every time I cut with someone whom I witnessed drop-starting the saw; I received valuable information at no cost to me; I used it with positive results; so I must ethically pass it on to your PSS, with nothing to gain except a better CSS, and maybe a few bucks for my time spent typing.

The CSS allows three acceptable methods for starting the saw that, when applied to nearly any situation, provide a safe and effective starting procedure; *the chain brake must be set before doing any of them.* The ground-rest, pictured on the left in the slide, is the method I used most when I first started using a saw; it seemed more stable to me, and my young body didn't mind bending down to the ground. As you see, the left hand is on the front handle, and the toe of the boot in the rear handle; some also place the right knee on top of the rear handle or on top of the cowling to create the two points of contact. I use the log rest method sometimes when I'm standing in limbs, but this method is usually used by operators out west who have those gigantic saws with the four-foot bars; the saw bar is rested on a log, back from the tip, leaned to the right, and the cord pulled with the left hand; very seldom a picture you see in Michigan with our twenty-inch bars, and you must take care not to have your finger on the trigger. The method I nearly always use is the knee brace method as I indicated above.

The rule is "Proper Starting." It is not "Never Drop-Start"—that would be a negative rule. I don't get along with "Thou shalt *nots*." I was never very successful at keeping those kinds of rules; I like thinking about what positive action I intend to *do*. This action will be the most difficult for experienced operators because they must reteach their brain and body for it to become a habit. Getting the right dress on your body, and getting the saw physically ready to participate in the operation are the easy parts you're probably already doing; the adjustment of your brain by another part of your brain will be the most work. If you are the kind of person willing to pick up the WMDH and go to work, you can do it in your PSS! You can change your mind, and do it *right* for the CSS!

When I think back on the first saws I owned, I did not treat those tools very well. As I became more experienced with chainsaw use, I began to understand the kind of power I held in my hands, and what I could do with it. I took better care of the saw; I placed it on a higher shelf in the shed—a special spot only for the saw, with all the related tools and equipment around it. It sounds strange, but if you really think about it, you may see the same kinds of thoughts in your mind. It's not really the actual saw that I admire and respect because I have the same regard for any chainsaw; it's more a "bonding" with the power; I even went through a period when I had to come up with some good "brain games" to convince myself the saw's power was mostly separate from my power. No other tool has ever been as significant an entity to my psyche. I use other dangerous tools; I own guns, and I really like my truck, especially now, when it's time for a new one. I have occupied myself with many risky pastimes, but that chainsaw and I have something weird going on together; I heard a guy say it well on TV last night: "It really weirds me out." I guess that's why Rule 2 is well within my standard operating procedure. I take care of my saw as if its power humbles me and its capabilities enable me, at the same time.

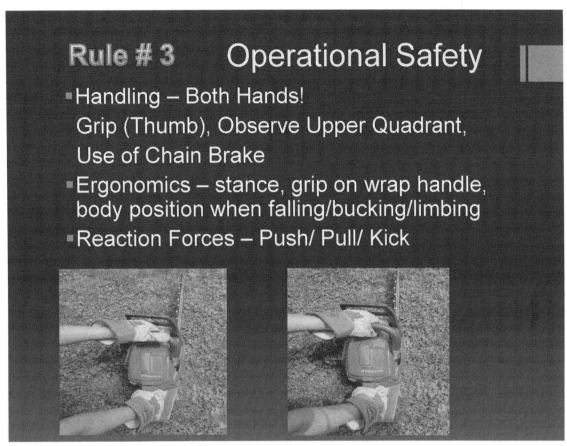

Slide 21: Operational Safety

RULE #3 – OPERATIONAL SAFETY

ALL OF RULE 3'S ELEMENTS are tried and true procedural techniques taught by all of the most advanced chainsaw trainers in the world; they have been proven to complement the saw's design and the physics of saw operation, and to decrease the numbers of all types of injuries among chainsaw operators. There are many more benefits to them. Remember, the CSS is a basic system; if you are involved in more complex applications, your Rule 3 may become very large.

Only four basic handling techniques exist; simple, right? If you can do all four of these things without missing anything the first time you try them, I would like to meet you; I think I could learn a lot from you about building my PSS. For normal people like me, these are very difficult to engrain into their subconscious reflex behavior. Whenever the saw is running, and the chain brake is off, you must have both hands on the saw; that would be your left hand on the front handle, and your right hand on the back handle with your fingers wrapped around both handles. Your left arm is your strong arm; it stays somewhat straight, but not rigid unless you purposely command it to be rigid. Your grip doesn't need to be locked in place; it can rotate on the back handle or move around on the front handle, as long as your fingers remain encircled on both handles, which means it would be within the rule to push the ignition trigger with your thumb if it were more convenient to do so, and to have your left hand anywhere on the front handle. (Remember the inertia brake.)

This leads me to a tangential topic: There is no such thing as a left- or right-handed saw; all saws are held the same way by all operators; all saws, whether they have a wraparound front handle or not, have the bar on the engine's right side; if you hold the saw with your right hand on the front handle, you bring that last tooth on the bottom of the bar several inches closer to your body; of course, you see that as an issue in your SAAC-RAM, right? If you take a close look at your saw, you'll also notice that the rear handle is offset to the right side of the engine to be more in line with the bar's center; this leaves a kind of "indent" on the left side of the rear handle that fits very nicely on the top of your right leg where it meets your hip—the saw's *home location*. Isn't life beautiful? Other people have done all the thinking for us! The brainwork has manifested itself into a physical object in our hands, produced by "the guys who make the big bucks"—the same stuff you paid for when you bought the saw; maybe you should use the saw as it is designed to be used and get your money's worth out of all those accessories you paid for. If you are a lefty, I have good news for you; your strong arm is the same as your dominant arm!

So, how do you move that branch in front of you if both hands have to stay on the saw? No, you don't give it a kick; I've cut a couple of pairs of chaps doing that. You set the brake before you take your right hand off the rear handle; loosen your grip on the front handle while keeping your left wrist straight or somewhat bowed out; as you let go of the rear handle, *push down* on it first, forcing the saw to rotate in your left hand and the front of the saw to rise. Hit the hand guard, in this case the parking brake handle, with your left wrist as your right hand proceeds to the branch. After you've removed the branch, you want to continue cutting; grab the rear handle, pull the saw home against your right hip with your right elbow "wrapped" around the back of your body; keep your left thumb on the front bar and reach out with all four fingers; grab the brake and squeeze. Your brain is going to think it has an easier and faster way to do this; if you see yourself doing it any other way, watch a video of a teacher, and go back to the right way to do it. (Gray matter must be forced into existence by self-control.)

Your strong arm's hand is very important; the front handle has a round cross-section for a reason; put your fingers together, curl them in, and touch the tip of your index finger to the tip of your thumb; what shape did your finger and thumb make? The left thumb must always be wrapped around the front handle, not placed up on top of the handle. If your thumb is on top of the handle and pointing to the right, you have just given away your strong arm's strength; any kick or jerk of the chain will have no problem being stronger than you. Your hand can be anywhere on the bar, but your left thumb has only one place to be—wrapped around that handle, whenever it *takes hold* and during all cutting. You will see experienced CSS members missing this one. It's good to keep in mind for those rare times when you have a teacher in the system who is particularly hard to listen to; they find every little mistake you make. When they are cutting, watch their left thumb; you might find a subject matter to turn that teacher into a student.

Do you remember the most dangerous thing about a chainsaw? Right—*it comes and gets you;* KICKBACK! I'll tell you more than enough about that later, but for right now, just believe me that the kickback's source is the upper quadrant of the bar's nose from a line at the point where the chain starts to drop over the nose to a point straight out the end of the bar's nose. In that 90° quadrant of a circle, the teeth are making the down-and-out movement. Use your AC to figure out what the reaction force looks like; see the reaction force vectors up and back, exchanging lengths as the teeth go around the corner, until the tooth at the very tip, which is going straight down for a split micro-second, is suddenly stopped and has an all-up reaction force at the acceleration of the chain; the saw climbs the wood and turns to a rotational force because you are holding on to the saw handle, which also accelerates the bar tip, due to centrifugal forces, with nearly the entire weight of the saw behind it. The only thing in your favor if you are standing in that arc is that it is slowing down because of the work being done to throw the saw. Now use your RAM to figure out how you instantly get out of the way if this happens to that tooth. The answer is: You can't! The mitigation you will find the most confidence in is: Don't be standing there, and/or have a good grip on the front handle. Of course, you have a chain brake for this; the brake not functioning is not the point; the fact that you allowed the kickback to happen is.

For this reason, the upper quadrant is my "focal point," the area I'm watching if I have nothing else in particular to look at; I follow it around with my eyes; I try to keep the angle of the bar's plane off my right shoulder; I see a resultant "kickback arc" where the saw would go if it were suddenly pushed up on that plane. What I am concentrating on the most during this observation of the saw's tip is: Don't let the upper quadrant be the first thing to touch the wood; don't let the upper quadrant be the last thing to come out of the wood; of course, it would also follow that I don't push the tip of the bar into brush where I can't see what it's touching.

If I had to do this whole chainsaw thing all over again, I would start with more work on my K&E of ergonomics. The pain created by the misguided steps of my youth is now most felt. I had a retiring firefighter tell me once, after watching me work at my normal pace, "Work methodically, paying close attention to each individual action. Try to be more meticulous; think, then do. Most of all, keep asking yourself, 'Can I keep up this pace for sixteen hours?' because you may find yourself in a situation where your life depends on your doing so." Of course normal chainsaw operation is rarely as demanding as when it is combined with a forest fire, but you could find yourself in hurry-up mode for an extended period of time if a bad storm hit your neighborhood. Learn to select your pace based on the complexity of the various risks in front of you, not on any particular cutting situation. Select the location of your step before you make it. Place your feet in line with the bar of the saw; a line from one foot to the other should be somewhat parallel to the saw's bar to put you in a position to best absorb the shock of a sudden pinch on the chain. Take your stance, establish your grip on the saw, and make the cut. Try to learn the most comfortable position for each cut while felling, limbing, or bucking with the following parameters: Use anchor points whenever you can: arm on hip, elbow on knee, body against a solid support. Be aware of the bar's position. Whenever possible, choose a location where your entire body is out of the "kick-back arc"; when you must cut while in the kickback arc, have a special signal for that in your PSS. (I hear a backup alarm in my head; no, I'm not crazy; I know because I'm healthy.)

The chain on the bar's top is moving away from you; if it is suddenly stopped by the "pinching" effect caused by the compressive forces in the wood, and only the chain is stopped, the rest of the saw weight continues to move, causing the saw to be forced back toward the operator; this is the *push reaction force*; if it happens at high speeds, the need for the thumb rap will become apparent. The saw can be pushed back until the bar leaves the wood, and since the last thing to leave the wood is the bar's tip, a kickback can result when the forces suddenly pull the chain from the wood's grasp. The opposite happens when the chain on the bar's bottom is stopped; the saw is pulled away from the operator, which presents the possibility of the bar's tip contacting other wood and causing a kick-back. It's easy to see how reaction forces are inherent when dealing with wood of high mass or wood under high bind; it is equally apparent that the danger being addressed by the "push/pull/kick" picture is kickback.

While operating the saw, try to maintain a mental concept that the saw is an extension of your body. Know where the kickback quadrant is at all times, but also be aware of where the entire saw is in relation to your body and the wood, especially the moving chain. A good SAACRAM will lead to heightened spatial awareness. Understand and picture in your mind the full length of the kickback arc and also the other half of the arc in the "follow-through" direction in the event you lose your grip with your left hand and the bar falls downward—that would be a bad place for your foot or leg to be; good thing you put those chaps on. Mentally establishing the spatial relationship between you and your saw as you both relate to the wood is what your job is as the operator; it's not as much physical power as it is thought processes and planned body movements—what I think of as "dancing with the saw." How well the actual cutting is going is up to the power in the saw. This thought process is aided by "bringing the saw home" to the top of your right hip pocket with a comfortable grip, so you can feel the saw run; then extend the bar to feel the teeth cutting, altering your stance in such a way as to maintain anchor points as much as possible. These techniques will become second nature for you quickly because you use them every time the chain is going to touch the wood. If you are a new operator, be persistent in the command of your body; monitor your actions closely, as if you were watching the "student you" cut, and continue to perfect the muscle movements through the admonishment of the "teacher you." (A fun mind game, but don't be too hard on yourself.)

If you've been running the saw for a long time, you are probably already accomplished at ergonomics, anchor points, and saw awareness, or you have a sore back. The elements you will have the most difficulty with besides getting rid of that drop start are the thumb wrap and setting the brake; with these, you may find that thinking of yourself as a beginner in the CSS might help you realize you may not "know it all." I had the most problems with the thumb wrap; I had to first learn to pinch my left index finger with my thumb, and hit the trigger only after I felt that complete grip circumference. I ran the saw like that for several days, and I did a lot of cussing at myself before I finally stopped finding my own damn thumb that seemed to have a mind of its own on top of the handle. Just remember: If any student sees your thumb up on the handle, they immediately become teachers who are good at spotting higher-risk activities outside the rules. If you are breaking even one small rule, you are operating outside the CSS, and it is the SAACRAM of other PSSs that will notice. (By the way, I didn't forget that hard thumb trick even after I mastered the thumb wrap; I still use it by pressing my thumb on my fingers a little harder when I'm making a cut while standing in the kickback arc; it worked for me, so why would I throw it out?)

> The CSS works like democracy; all for one, one for all (E pluribus unum). Each *registered* voter gets one vote. We all elect the person to best represent our combined effort: the operator. The saw crew debates the risks involved in our chosen activity, then decides on the best course of action by voting for the best representative to carry out the action under our scrutiny. Where will the most fingers be pointed if something goes wrong and people get hurt? That's where politics takes over; this is why there can be no "official" operator in the system; the vote is held at the tree with each person's Go or No-Go. When the work is done, fingers are pointed at the stump and the pile of firewood as evidence of how well "we" did!

Since kickback is one of the most dangerous aspects of chainsaw physics, it gets the most attention. Instead of spending time listening to all the gory stories and discussing all the negative possible outcomes from a kickback, I used this slide to spend some time talking about the various methods employed by the CSS to mitigate that very significant risk. The system uses positive action born of logical mental processes to remove the negative aspects of running the saw, which, in turn, builds confidence and assurance of positive results, i.e., safety.

I think I beat the first two bullets to sawdust on the last slide, but what about "speed-accelerate/initiate"? The chainsaw has basically two speeds—wide open and dead stop—where the probability of a kickback is lowest; you don't want the chain frequently increasing and decreasing in speed while in contact with the wood. Let's take a look at our AC to

Kickback Avoidance

- Grip – Thumb wrap, Both hands, Strong arm
- Chain – Observe Upper Quadrant, Speed - Accelerate/Initiate, Stand out of Arc
- Use smooth handling - below shoulders
- Watch the kerf, plunge with lower quadrant and wide open
- Hold the saw close - Use anchor points
- Methodical vs. Aggressive

Slide 22: Kickback Avoidance

explain to our brain how this works. Since F = ma, if the chain is slowing down, that's decreasing acceleration; there is a better chance that the mass in the wood will win the battle with the deceleration in the chain, and *force* the chain to reverse direction and climb the wood instead of cutting it. The physical method by which a chainsaw cuts is nullified if there is no wood above the tip of the bar to provide enough force to allow the tooth's cutting edge to penetrate the wood fibers. If there is no wood above the teeth going around the bar's tip, and only air above the bar, there is nothing to stop the bar from climbing the wood; the result is a kickback equal in force and in the opposite direction of where the chain was stopped. Some reverse reactions are small, at a low resultant F; some are big, but even a small kick has the *potential* of jerking the saw from your grip; your "m" (mass) is added to the saw's "a" (acceleration) to resist the wood's "F" (force). There *are* times when you might want to "feather" the trigger, like when you are approaching the ground with a cut, or taking a small amount of wood off a too-thick hinge. In most cases, however, fully depress the trigger; then touch it to the wood at the instant it reaches full speed. As the chain is just about to exit the cut, let off of the trigger so there's no speed left in the chain as the cut is completed. You shouldn't hear any high "rev" before or after the cut; it should sound like a smooth transition from air to wood and from wood to air.

"Below Shoulders" means a chainsaw is not meant to be used over your head; that presents the same problem as reaching too far out with the saw. With no anchor point for extended arms, the operator yields to rotational forces if there is a kick; only raise the saw up until just before your right elbow leaves the side of your body; once it leaves, that's work for some other tool up there.

The kerf is the wood taken out by the teeth's cutting width; as with all saws, the kerf's width is wider than the bar itself, which affords easy movement of the bar through the wood. The cut-out slot gets its own name because it is a very important aspect of AC when cutting. The operator can fight the saw by applying forces at 90 degrees to the bar's plane, thereby forcing the drive links and bar to rub on the wood. The kerf is also the best visual confirmation of the wood's tension and compression reactions while making a cut in wood under stress, which will be covered in extreme detail later. I'll also talk more about the plunge cut later; this is actually a misnomer in this slide since a "plunge" is part of the cutting method known as a bore cut, as is using the lower "initiation quadrant" of the saw to start it. It will become intuitively obvious why these processes are listed on a slide about avoiding kickback.

It's not so true nowadays, but when I was younger, I was a very aggressive worker. I always tried to get any work done as quickly and efficiently as possible, as if I were trying to balance a scale of quality and quantity; the more I learned about doing a particular task, the faster I tried to do it. While developing my PSS, however, I found that giving myself time to think about new actions or activities first nearly always decreased the overall time spent on a job, since I spent less time correcting mistakes. I started letting the risks presented by the work determine how fast I could get the project completed; breaking down complex work into many small, logical steps ultimately resulted in decreasing the number of close calls I needed to mentally process at the end of the day; in other words, a lot less job-related stress. I developed a methodical cadence of working that allowed me to work just as efficiently, and still call it as quick and good a job as I could do. As it turned out, it was always more than adequate, mostly because the job got done without anybody getting hurt. The surprise was I was just as proud of my work; I had earned my pay when the job was completed, and the method in the methodical movement actually afforded my brain an opportunity to produce complementary endorphins; in other words, "I felt good about my work."

> You will never possess a stronger camaraderie than the one you gain with another who is concerned most for your wellbeing while occupied with navigating through a dangerous situation. Running a chainsaw to cut down a giant woody plant is a dangerous situation, times two. The system will help you save each other from injury and thus strengthen your bond, which could possibly even benefit you in other occupations!

Additional Handling Considerations

- Watch for rocks, wires, or objects other than wood
- Never overreach, but cut nearer end of bar
- Pull the saw smoothly out of the cuts
- Cut one log at a time
- Use caution when entering the bar into a partially completed cut
- Use a correctly sharpened and tensioned chain
- Establish footing before initiating the cut
- Anticipate a reaction from the cut
- Initiate the chain then the cut
- Use bumper spikes (dogs) for leverage
- Use wedges to aid bucking
- Use a proper size saw – carry correctly

Slide 23: Additional Handling Considerations

This slide lists additional things to watch for and do while cutting to help avoid a kickback and diminish its effects. This list is not exhaustive; it changes with the application of the saw in your cutting area. Most of these bullets are self-explanatory, and are expounded on somewhere herein, but I usually get questions on:

- **Cut one log at a time:** Logs piled up should be removed from the pile before they are cut up into firewood; crotched branches should be cut one at a time since they may contain different stresses: one may be in compression, the other in tension. In both cases, a higher probability exists that the kickback quadrant could come into contact with a high potential energy surface.

- **Use bumper spikes for leverage:** These are the sharp spikes on the saw's housing next to the bar, which can be "planted" into the wood to provide a leverage fulcrum; it also infers that you are aware if these are on your saw since they tend to be *sharp*.

I mention more about the wedges later; suffice it to say here that, like the hinge, the wedge is another tool that uses the wood's properties to aid the operator in manipulating the wood.

The "proper size saw" is the one that accomplishes the plan of work without too much excess power, bar length, or weight, all of which can increase kickback force. This thought could also be extended to include the proper PSS, of the proper operator, of the proper saw, for each cutting activity. The correct way to carry the saw is with one hand on the front handle, preferably the left, extended down at your side with the bar pointed backward, on the downhill side if you're walking on a contour. Continuing with the parallelism, the correct PSS must be carrying the correct saw in the correct way if such a saw is available; if not, the combination requires more SA to accomplish the increase in AC for the RAM.

There's a lot of information on this slide, but like most of what you will learn in this book, there is no dire need to memorize it; just read it carefully as if you were adding knowledge to your PSS; the information will be there when you need it. Trust me; rather than accepting a fear of the unknown, your brain will find these words stored in your memory when they are needed.

I copied this slide from a PowerPoint my predecessor at Bay College was using when I took his job. I normally don't like slides with a bunch of text. I prefer a small amount of words and more pictures; it's less mental work. In this instance, however, it is appropriate; it is a list of items that an expert chainsaw operator and teacher of safety deemed worthy of being in print. He is giving you examples of important considerations in his SAACRAM—confirmed by hours of cutting and sharing of information with other experienced teachers and students. These are the kinds of things that witness accounts of accidents contain; you will hear your own to add to these—brief observations that will be linked to a picture of practice in your mind that always tell the same story. They are just some of the ever-present origins of risk—mitigatable because you first recognized them, you figured out a way to get out of the way of them, and you remembered how you did it because you spent time teaching it to yourself or someone else. If you are a beginner, you don't have a list like this, but you can use these few examples as a start to your list of things you automatically include in your PW when running your saw.

Until you learn that a black spot on the trunk of your tree can cause your saw to kick out of the cut without even coming close to the kickback quadrant, you probably wouldn't think that a wire nailed to a tree when it was a 3" diameter sapling could possibly still be solid in the center of an old 20" diameter. The chain comes to a sudden stop and kicks straight out of the cut at a time you felt comfortable standing in the kickback arc and maybe loosened your grip on the front handle—an outlier (something with low statistical probability of happening) happens!

Tasks and Techniques:
Limbing   R408.15333 – Rule 5333

- Two levels – down and standing
- Tension/Compression concepts
- Mini size-up, stance location, handling, fell reaction
- Spring Poles – shave 'C' side
- Observe the kerf
- Storm Damage = !!!

Slide 24: Tasks and Techniques - Limbing

The next several slides attempt to deal with Rule 3's various applications: handling the saw in all the following procedures with routine adherence to the elements of the rule, combined with the quality of your SAACRAM and the integrity of your PSS, will see you through learning them safely for the first time, or as it may be, incorporating your current K&E into a respectable/teachable CSS. The best way to learn this is to watch other operators, or to evaluate the way you've always done it through the rule; look for ways a particular handling practice stays in the system, and the ways it does not; look for the little things: the stance, the thumb wrap, and the chain brake. These picture stories being played before your eyes contain enormous amounts of valuable and instantly recallable information. Many things other operators do with a chainsaw get the job done safely, but that does not mean they did it the safest way; it may just mean they were lucky this time—that they didn't get a kick when their thumb was on top of the bar. It's been my experience that people who run solely on luck to stay out of the way of injury end up hurt.

We call cutting branches off a tree "limbing." If the limb is touching only the tree it is attached to—the most probable instance in a standing tree—it is very different AC than when the same limb touches both the tree and the ground after felling. Stresses in the limb's fibers are much more predictable in a standing tree, and very unpredictable in a limb that contacts the ground or other branches. A small diameter branch, one that can be cut fully through by the chain before it begins to fall, can be severed with one cut from the branch's top near the tree's bole. A larger diameter branch on a standing tree may splinter on the bottom before the chain can complete the cut. Splintered wood and chainsaws do not mix; splintered wood has a high probability of pinching the chain. In this case, you would need to make a small cut on the bottom of the branch first, usually about 1/3 the diameter; then finish the cut from the top. In effect, cut the wood that will splinter first, thereby removing the risk. If that cut from the bottom goes too deep, the branch can bend down and "pinch" the chain, and cause a "push" reaction force. If you're "under-cutting" a large limb with the top of the bar, just behind the kickback quadrant, there is an increased chance of a kickback if the chain is bound in the cut or the chain is "dragged" off the limb while the chain is still moving. The action would be to place the kickback quadrant onto wood with the chain still moving or the chain stopped and the bar moving back; the reaction force will be to push the saw toward the operator. If the potential energy in the wood and the kinetic energy in the saw are sufficient, they could cause a large enough kick to reach the operator; close adherence to handling techniques and a special concern should be on the operator's mind when "under-cutting" a limb, and while limbing in general, since this is when most pinches and kickbacks occur.

If the tree has many small branches, as with branchy species like balsam, spruce, or pines, several branches may be cut with one pull of the trigger. The higher risk option of cutting one branch at a time from the bottom and accelerating the saw with each cut introduces the kickback quadrant into branches with each cut, with the added risk of a slowing chain first contacting the branch above on the kickback quadrant. The safest way I've found to cut these many small branches is to reach up, keeping your right elbow anchor point. Make a careful cut to establish a space for the bar; line the bar up parallel to the edge of the tree's bole; stand out of the kickback arc, and with one pull of the trigger to full rev, let the saw fall through the branches and zip them all off with one cut; then turn about 90 degrees and repeat.

Limbs on a tree lying on the ground or against other trees are much more complicated or, in system terms, more complex with higher risk; your SA must *see* what it is looking at, and consider each cut individually. A limb only touching the tree's bole can be considered similar to a limb on a standing tree; whereas, a limb that also touches the ground or other branches will have opposite stresses. Again, smaller branches may be cut with one cut, larger ones with two cuts: first, on the side being pushed together first (under compression), and the finishing cut on the side being stretched (under tension). Limbs may also be pushed into the ground when a tree falls, making them very difficult to cut through without pinching the chain; it may be best left there to hold up the tree's bole until the rest of the branches are limbed.

Tension and compression concepts will be covered in later slides; suffice it to mention here, they must be understood and mitigated while limbing if you are planning to process a felled tree, and at the same time, look like you know what you are doing; if you try to learn in this application with "trial and error," you will be spending time trying to pull your pinched chain out of a branch's grasp, or worse yet, cutting your saw out of a large limb with an ax.

A "size-up" is your SAACRAM being applied while you are cutting; a "mini-size-up" is meant to indicate that the total objective is composed of many small challenges; the large assessment of safely felling and processing a large woody plant can only be accomplished efficiently if SAACRAM is applied to each and every cut. The most important element of wellbeing for you and your coworkers is the cut you are presently making; like all mental processes, recognition and mitigation of each smaller risk will become instinctual with practice each time you operate the saw. Like frames in a motion picture of a CSS operator, each cut is part of the complete story, with a safe, more productive, and stress-free ending.

Even with many experienced operators, push and pull reaction forces are common when limbing. I tell my students in field exercises: If you can limb the entire tree without pinching the chain, you understand the tension and compression found in a single segment of wood. Since reaction forces are common, being ready to receive them is logical; try to keep the line from your one big toe to the other somewhat parallel to the bar; as part of your mini-size-up, locate where your feet will go, take your stance, and make the cut. Watch your handling while you're moving from one cut to the next. Remember the two-hand rule. Set the brake if the move is more than a few steps. Maintain your right hip pocket anchor point and stay out of the kickback arc as much as possible. If you should stumble on branches, push the saw out away from the direction you are falling; I once saw an operator cut the back of his left arm when he fell in the bar with the brake set. You shouldn't be tripping on branches, though, if you have good SAACRAM; you should mitigate the trip risk before your feet get to it; one of my first instructors told me: "When you have one of these in your hands, you don't have to take 'shit' from anything made out of wood."

Use your AC to anticipate where the most stressed limbs will be in the felled tree; a tree that remains attached to the stump will have fewer stressed limbs than one pushed to one side or the other off the stump; you should wait a while in your safety zone after a tree goes down anyway; use that time to let things settle; look the new "down-sized" cutting area over and develop your plan of work for how best to limb the tree. You could do your limbing on the tree's left side, starting from the stump; the saw's bar is on the right, and the saw is held on the body's right side, so this is the best ergonomic method. Work to the top of the tree limbing on both sides of the bole while leaving any branches that may be acting as pedestals to help hold up the tree; then cut the tree up (bucking) back to the stump, removing the pedestal supports as you go.

"Spring poles" are small diameter standing trees that have been bent over to the ground by a falling tree, or they can be branches on a felled tree or small trees lying flat on the ground that are under extreme bending stresses but have not splintered or broken. I have this bullet in this slide to initiate the topic of tension and compression concepts in wood. There are some good videos on YouTube (search: spring pole chainsaw) that show how to mitigate the risk of a spring pole; remember to watch these videos as a CSS member. Even though the operator in the video may show you an adequate method, watch for actions that indicate the operator is a competent CSS member, or a work in progress. Remember, if success comes at the cost of breaking a rule, like the higher risk thumb up on the front bar, the operator didn't hit "perfect," so he needs to adjust his PSS.

The "kerf" is the slot in the wood left by the teeth while the saw is cutting; all saws have a kerf that is wider than the bar—on your chainsaw, the width of the teeth must be wider than the bar in order for the bar to pass through the wood without friction. (AC right here should tell you that this is also the reason you should not apply force to the bar at 90 degrees to the arc; it causes the chain itself to rub on the wood.) If the wood is being compressed, the kerf will get smaller in width; if it is under tension, it will get larger in width. Simply watching the kerf relieves your brain from a lot of AC work while looking at a mess of tangled trees and branches, as can be the case especially in storm damage work. If the bar of the saw is all the way into a log, the kerf is very easy to read for (T)ension or (C)ompression; your eyes are genetically adept at seeing two vertical parallel lines come together or go apart—something to do with saber-toothed tigers in the forest; the smallest change in the width of that kerf is an instant meter of not only the presence of T or C, but their rate of change. You will see either T or C or neither, but the worst case here is when you see both; they are opposites in the same kerf, and the one that pinches is the one of greatest concern; C can take the saw away from you; the biggest problem with T is that it can move faster than your saw can cut; it turns solid wood to splinters at the end of the cut.

If the cut's diameter is small, so the bar is not all the way into the wood, you can still read the T/C gauge on the side of the bar since the bar is not as wide as the kerf. There is a space between the bar and the wood that must react to T/C the same as the whole kerf. If you are cutting with a "pulling chain" nearer the tip, you can learn to increase your focal point from the kickback quadrant to include the kerf width—two things you're always watching when you have nothing else in particular to look at. I realize many of these concepts are difficult to visualize and analyze, especially for beginners; when you are practicing, your brain will find this information as you need it, and in the CSS, every time you cut, you *are* practicing; just cut with close attention to the rules.

TnS; Teacher 'n' Student

Everyone in the CSS must be willing to be a teacher and a student at the same time. In my Navy psych school, we were taught this psychotherapy technique: You have to be both TnS (like conjoined twins) at the same time because your brain has two halves; they look physically the same, but they have very different functions; your right hemisphere (RH) is essentially leading your consciousness into the future, and the left hemisphere (LH) is holding on to earth for dear life. Essentially, what we all do to survive is go around in the present with our RH, and whatever draws our RH's attention the most, our LH moves in on, and devours all the survival information. We can't know if we are the teacher or the student until the dinner is served and digested. This definition of TnS was not created for the CSS; it exists in every human brain, and most other brains; two sides connected by communication cables plugged into a stem leading to the body, where the LH is the only one doing the talking because the RH understands only in pictures, acronyms, and stories. A successful student learns to trust his RH, and a wise student confirms it with his teacher, who is the LH. It requires that each be both teacher and student simultaneously until the student learns the task. One side gives logical information; the other gives acceptance, compliance, and assistance. Teachers learn how good their demonstrations are when they are willingly critiqued by their students, based on what they "did," not the thought about what they "said" they could do. In your brain, the LH and RH meet at a place between white and gray matter; when you have a chainsaw in your hand, your PSS meets the CSS at the stump. The "said" and the "did" are the facts before you, the plan of work, done right.

Brushing is cutting something attached to the earth; slashing is cutting it up after it has been detached from the earth; same bush, different challenges.

Look the cutting area over before you get started. Come up with a plan of work that acknowledges the various challenges at hand; it always makes you look smarter when you look things over first before starting the saw. The cutting area is smaller while cutting small trees, but it can move around more quickly, so be sure to move your plan with it. You can do that best by setting your brake; if you need to move large distances, shut the saw off.

"Look up, down, and around" is just another way to remember to use your head—to think before you leap; don't become so focused on a small cut that you forget what other people are doing. There are lots of small cuts to make with the potential of holding many different stresses—binds, twists, and bends—so the possibility of kickbacks, pushes, and pulls is greatly increased. I would definitely use a different tool than a chainsaw to cut small diameter brush if there is one available—what they call brush-cutters and clearing saws. If you see a lot of brush cutting in your future, buy one now so you can start building your safety system for it. In storm damage, you may find yourself cutting slash above your shoulders; this task is very difficult to accomplish safely because the AC and RAM is difficult; find a way to bring the slash down before cutting it; don't reach up to cut! These concepts are mentioned here because brushing out an escape route is a requirement of Rule 4. Cut the tripping hazards out of the way first; then cut the tree—the logical method of operation (MO).

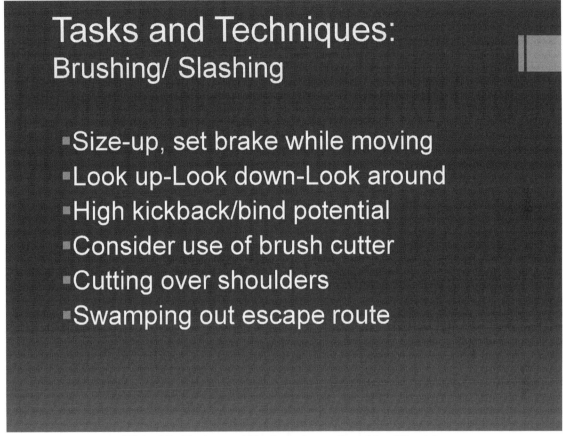

Tasks and Techniques:
Brushing/ Slashing

- Size-up, set brake while moving
- Look up-Look down-Look around
- High kickback/bind potential
- Consider use of brush cutter
- Cutting over shoulders
- Swamping out escape route

Slide 25: Tasks and Techniques – Brushing/Slashing

Here are the proper dance steps when using a chainsaw in a brushing situation:

1. In an 8-10 foot radius cutting area, stand with your feet at a wide stance, a line in each foot from the heal to the toe separated at 45 degrees with the center of the angle directly in front of you.

2. Now slide your right elbow anchor point down to your right knee as you crouch over your center of gravity; as with many branches on the side of a standing tree, make a careful cut to open a space for the bar's tip.

3. With your right thumb on the trigger, and your left thumb firmly wrapped around the front bar on the side of the saw, sweep the cut to the left through the 45-degree arc, taking all the brush in it with one cut.

4. Brush with the saw at full rev, and let the chain come to a stop.

5. Keeping both hands on the saw, pivot, and repeat, starting where the last swipe left off and keeping the 45-degree angle in front of you.

6. Remember to set the brake if you need to remove brush by hand as you advance the cutting area into the next cut.

7. Stand and look around periodically; straighten your vertebrae.

Cutting Area

If you are on a trail crew or the like, perhaps several saws are running, involved in brushing and/or slashing at the same time as you advance down a road or street. Is the cutting area around each saw, or around the entire crew? Yes!

The cutting area is established by the identification of an operator confident enough in their ability to safely control it. The cutting area moves and/or changes in circumference and height with each different application of the tool. If there is more than one operator, the cutting areas must be monitored for overlap. An overseer should be present who has communication with the overlapping/adjoining cutting areas; they should know who the operator and SP are in each CA, what their K&E is, and what type of operation is being conducted. They should have contact with the SP in each area by line of sight or radio. A mini-tailgate safety session should be conducted to work out communication parameters. The overseer is usually the legal authority for the cSS, so they should also make sure operators are taking proper charge of their respective cutting areas and not stepping on other operators or parts of the crew. The overseer should have some kind of permission from an operator to enter a CA when the saw is running, such as eye contact or communication relayed by the SP.

If the only work to be done is brushing small diameter stems, your SAACRAM should be searching for a lower risk tool, but if a chainsaw must be used, this is a good situation in which to practice ergonomics, saw handling, thought processes in mini-size-up, and communication skills; "Walk the walk and talk the talk" as they say. The wood's forces are reduced because of decreased mass, and the subject trees' heights may allow for a closer involvement between operators, SPs, swampers, and possibly even overseers. These types of projects can be good teaching opportunities to build a healthy cSS when cutting small, non-complex trees. If your cSS is composed of your daughter and son cutting the brush along the north line of the pasture, I guess that would make you the overseer, the property owner, the teacher, and the boss. (Unless the wife came along; then you might end up being just a swamper.)

Tasks and Techniques:

Bucking R408.15337 – Rule 5337

- Situational Awareness – have an escape route
  - Overhead, area, footing, hazards, plan
  - Tension/Compression (Cut C first)
- Techniques
  - Up-hill side, binds/pivots, use dogs, cut off-side 1st, watch kerf, wedge/pie cut, ground clearance, spring poles
- Binds
  - Top, Bottom, Side, End
- Blow Down – Special significance on bind

Slide 26: Tasks and Techniques – Bucking

Bucking is cutting up the tree into a product after it has been limbed. *Situational Awareness* is obviously an important factor for the various trainers who compiled these elements of limbing, brushing, and bucking; they keep mentioning it over and over with various terms. While bucking, you are creating large heavy pieces of wood that can move toward you when cut, so have a place for your leg or entire body to move to in the event the wood comes your way. When you drop a tree, or a storm does it for you, look the cutting area over for the best places to execute the limbing process to create the most advantageous approach to the bucking. (AC and RAM say that larger mass is higher risk, so that must be mitigated first; in this case, optimal limbing sequence in preparation for bucking.) Look for the unexpected risks, or those caused by the tree coming down through other trees; in storm damage, all sorts of materials may be mixed in with the wood—things a chainsaw is not designed to cut. (Increased complexity + increased risk = increased awareness that knows what it is looking at.)

You must pay very close attention to tension and compression concepts when bucking. It's simple to cut your saw out of a branch with an axe, or pull it out using all your strength. A large diameter tree won't give it up so easily; the wood may win the war of wills, and you may end up pulling a muscle in your shoulder or back. When cutting large diameter logs, I always carry wedges: two in the pocket of my chaps for felling and one in my back pocket for bucking; then I actually use them as tools to make the work easier and safer, to hold the kerf open, and to provide the wood with something to compress besides my bar! There are actually wedges designed to be used for bucking that are easily pulled out of the kerf, and wedges designed for felling with cleats on them for holding to the wood.

Remembering to "Cut C side first" is very important when attempting to cut a log with any type of saw. If you cut from the T side first, and you continue cutting in, things may go right for you most of the time, but there will be times when you don't make it to the end of the cut before the wood splinters; splinters are the enemy of saws! A splinter is usually composed of a bunch or radial fractures in the wood; the wood fails first in the weakest direction—the radial direction—because it is easy to split firewood. The stress in the wood is transformed for one continuous spectrum from C to T into many small pieces with small Cs on one side and small Ts on the other; this causes a jerking action in the cut; each jerk is you trying to cut through a small C. (I did not say you were a jerk, but the chainsaw can make one out of you.) When you cut the C side first, you take away the wood that is going to splinter; it's the same principle as when you face the tree in Rule 4; you take away the wood that is going to splinter. This technique is not new; when the Pilgrims felled trees for their forts, they faced the tree with an ax first!

The list under "Techniques" includes some tricks most safety instructors highlight in their training; they are methods that consistently end up helping the process; they are worthy for "regimentation"; they are common sense actions you regularly include in your favorite moves. If one works, do it every time. In the CSS, if you see someone doing it differently, teach or graciously receive instruction! Gravity is a force vector you can count on being there; the larger an object's mass, the more potential energy it contains, and the more kinetic energy it carries in the form of force—work done on your leg. It's a very good idea to work on the uphill side of a large log, but you also must keep in mind the wood's properties and stresses. A small diameter tree will bend to easily indicate T and C stresses; a large diameter tree will usually resist the bending because of its mass; the T and C will need to be read by the position of the tree on the ground. A stump, berm, or another tree can give the tree a pivot point; the mass in the log that you are standing uphill of could be stronger than gravity and move uphill. You have to see the pivot point (SA); you need to calculate without a calculator what its effect (AC) will be; then you need to cut the tree up in a way that controls the release of the energy without your leg being in the way (RAM).

I mentioned using the bumper spikes, here called the "dogs," as leverage to lessen the level of force your muscles need to produce to make the cut; ergonomics says you are always looking for an easier and smarter way to do it, like cutting the off-side of the logs cut in from the other side for about one-third the diameter so you have the option of standing back a little from the log when you get the log's reaction when the cut is completed.

A very valuable piece of your mental toolkit is your T/C gauge: the kerf. The kerf can be held open with a wedge when cutting a log from the top that is resting on the ground. If the log is lying on the ground for its full length, cut from the top until the kerf starts to close; place the wedge in the kerf to take the compressive force, and thereby hold the kerf open for your bar and chain; then cut to the bottom of the log. Watch out you don't run your chain into the ground; keep it parallel to the ground as you cut down. "Aim" to make it perfectly parallel, and stop cutting at exactly the right time before it touches dirt. If the log is suspended in the air, you may be able to bring it down slowly by cutting a "pie cut" on the C side; then cut up from the T side carefully to leave a small amount of wood in the middle of the log to bend, splinter, and slowly displace the force of gravity; this is actually a "face cut," a "back-cut," and a "hinge" on a horizontal tree, which will become more apparent in Rule 4. (If you're a beginner operator and you can't wait to get to Rule 4 right now, you are going to make a very good CSS member; I believe I would really enjoy cutting with you.)

I already mentioned spring poles. I left them in this slide so I would remember to mention that spring poles are not always small diameter trees and branches; a 6" diameter log can also be a spring pole if enough force is applied to it. If you consider that a true statement, you can also believe that any size stem could be one; the larger the mass, the less visual indication there is of bending. Your AC needs to kick in when your SA sees a tree wedged between a bunch of other trees. (Did I hear someone mumble "storm damage"?)

I like to think of cutting in storm-damaged scenarios as playing a gigantic game of pick-up sticks with all the sticks under stress; I start small and work my way to big; I start high, and work my way to low so my kickback quadrant is clear; I start simple and work my way to complex; I start slow, and work my way to fast—all are techniques that make you good at picking up a stick without another stick moving. Use this mental picture as a tool; follow Rule 3 the best you can and you will win the game. (You will also be a super-hero to some kid who watched their parents go nuts over the trees across the driveway and would love to play that real-life game you call work—a challenge with real-life risk.)

You've heard people say, "If you want to experience life to its fullest, you must get outside your comfort zone." That makes for a good saying, but it is misleading, and, therefore, creates false hope for avoiding injury, which is the opposite of comfort. A more logical way to teach this concept would be to say, "If you want to learn, you must *expand* your comfort zone." There is a reason you have no stress in the zone: You can only trust the zone with comfort based on the truth content in valid reasoning—by logically considering the *knowledge* level of your common sense and any weakness in your instinct, without bias, as if you are your own instructor. That location outside your zone can be occupied by you with confidence, but confidence in what? The best way to build comfortable and appropriate confidence is to take small repetitive steps, carefully examining each new ground, then confidently occupying it; your confidence in that ground is sufficient to be used as a base for the next step; you know it's solid, so you successfully add it to your zone; your comfort zone expands ahead of you. This is an ongoing process we call "practice." It doesn't need to occur in a controlled zone in reality; it needs to be *experienced* in your mind, where the comfort zone exists. In the CSS, this zone is in reality your cutting area; in your mind, it's a combination of your SAACRAM and your ability to abide by the rules. If expanding your comfort zone is simply starting the saw, practice the rules first by putting on your chaps, hard hat, and gloves; take a look at yourself in a full-length mirror; tell your mind that this is what a chainsaw starter looks like. Imprint that picture in your mind; take another picture of how you will hold the saw; practice your method for holding the saw over and over until the actions are added to your reflex, instinct, and common sense; then use the rule, and start the saw; you are extending your comfort zone wisely.

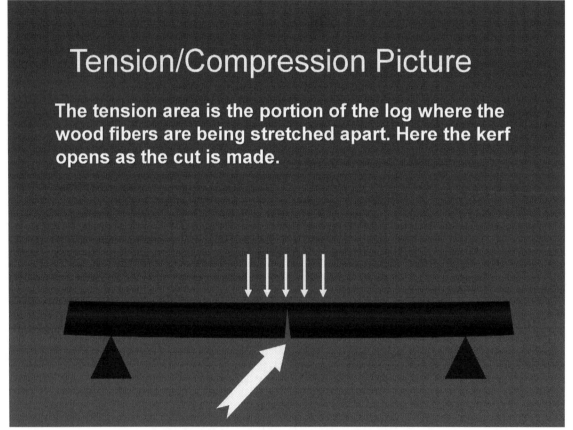

Slide 27: Tension/Compression Picture

This slide and the next two were in the PowerPoint presentation I inherited from my predecessor at Bay College. I was going to take them out until I realized that when cutting for extended periods of time in storm damage, these pictures are very handy to have in mind. My brain cannot be depended on to instantly figure out where the T and C are in a log, so I often find myself visualizing this picture to figure it out before choosing where to start the C cut. Since I see myself as an average person, I give the picture to you to place in your memory for the future. I believe you will find it useful, assuming that you're not a "genius operator." If all this information contains too much redundancy for you, please remember you are simply gleaning it so you know what you are handing your student.

New Operators

Most new operators should expect to spend as much time as they can as a SP. If you have good SAACRAM, and are trying to get better in the system, you will be on your way to becoming a safe and productive operator, who even has some fun, especially in seeing his "old" teacher standing in the safety zone watching.

It's amazing to me how fast you can interpret the look on someone's face; their face and eyes are speaking a separate language we all understand, mostly in our subconscious mind, but the understanding can only increase in value when it is exercised between two people while being enhanced through cooperation of action in a high-risk situation. The inquisitiveness in the eyes of an eager student is a lasting endearment to an old man. Your question alone can answer my question, but the only way I can truthfully answer your question is to tell you how to *do* the answer, then hand you the saw, tell you to do a good job, and go to the safety zone (SZ) and pay attention to you!

This next slide depicts a log supported very nicely on both ends. It's easy to read; you cut in about one-third the diameter from the top, watching the kerf closely for the first sign it's closing; then line up the bar on the bottom of the log with the cut on the top and cut up until the log is severed. This can only be made more complex: Say there's brush under the log, there's no gap under the log, the log is still attached to the stump, or other trees are pressed up against the log—you can see how easily this could get very complicated.

If I were a beginner practicing my bucking, I would purposely set up some logs so they looked like this one; maybe I'd put the supports under it, and cut some very simple examples; once I had the simplest example down pat, I would apply the technique and the muscle memory to a more complicated situation. The CSS should allow easy access to this plan; if you are volunteering for a county conservation district, there will be times when an operator on the crew will fell a large diameter tree; ask that operator if they will watch you buck the tree up and critique your work; after all, you must be good at limbing and bucking on many different complexity levels before you fell your first large diameter

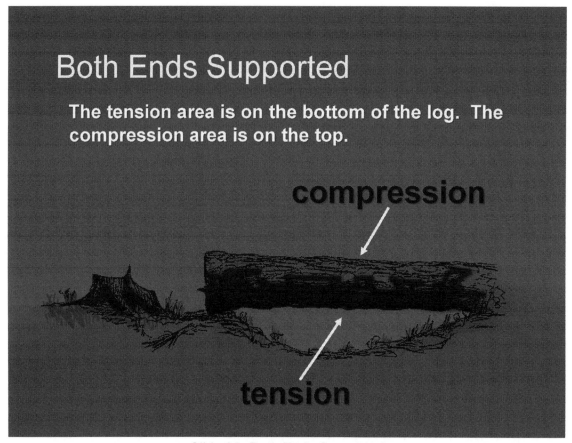

Slide 28: Both Ends Supported

tree. The tree you drop is work that you created, an embarrassing place for a No-Go. If you do find yourself in that situation, find an experienced operator and verbalize what you intend to do: your plan of work; then demonstrate it. You become your own student under the watchful eye of a teaching SP.

Practice, practice, practice; the more you repeat it, the more you exemplify it, the more you become it.

If you have enough passion to learn to excel at it, you will share it. If good comes out of sharing it, more will ask you for it—the passion will spread without you, and because of you.

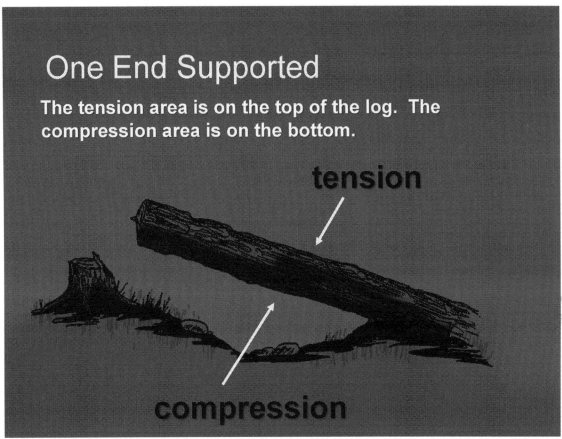

Slide 29: One End Supported

I'm sure that at this point you are convinced of the importance of understanding T/C concepts using very fundamental depictions. When you teach, even if you are an operator with previous K&E, you should start with the easiest concepts so you can foundationally identify the quality and quantity of your student's unique experience, especially if your student is young in common sense. This, again, is a simple scenario, but many more complicated cuts can be explained only when the basic cut is understood. Of course, here I would cut up from the bottom for a short distance, realizing that the kerf in this situation can't be seen. I'd probably determine the distance to cut up as indicated by the log's condition or position, or perhaps by how it responded to previous cuts. Ways exist to cut this log so it does not drop when the wood is completely severed; after the C cut is made, the T cut is off-set a distance to the right of the C cut to form a step for the falling log end to rest on. This cut is handy to keep in mind with any wood under stress; in this situation, gravity and the wood's mass are the source of the potential energy. Maybe you don't have a good option for a safety zone when the log drops to your feet, so you want it to stay put for now.

Take a look at the "Mortise and Tenon" cuts on YouTube. Complex cuts like these can be used when more control is needed to compensate for the wood's cutting reactions; to use most of these cuts, the operator must be proficient with Rule 3, or attempts at getting "pretty" could result in ugly scars; start simple and learn your way to complex in small increments.

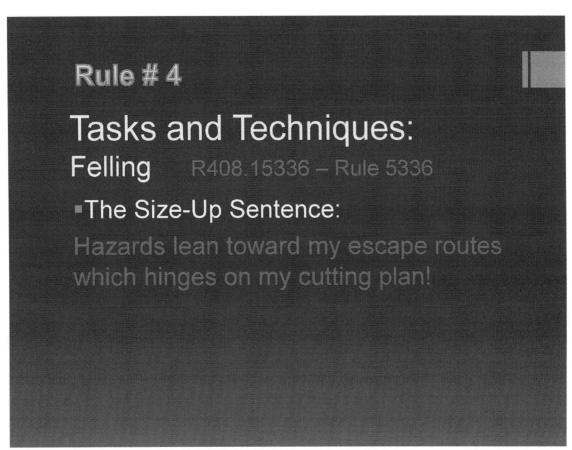

Slide 30: Tasks and Techniques

RULE #4 – TASKS AND TECHNIQUES

THIS RULE, LIKE THE OTHERS, is a habit that your body forces your brain to repeat; your brain then redirects your body to perform it; it's a preplanned pause in the physical action to allow your brain SAACRAM processing time. When I'm talking felling, I'm thinking larger diameter and higher complexity trees; the smaller ones with easy analysis are the ones you use to practice and perfect your PSS. That doesn't mean you forget the rule; it means you think more about the rule as you extend your limitations in a minimally dangerous, carefully chosen cutting area. *Aim for perfect; then adjust.* In fact, many of the abilities required to master the actual felling techniques can be learned by cutting on high stumps left by other operators explicitly for the purpose. The analysis can be done on any tree you see; I always enjoy spending time walking in the woods staring up at large, complex trees; doing so increases your chainsaw SAACRAM whether you cut them or not.

When I did my C faller recertification in Kentucky, the instructor told me that when I cut for my test the next day, I had to cover five elements; if I missed any of them, I would fail. These are all long-standing practices while felling a tree, and I used them most of the time, but I had never realized how important they were until a teacher held them in such high regard. He told me, "You will have to verbalize everything you are thinking during your size-up, and make sure you tell me as much as you can about each of these five elements; mark where the tree will fall, and successfully place the tree in order to keep your certification. If you miss setting your brake any more than three times, you fail. If I see your thumb up on the bar any more than three times, you fail."

Now I'm sure I am a lot like you in this; I have never been into failing, especially when a blatant challenge is detailed in front of witnesses. My stubbornness kicked in that night, so I practiced brake-setting until the back of my left hand was red. I made up a sentence with my vivid imagination that included the five elements; I even had a picture for it: Me at the base of my subject tree. Several snags in the lay leaning to where I had my escape route caused me to change my plan. I talked my brain into believing this situation was of life and death importance: "I'll show those guys what Hiawatha operators can do." When it came my turn to cut, I kept repeating that silly sentence to myself to make sure I hit all the elements in order. I did not forget to set the brake; every time I took my right hand off the rear handle, I pushed down hard, deliberately. I did not put my thumb on top of the bar; I made sure I had my index finger wrapped around that handle so it could pinch it hard until it hurt. I passed the test that day and got my C Faller. I had to do more than demonstrate my cutting abilities; I also had to verbalize and demonstrate my safety abilities so I could prove that I could teach it. When you use a chainsaw to fell a tree, safety *must* come first if you intend to cut trees all your life, and you expect that life to be long and healthy.

So, did I go back to cutting the next week on the job and forget all that stuff? No, it became my PSS; even to this day, more than fifteen years later, I still find myself saying that sentence when I'm looking up and down a tree, or verbalizing what felling is to a student. Now there is no way that I can know for sure—safety gives an invisible reward—but it is very possible that my strong desire to pass that test was my self-preservation instinct prompting me to take the training as a "life or death" ultimatum—the frame of mind it put me in, the regimentation it placed me in, and the precision and accuracy it insisted be in my actions allowed me to realistically evaluate my own ability, as if from outside my body, and constantly improve what I would someday teach: the CSS.

CSS chainsaw operators have a practiced ability to see details in the size-up that normal or even more experienced people do not see. They are practiced at the art of perception; they do it all the time in their daily lives as they exercise their SA. They have an uncanny ability to resolve problems that individual trees present because they have trained their analytical mind to respond correctly with their AC; they don't let pride stop them from saying "This is a No-Go" because of this reason or that; they'll willingly say, "We can't mitigate that hazard with the resources at hand." The five elements of felling are in the sentence as shown in the next slide; it's a simple method for memorizing and teaching (verbalizing and demonstrating) the application of a mature chainsaw operating SAACRAM to beginners and SPs.

I can usually tell a good chainsaw operator before they even pick up a saw. They have good SAACRAM, but that's not what they call it; they call it common sense. It's the reason that kind of person is rare; everything about them says "uncommon"; they help the rest of us define the center of our individual sense. How do you teach this type of character to a beginner? Is there such a thing as a beginner who is also a leader? Could leadership also be called "concern for others"? If I am looking at a chainsaw for the first time in my life, and I see you sharpening the chain—you're grabbing the chain and rotating it bare-handed—I get your attention and throw you a pair of leather gloves; you stop, smile, and put a glove on and proceed; does that make me a chainsaw operator, a SP, or a swamper? We are all in the same situation whenever we enter a cutting area together because we are working the same plan: one where we *all* get out of it in one piece. We all control what we let our mind ponder; if we see something, we say something. We collude against injury with our trained focus on the chainsaw and the wood; my casual SAACRAM response to your bare hand sliding along the chain, as a first and only responder to your injury, because it never happened. I stopped the bleeding before the cut—it's like leading you down a safe path from a future course I have already walked, with simple risk mitigation.

They're all in this next slide: the five essential thought processes you must cover every time you cut a tree. For a small diameter tree, it might take just a few seconds; for a large diameter, complex tree, it may take a half hour or more. I have felled trees in family members' backyards where I visited the tree on several different occasions after agreeing to drop it, and I have even met my SP (usually my brother-in-law for family cutting) at the base of the tree so we can go through these five processes together; we talked about different cutting plans, available equipment, weather, who would get the wood, and scheduling when to do it, with no chainsaw in sight.

I don't know why I call it a "mantra"—it was the only word I could think of that helped define this thought process's importance; it's almost a spiritual experience: an operator, the WMDH, a tree that has served the residence well, but reached its demise—everything as it should be except the part where someone gets hurt, or a house gets demolished! The word infers that there is a dedication, an allegiance, but to what? If it's just to save my own ass, and that's it, isn't that just paranoia, lack of self-confidence? I suppose it is if all this thinking is done for any other reason than to support the CSS, to take control of this sacred privilege and drop this sucker on the mark. Can you understand now why this crazy old brain would take it as a personal affront to stand there and watch some yahoo walk onto my turf with his pa's old saw, dressed in shorts, his dirty hat on backwards, and start

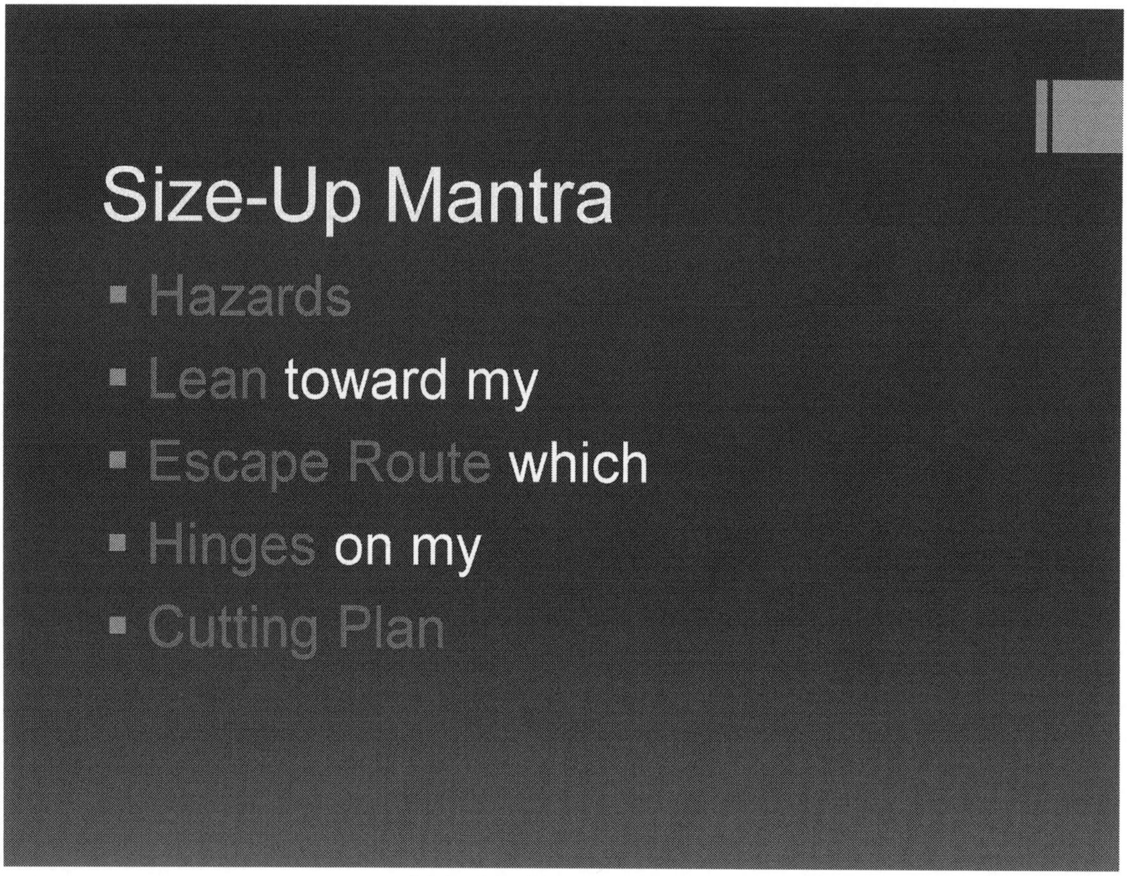

Size-Up Mantra

- Hazards
- Lean **toward my**
- Escape Route **which**
- Hinges **on my**
- Cutting Plan

Slide 31: Size-Up Mantra

cutting on my mother-in-law's tree without even looking up at it? For the sake of my respect for all my fellow operators in the CSS, you had better bet I'd be over there teaching that guy with a very stern look on my face. It doesn't matter to me if he's the owner of the local tree trimming service or an arborist with plaques on his woodshed wall, I know when someone is *not* in the CSS with the slightest glance, and until he agrees to line up with the rules, I'm making that *my* cutting area! Does this make me a bad person? Not for this chainsaw operator, it doesn't. I blame my behavior on the CSS; it's the system's fault; I'm just trying to improve my PSS. My mother-in-law knows this; that's why she called me to cut the tree; that, and the fact that she's always looking for a "better deal."

You *must* have these five elements of the felling size-up memorized! In the slide, my list of five elements adds up to a sentence: Hazards lean toward my escape route which hinges on my cutting plan. I used that sentence because that's the way I remember things; you might have other methods for memorizing a list, which is fine as long as it makes you sure you didn't miss any of the five; they are all very important, and missing one can be the most egregious judgmental error in chainsaw operation. As you've already learned, it's simple to measure how unsafe it is—just add up all the operators who are injured and killed each year in the United States because they skipped through this thought process.

I learned this "make a picture" memorization process from a Dale Carnegie lecture I once attended; I actually see my subject tree with some <u>hazard</u> snags on my lay that are <u>lean</u>ing in the direction I plan to go to <u>escape</u> the stump, which causes me to change the <u>hinge</u> in my <u>plan</u>. One of my students said he uses H.E.L.C.H.; I like it because it allows "hinge" to be first and the hinge is the most important element of the felling procedure, but the sentence follows the natural sequence of the process very nicely, and completely by coincidence, I might add. I find many trainers use the same thought process without conferring with me at all; that's what I refer to as common sense; we all came up with the same result at around the same time without having a meeting—something a well-practiced CSS does all the time.

Wood is as strange a material as a chainsaw is a unique tool; it can creak and snap to indicate it is about to fail in its ability to hold together, or it can quietly, unperceptively exhibit sudden failure. A spring pole is called such because it stores energy in a static state like an expanding spring with a load that is tied down by a wire, a few longitudinal cells. That, in itself, is a problem, but in addition, catastrophic failure of the wood can occur with removal of very small quantities of wood holding the energy from release. Maybe a better name would be snap pole because it happens so fast you can't get out of the way; it can contain enough force to take your saw away from you and hit you with it; it can have enough power stored up in it to hit you upside the head and knock you out, or worse. When the wire is cut, the result is surprising; operators have been killed by the sudden release of power from a branch or an entire tree (barber chair); it's like the tree has its own form of kickback. There is also this ever-present truth: if wood has a physical property or characteristic on a small scale, like a branch, a facsimile or larger version of that same action exists in the tree's high mass sections; they don't have to move as fast to apply the same force; the same physics are being applied, just at a larger scale; the whole tree spring pole just has less bend in it. It is possible to split an entire twenty-foot-long section of a 20" diameter tree with a few inches crosscut at the middle of a bend in the log; I've seen it many times and had my saw ripped from my hands a couple of those times.

When I first started firefighting, I was always amazed by the experienced people who, when faced with high-flame lengths in a dangerous situation, could very calmly run through a list of priority actions followed by detailed instructions for each individual on site; it sounded like they were repeating a list of things to pick up at the store, but they were surrounded by a wildfire. I later figured out that these people didn't have extra-sensory perception and nerves made of copper wire; they had a memorized, practiced, and

Size-Up Thought Process

Applicable to any dangerous activity

- Hazards - what in the area is of concern?
- Lean - what are characteristics of the subject that affect the outcome?
- Escape Route - where do you go for protection?
- Hinge - where is my control?
- Cutting Plan - what is the best and safest way to accomplish?

Slide 32: Size-Up Thought Process

rapidly recallable list of things to think about already programmed into their brains for handling complicated and confusing issues.

The five elements of the felling size-up are not exhaustive; other things may need to be thought about before dropping a tree, not the least of which is the operator's/SP's level of K&E and SAACRAM savvy. These elements are a common sense approach to exercising SAACRAM and the CSS's rules in a regimented/teachable format, within a stress-provoking environment. The logic is not unique to chainsaw operation except in the definitions of the words. The same logic is applicable for analyzing any dangerous work or activity. Try it; think of some dangerous activity you are regularly involved in; then run through the words in white after each element; apply them to that activity, and see if, indeed, these are exactly the kinds of thoughts that go through your head each time you do that activity.

Mentally place yourself behind the wheel of your favorite ride as you cruise down a four-lane freeway; now think about what goes on in your mind to respond to the apprehension you feel entering a maze of intersections in a place you've never been at 75 mph. I've found this little brain game to be very useful in many complex and/or dangerous situations in life; in the CSS, however, it is not a game; it is Rule 4. It gives you a format in which to teach this amazing ability to turn apprehension into confidence that you have a safe product.

The elements are also a very good topic for V&D (verbalize and demonstrate), whether teacher to student, or student to teacher, on any aspect of cutting, from taking off a limb to felling a complex tree. Discussing your thoughts with your SP/student not only solidifies the reasoning in your own head, but it recognizes your helper as a valuable component of your plan. In fact, it can be used to analyze any action, whether low or high risk, because this is the regimented communication to determine risks and their levels. It's a system you use to make your safe plan of work; then you find reasons to change that plan to mitigate newly recognized risks—like a system within a system, or an incident within an incident. Nearly every injury can be linked to a lapse in communication or expectation; these two birds can be taken with the one stone, so talk about it. If you run into a risk that prompts you to change the plan mid-action, but you can't do it safely, stop and come up with a new plan of work together, just you and your SP, talking about the same mental list.

The amount of detail in a photo is determined by the number of pixels; the more in a frame, the better the photograph's clarity, but the human eye automatically increases and decreases what it's going to preserve as the consciousness takes the picture. All the shots your brain camera takes are initially seeking the minimum number of pixels needed to make the picture recognizable, based on what draws the most attention in front of it—the prettiest, the best, the fastest, the brightest, the loudest, etc.; then it goes on to its next frame. That continues until a picture's similarity to the next one taken continues at the same "sense level," causing a chemical release in the brain: done, remembered, stored for future use. If an item of future importance is not clear in the picture we have recorded, it won't become so until caught on many succeeding frames; like adding pixels, we stare at it; this is what some call "freeze." Additional information could come in quickly—a fist goes up for the fight—or your consciousness may not like what the new picture is exposing and you take flight in the opposite direction. The easiest and best pictures to hang on the wall are the ones with surprise on the face, like when you figure out what I'm talking about; I just gave you a picture to remember, so frame it, and hang it on the wall. Every time you look at it, you increase your perception's accuracy because of your new perspective. When you need to recall what you thought you forgot, it will become crystal clear to you because of your ability to add the pixels.

Under legal authority, we are all huddled together for a group picture with a beautiful wooden frame; under ethical authority, we are all portraits hung side by side on a beautiful wooden wall, our students on the opposite wall, staring at us.

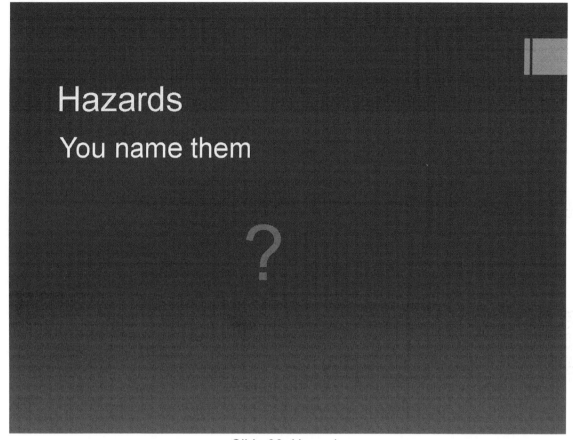

Slide 33: Hazards

I use this slide in my class to see if the message is getting through to my students—to get a feel for their level of K&E, and to wake them up for a few minutes. Actually, by this time in the lecture, the students are usually very attentive; they are recalling all the close calls they had while dropping trees, or revisiting that story about how some guy out on a farm killed himself back in '08. I will go around the room and ask each student to name a possible hazard while cutting down a tree. I'll usually get through a few sitting near the front of the class with responses like widow makers, telephone wires, the outhouse, my stupid dog—things like that—before I stop and let them off the hook by stating, "You could say just about anything, and I could dream up a scenario where it could be a hazard while cutting down a tree with a chainsaw." Of course, after making such a bold state-ment, I get instant challenges like: "elephant, pancake, sea anemone," yelled out by some smartass. After having some fun with that by showing how they could be hazards—cut-ting down a tree at the zoo; I ate fifty of them for breakfast; I have a coral cutting saw with a long snorkel—I point out the reason for the exercise: Nobody can possibly predict the hazards that could be encountered in felling any tree until they are actually in the cutting area; it's something that must be done in the moment, on scene; there are simply too many variables present in even a simple drop, let alone a complex one; you have to be there with an eye that can see what it is looking at and understand the risk indicated by: a scar on the side of the tree, a large branch extending off one side of the bole, a sudden change in topography in the lay, or an ambulance coming at you with its siren blaring.

So how can any average brain like mine possibly anticipate even the simplest set of risks? Next slide!

> "The fear of death is the most unjustified of all fears,
> for there's no risk of accident for someone who's dead."
> — Albert Einstein

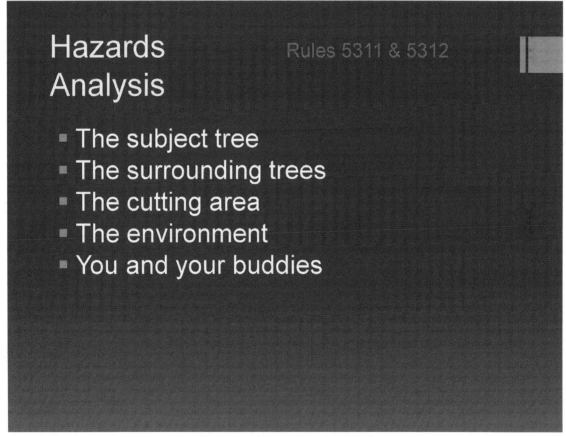

Slide 34: Hazards Analysis

Surprise! There's a mini-system for sorting out all the risks! Alternately described as a systematic method, it's used by the operator and safety person to analyze and discuss what risks are present, how *they* are pertinent to our perspective, how they will progress during the fall, and how *we* will proceed to mitigate them.

Start at the base of the subject tree: Check the ground condition for type of soil, moisture content, whether there is a sloping surface, and what type of clearing and clean up you'll need to do around the tree. Look for the roots to see if they are exposed, or pulled up out of the ground. Check what is on the ground that could have come off this tree. I start my SAACRAM scan up the trunk by letting each visible mark or defect share the information it holds, just as I always do when practicing my perception (SA), and comparing what I am looking at with any past K&E memories that may be stored in my PSS—things I've seen and done in the past. I constantly ask myself questions about it, or you may hear me speaking it out loud with my SP or teacher: Is the bark tight or loose? Is the cambium alive, dead, or rotted? Are there signs of insects, scars, or fractures? I work my way up the subject tree, paying close attention to the place where the face and hinge will be and whether any branches need to be removed to clear my work area. I continue lifting my eyes, letting what I see "talk" to me: Are the branches dead or alive? Are there leaves on the tree or not? Is the tree dead on top and alive on the bottom, or vice-versa? I check the size, condition, and location of large branches, crotches, and defects in the bole.

From my subject tree, I move out to any surrounding trees; first to any trees that may be touching the subject tree, then to any trees or branches in the opening where the tree will fall: *the lay*. Will the location of the surrounding trees place restraints on my cutting plan? What is going to stop me from putting it in my lay? I check the condition of the surrounding trees: Are there branches on them that are entangled with the subject tree? Will trees in the lay break if struck by my tree? Will they stop it from falling, causing a hang-up?

I move my SAACRAM out to the cutting area looking for people, and the things they leave behind: other workers in the area, hikers on the trail, curious children or childish adults, pets, power lines, roads, houses, barns, fences, fruit trees, other healthy trees—you get the idea. You need to recognize everything that is *not* your subject tree and sort them out: concern/risk/relevant hazard or not!

I continue outward from the subject tree to the environment with my body usually still located at its base: Which direction is the wind coming from? Is it variable or gusty? Is it with me or against me? Is there a weather front moving in? Is it now or has it been rainy, snowy, dry, or hot? What is the area's topography? What is the general health of trees in the vicinity?

Finally, I constantly consider myself a hazard to others' wellbeing: Am I extending my limitations too far with this drop? How long have I been working? Am I getting tired? What is my attitude toward this tree/situation? Then I consider my coworkers: Is the drop too much stress for my SP, or should I teach? Are the boundaries of my cutting area the right size and well established? Do I have a good safety zone? Am I below .08 after drinking last night? Are there any No-Gos here?

I know what you're thinking: *All this brain work to cut down a tree!* Wait a second; you do remember that this is only the first element of the five, right? There is still a lot more thinking to do, but let me assure you that mentally processing an average tree—one that's away from any infrastructure, with some "forward lean," in a relatively open area—will not take more than a few seconds, going through the entire fourth rule in your head once you have practiced and developed your PSS, have a K&E base, and are not extending your limitations too much. These thoughts are processed through your brain very quickly without stress; what I mean by stress in this instance is that aching, uneasy, and anxious feeling of not knowing for sure what is about to happen. In fact, if you feel anything except confident that your tree will do anything but end up near the center of the lay, if the complexity of the drop is forcing you to think too much, that's one part of your brain telling another part of your brain that in its search for information pertaining to this dangerous activity you are about to attempt, it found more reasons why you *shouldn't* do it at all; ask your SP for input, or another operator/teacher in the area. If together you can't mitigate the risks, that's a No-Go—you need additional equipment, alternate methods, or more K&E—so you go on to the next tree, or go home, whichever the case may be; the anxiety is gone; you go back to thinking about it!

If the corporate safety system (cSS) says the tree must come down or you don't get paid, hand the saw to the teacher and ask for a V&D for you and your SP; it's your employer's legal and ethical responsibility to provide training before making the accomplishment of a dangerous activity a condition of your employment; the law is on your side; the CSS is on your side, because *you, the operator,* must determine the risks in cutting down a tree with the WMDH. No job is worth losing all future jobs because you are physically unable to work! Get into the CSS. Teaching your employer as you bring them into the system equals risk/hazard mitigation.

> Your dictionary will define a "hazard" as an "unavoidable risk"; the "un" must be removed systematically.

When you cut down a tree, particularly a large tree through other large trees, you change a lot of potential energy into kinetic energy; you do work with the subject tree; the environment was pretty much in an energy equilibrium until you showed up with all that power. Who would you say is responsible for analysis of the results and cleaning up that mess? Exactly. But you don't need to do all the work. I have on many occasions taken advantage of a tree lying on my mark to provide a student/beginner with the opportunity to practice their PSS. If you're approaching my age, and I assume not many readers are, and still cutting, you might even get away with sitting on the stump to watch and comment.

If you're the type who thinks all kinds of cutting is fun, not just felling, simply cut the tree in half; give your student the limbing half, and you take the bucking, or vice-versa; just watch for the overlap of your CAs. Before your student starts felling large complex

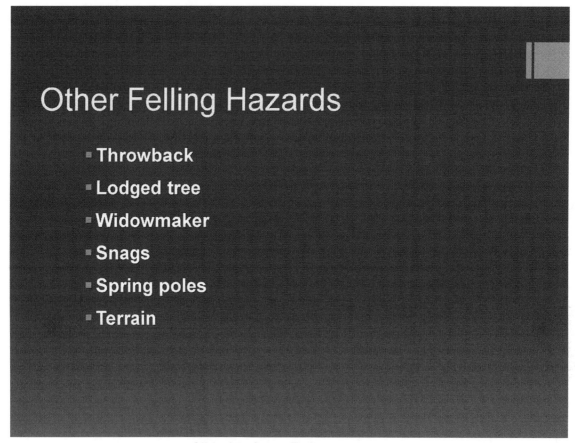

Slide 35: Other Felling Hazards

trees, they will need to know how to clean up their mess by doing complex limbing and bucking of their own tree—an activity, incidentally, that results in more cuts, breaks, and bruises than felling.

When you're standing there looking at the tree you just fell, waiting for things to settle, take a moment to think about how your PW matched up with your WP, and if your drop was totally successful. Pat yourself on the back if your PW = WP. Enjoy the remnants of the endorphins in your brain, and put the picture in your frame. Take advantage of the rush you get from watching that giant woody plant go exactly where you wanted it to; it's what makes a lifetime chainsaw operator. If you're like me, you'll get hooked on the high. I sometimes tell my students that my drug of choice at work is the one I get when all that kinetic energy is put to work exactly on my mark, and it went exactly as I planned it. I control the dose and the chemicals released in my brain with the CSS; I like dopamine and serotonin. (Wikipedia: Serotonin [/ ˌ s ɛ r ə ˈ t oʊ n ɪ n, ˌ s ɪər ə-/] or 5-hydroxytryptamine [5-HT] is a monoamine neurotransmitter. It has a popular image as a contributor to feelings of wellbeing and happiness, though its actual biological function is complex and multifaceted, modulating cognition, reward, learning, memory, and numerous physiological processes.) I don't like cortisol; it makes me nervous and has negative after-effects.

Throwback usually happens as the tree is on the way to the ground when part of the subject tree strikes another tree or obstacle; due to the springing action of the longitudinal cells in the wood, branches can load energy into various segments of wood and send them flying through the air. In my head, it's like the tree is making one last attempt to get you. With the right branch configuration, combined with the proper physics, the branches might also load up with potential energy, and spring the entire tree back over the stump, straight back in your direction; if the tree has a large crown of branches, you definitely do not want to be standing there at the stump looking; most likely, your brain will not have time to move you out of the way, the same way the white ball doesn't have time before the cue-stick hits it. If there is a weak section high in the subject tree, and the top of the tree strikes another tree on the way down, the stem can break at the defect and bend over backwards like a folding jackknife to come back at the operator, but you would have already recognized the possibility of that happening because you saw the defect on the tree and the tree it could possibly hit on the way down when you did your size-up; you took to your escape route in earnest—your mitigation for that risk.

A lodged tree is a section of a tree that was somehow severed from the stump and is leaning up against other trees; all those small diameter, springy branches up there are stuck together, holding the lodged tree vertically, just waiting to be loaded up with potential energy by the kinetic energy released with the subject tree. The tree loads up; then the springs release their energy to fell the lodged tree in your direction. A student once gave me a personal account of how this happened to him on his forty, where he regularly cut alone. The lodged tree hit the ground beside him, bounced up, and landed on him, pinning him to the ground. He said that as hard as he tried, he could not free himself from the tangled branches; he lay there yelling for help for quite a while until, only by chance, his nephew was on a walk with his girlfriend nearby and heard his cries for help; a small diameter lever/pole moved the tree away to free him, without a scratch on him. I suppose that nephew was glad to volunteer to be his safety person whenever he cut after that, just to prevent his future walks from being interrupted.

I make sure in my seminars to ask: "What is a widow maker?" In nearly every case, I get the answer, "A dead branch stuck up in the branches of the subject tree." Of course, I expect this answer and am always ready to use it to teach my students how to think more like a CSS operator. A widow maker to me is anything that kills a married man; thousands of them are out in the woods, and at least a few in every complex tree—it's why they are defined as complex. To be a safe, confident, and productive chainsaw operator, you *purposely* need to start looking at every small part of the environment for its potential to become a widow maker. This is not a hard thing to do once you make the conscious decision to do it every time you think of doing it. Your brain is already doing this automatically; it searches environmental information that represents negativity; it's part of natural survival instincts. All you need to do is bring that thought process into your cutting area with you. Use *it* as a tool; just like the chain-brake is a safety feature added by the manufacturer to the saw, your conscious effort to identify a defect, an indication of rotted wood, an increase in the breeze, or a root protruding out of the ground on your escape route—all these hidden widow makers—will be recognized without thinking about it by this safety feature attached to your PSS in the "factory" called your brain—an automatic widow maker identifier!

The more you consciously practice this feature in daily living, the better refined your memory recall will be. Your instinctive reaction learns what to look for; it automatically calculates the statistical probability that a particular widow maker will be significant; it becomes apparent. If you are very close to it when you get the notice in your consciousness, the result is stress—fear chemicals are released in the brain. If, on the other hand, a trained, well-practiced eye sees it when it is still a statistical outlier, different chemicals that make you feel challenged are released in the brain to find all pertinent memory—but it can't find the memory if it's not in there. Practice and K&E in the PSS are what puts it there. The nice thing about the CSS is that you can use these great powers to also watch out for everybody else in and around your cutting area with little extra effort; to increase these perceptive abilities, teach them as you do them.

Snags are broken off trees, like tall stumps; they can look innocuous, but they can be unyielding to a falling tree, act like the center bar of a "teeter-totter," and send large trees flying. I only listed them in this slide because I have a "recallable picture in my PSS" of a very surprising outcome when an 8" hard maple that I was felling using a conventional face notch (45 degrees) struck a 12' tall, 7" diameter spruce snag dead center at just the moment the hinge broke off the stump; the butt of the trunk flew up into the air and swung off to the side with such force that it looked like a helicopter blade. This was a completely unforeseen outcome for me—a sudden surprise producing a chemical reaction in my brain that translated into shaky responses in the muscles and thoughts like "Maybe I should find another job." I saw the snag out there in my lay before I made the release cut, but I logically determined there was no way such a dead-appearing stub could possibly be strong enough to stop a large green tree; I was in too much of a hurry to walk over there and cut it. As it turned out, that spruce was nearly all green wood with annual rings of a couple of millimeters; it was definitely a big, strong problem. I didn't get hurt because I was nearly at the end of my escape route when this happened, but my PSS was gravely injured; I had circumvented a standard procedure of clearing out the lay of possible hazards. (As I many times did when pushing for miles of property line.)

So why am I taking the time to type this up? Since you are this far into this book, I know you are already a CSS member; I am putting a picture in your brain as your teacher that will tell this story to *your* PSS the next time you see a large stump-like object near the mark where you want to place a tree. You may even hear the voice that is speaking to your brain right now, as you read this; it will say something like, "Remember what Chuck said in that book? You better go cut that stump out before you drop this tree." At that moment, the quality of your PSS will be revealed to your consciousness by your behavior;

your reaction to that voice—that "revelation" of safety, the memory I give you in these seemingly forgotten words—will be handed to you as your PSS pass/fail grade, depending on whether you assumed the role of teacher and made yourself go over there and cut that snag. The result will be, in actuality, that I experienced the hidden outlier for you, and you responded as a well-behaved student; the accident didn't happen, and you feel proud of your excellent grades.

I mentioned spring poles previously, but have it in this slide because their presence may be the result of you felling a tree, or of a storm felling a tree. I use a dry erase board in my classroom, and at this point in the lecture, I draw a picture to teach what tension and compression are doing in small diameter cylindrical objects made of longitudinal elastic cells. That would be much more difficult in this venue, so I'll trust that if you still don't have a good picture of what a spring pole is, either you'll watch the video I suggested when I mentioned these high potential energy objects before, or you will consult a teacher. The reason T/C is a problem is because it happens under the bark; the only way to understand something that cannot be physically examined is through knowledge of that thing: how it works. I have the *Textbook of Wood Technology* on my desk, but you don't need to have all the facts to understand what's going on in wood; you only need to know enough to predict a reaction force when you touch it with a speeding chainsaw.

Let me see if you can do this: Take another look at Slide 28. A large log supported on both ends has tension on the bottom (cells are being pulled apart), and compression on the top (cells are being pushed together). The maximum T and C, of course, would be on the outside edge of the wood, top and bottom, but since these are opposite forces, one pulling, one pushing, there must be a point between the T and C sides where there is zero force. That zero location is not a point or a line, in a cylindrical object; it would be more like a ribbon with increasing T on one side and increasing C on the other; the amount of bending in the branch or stem, without it fracturing, would determine how close the ribbon gets to the branch's compression side; as the bending is decreased, the ribbon would move toward the tension side. If you can imagine that ribbon as you look at the downed tree, or the mix of down trees in storm damage, it will make it easier to read the kerf reaction between the bar and the wood. A sudden snapping reaction of a branch or stem if you touch high tension not only presents the chance of your body being struck, but of the saw being thrown into your body. Watch that you don't try to cut too far in at *90 degrees to the edge* of the ribbon; that would mean increasing C in one half the kerf and increasing T in the other; just as with trying to cut into full compression, you can't make that cut without a pinch; you need to watch what the entire kerf length is doing, opening or closing: not both.

I know I used a lot of digits explaining T and C concepts. I will explain my intention in this: I'm not worried about partial pinches and small kicks. If you are very good with Rule 3, you can continue increasing your K&E without stress because the rule is designed to make you ready to accept a small kick or a minor pinch. If you have knowledge of how the wood's physics work, you can turn your experience into understanding; you will begin to look like a proficient CSS operator if you're not one already; beginners can have confidence in this thought process too; *you*, as student, will trust that *you* are telling the truth because *you* can *do it*; *you* can limb and buck an entire tree without once pinching the chain or having the saw suddenly jump up out of the cut. *You* will become a picture of the best-case scenario (BCS) for *you*, the teacher, and *you*, the student.

Terrain simply means your cutting area will not always be on flat land; whenever cutting on a slope or any kind of uneven ground, Rules 3 and 4 will need to accommodate higher and more complex risks. You add the complex element called gravity; it has a force vector to the center of the earth, until it meets a slanted surface; then there are force vectors on the horizontal that move very large objects sideways with ease. If you're dropping a tree into a cut-bank or steep hill, the terrain, in the right place at the right time when the tree is stopped, can throw the entire tree in your direction—something that would seem impossible to an untrained mind. This throwing happens because, contrary to popular belief, gravity does not "suck"; it warps time and space in waves.

Slide 36: Hazards (Utility Pole Image)

Several following slides are pictures I took of a tree I cut for my brother-in-law on his ranch. This is the same ranch I worked in my teens—my first minimum-wage job. That's right; I married the boss's daughter! Now, my brother-in-law knows how to run a chainsaw, and just like everyone else in my world who wants to run a saw in my presence, he has been introduced to the CSS, but being a good member of the system, he has the obligation to his PSS to recognize when he encounters a No-Go. (He just doesn't know it's the CSS; he thinks it's his picky, safety-conscious brother-in-law.) Of course, he gave the reason for the No-Go, as should all who meet one; he was very concerned about that transformer on the power pole; if that thing goes down, so does his water and freezer, and possibly his livelihood. So I wasn't there to show off my superior abilities; they're obvious enough. I wasn't there because he's my wife's brother; I was there to relieve a CSS member of stress; I was there to teach him how to improve his PSS. To accomplish that, I spoke out loud the CSS logic and methods being collected by the conscious observations in my mind (my SAACRAM verbalized): what the risks were that I saw, how a method or action would mitigate each risk, and why I was confident that the tree would go exactly where I wanted it to go. It was not so much about the K&E in my PSS as it was about the maturity of *our* CSS—the one where I am the operator and he is my SP. Maybe the next time there's a tree like this on the ranch, the roles will be reversed; he will do the V&D part; maybe he won't find a No-Go; he'll be the operator, and I the SP.

The subject tree is the 24" diameter hard maple in the photograph with the heavy lean just to the right of the power pole. When I first target a tree for felling, I ask myself, "Where does the tree want to go?" If I can put the tree where it wants to go, that is where I put it—the place it would go if it just fell with no other forces applied to it other than gravity and a hold on the stump! What I am determining by my observation is whether a plumb-line from the center of the tree's mass is on the same side of the stump as where the tree wants to go; another way of stating that would be: Does it have forward lean? If the center of mass is on the other side of the stump (hinge) the tree has back lean; felling a tree with back lean is a much different scenario than dropping it with the lean; there will be a significant RAM and a more difficult AC. I call this place where I intend to place the tree my "preliminary lay"; I base my size-up on the assumption that the tree is going there. If at some point in Rule 4, I decide I can't put it where it wants to go, I go back and start my size-up at the beginning with a new chosen lay; of course, the second time through goes faster. Once a different lay is chosen, it's like dropping an entirely different tree—most of the physics, and thus the risks, change.

As you can see in the picture, this maple has a heavy lean to the left, and that "fall path" can take the tree with ease, so I chose that location as my preliminary lay. The first big risk I must consider in a heavy leaning hardwood is "barber chair." (Go on YouTube and punch in "barber chair tree felling" and you will see why this is a big concern. Remember, you may see some operators who really seem like they know what they are talking about, but what they do says they are not CSS members.) Hardwoods, on the cellular level, have a different kind of reaction wood than conifers. They compensate differently than softwoods for natural lean to stop the leaning tree from drooping to the side; this is also how branches are held up. This specially grown wood is called tension wood; its longitudinal cells have different physical properties than normal cells; they resist bending and have a higher tensile strength, but are more easily split apart. The problem with these adaptive cells is they are formed only on the upside of the leaning tree, creating a transition layer running vertically up the stem to create a plane (like the ribbon in T/C) that is highly susceptible to radial fracture up the tree's bole, like that piece of firewood that splits in two when you just touch it with the maul. When the tree begins to fall, while the hinge is still too thick to bend, the forces are transmitted into the bole, splitting the tree up the middle and sending the bole's top half back at the operator like a giant pool cue; that's the wrong time for the operator to suddenly attempt to be "on the ball."

As soon as I looked at the tree, a cutting plan immediately came to mind: "**O**pen face, **B**ore cut, with a **S**trap!" (OBS) (YouTube: "open face chainsaw"). This is a safe and effective method to take out the center of a tree where the barber chair initiates so the risk is removed. I also use it when I want to drop a tree against the lean (a tree with back lean), since it allows wedges to be set to hold the back-cut kerf open before the strap or "holding wood" is cut, thereby stopping the tree from sitting back on the saw's bar; I use it on a tree that appears to be standing straight up, with the center of mass directly above the hinge; on a tree with a lot of complex limbing; on a tree where there are people and/ or animals around, or when the property owner/boss/John Q. Public is watching me cut. The OBS gives me control over when the tree goes down; it looks a lot cooler too (it looks like I know what I'm doing because I do) when the tree starts down right after I check my CA and yell, "Tree coming down!" and I cut the strap. If I use just a back-cut on a forward-leaning tree, the tree falls when the hinge is thin enough to bend; it falls when *it* wants to; I'd much rather have control over when it falls. Despite all these scenarios when I use it, there are a few times when I don't—usually only on small diameter, forward-leaning trees that cannot accommodate the face, the saw's bar, and a strap; otherwise, an "ITAP" is involved in my cutting plan. (I'll explain ITAP later.)

The top of the slide says "HAZARDS," so let me get you started by telling you I carried my saw to the subject tree, which was at the bottom of an eight-foot slope, kicked away some snow, and noticed several scars at the trunk's base. Take a look at the picture and see if you can find some other hazards I had to deal with; I should also mention that Grandpa was there watching.

After I exercised my right to look the entire cutting area over for hazards, I moved back to the location where the picture was taken, 90 degrees from the lay. From this position, I was trying to determine how much forward/back lean was in the subject tree. This lean is based on the tree's mass, so what I am attempting to determine is whether or not there is more weight in the tree ahead of the stump in the lay's direction. I look at the shape of the tree first; I take a mental plumb line from the outermost branch to the left and one on the outermost branch on the right, come to the middle between them, and imagine the plumb line to the ground. You can see in the slide how that line ended up seven feet from the stump in the lay's direction, so it has a "seven-foot forward lean." I have also used this method: Hold your arms extended toward the tree, palms facing the tree, and thumbs pointing at each other; encircle the crown with your hands; touch the outside branch on each side with the bottoms of your index fingers; look at the gap between your thumbs, and bring your thumbs together, touching at the midpoint between them; now drop your arms so your thumbs go straight to the ground; visually mark that spot; now move that location closer to the stump or away from it as you scan your eyes up the tree, estimating the weight of the branches on each side to determine which side weighs more; where your mark ends up tells you the forward or back lean. You don't need a calculator or some expensive measuring device—the measuring device is in your brain; you just need to get it calibrated with practice and success; soon you will be able to look up and down a tree a few times and have a good idea of where the lean is.

In our picture, if the tree had many large branches extending off the bole to the right, your AC would tell you that these would pull that center of gravity toward the stump, depending on how much weight they had pulling down with a cantilever effect on the tree; a tree with the right-shaped crown and the right arrangement of branches could have a bole leaning to the stump's left with the center of gravity to the right; when operators don't see that, and mistakenly use a straight back-cut, they get the bar of the saw stuck in the tree—a very big problem if it is a big tree, and they only have one saw.

The subject tree has a somewhat symmetrical crown, so I stayed with the seven-foot forward lean.

> To understand what you are doing with a chainsaw—and understand you must, in the CSS in order to perfect your AC—you must know how wood works, how it grows, how it deteriorates with age, and how to predict what will happen when you try to reduce it to small pieces. The best way to do this is to use your analytical mind, your engineering mind, your biological mind, to learn about your adversary, and learn not just about trees, but about wood. Find out what xylem and phloem are; why wood is very strong in tensile and compressive strength, but very weak in radial strength; and how the amount of water in the living tree increases its ability to bend, while the presence of water in a dead tree indicates rot. To understand something large and/or complex, break it down into the smallest parts, and define in your mind the words used to describe it.

I had an instructor tell me that every tree has two leans; that is not true until a chainsaw operator comes along and decides to fell the tree in a place other than where the tree's physics say it would fall on its own. The laws of energy preservation must be followed by the tree; since it has *no* choice, there cannot be two possibilities. A bit of a paradox then is: unless the center of gravity of a tree is exactly in the center of the stump (no lean), it only has one lean at a single vector in the 360 degrees of possibilities; if the operator chooses to drop the tree any place else, it will have side lean away from the vector the operator chose.

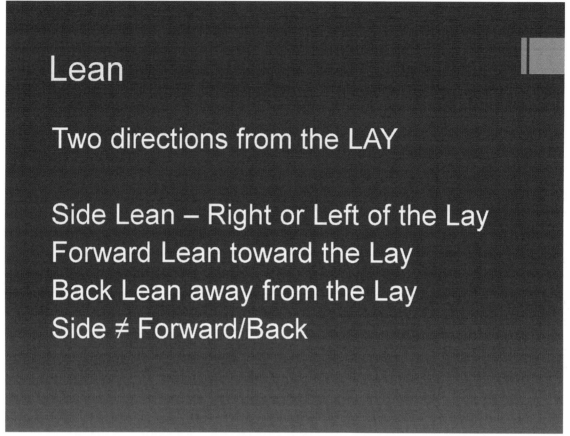

Slide 37: Lean

We don't have to consider these laws of physics that strictly, however, because we can *carve* a board (the hinge) into the stump with our chainsaw that will break first along its long edge; that's what boards would prefer if they had a choice of where the forces were applied; it's less work, and everything takes the path of less work, not just Chuck. The hinge will reduce many possibilities to one, and hold that chosen directional vector to the ground, hopefully with enough potential energy (mass) to counteract the force applied by the offset center of gravity in the side lean, which produces a force vector pointing at the small edge of the board, trying to rip the hinge like you would a piece of fabric. The side lean measurement, right or left of the stump as you stand at the stump and look down the lay, is not based on the tree's mass, or where it wants to fall, because the hinge will determine that within the physical restraints of its length, its width, and the vector that is 90 degrees to its long edge. The side lean is estimated based on the "geometrical center of the crown," which is aimed with the placement of the hinge; it is aimed at the center of the hole where the crown can safely and conveniently go, with the added adjustment of the amount of side lean in the total tree, since the hinge holds that lean to the ground.

If you understood all that the first time you read it, and you are sure about how to do this, you're either a lot smarter than I am or you have plenty of K&E; if you didn't understand it, you can most likely still conceptualize it in your mind because your brain knows what a tree looks like, and it understands how gravity works; you just need to see it done so you can lock down the definition of all those words and associate them with a picture in your PSS; if you can do that the first time, you are very much needed by the CSS as a teacher and a student. I had to think through this and do it many times before it became routine. Watch that YouTube video again: "How to Fell a Tree With a Chainsaw," by Husqvarna; fast forward it to where the operator measures the lean.

So we do have two leans to account for: forward/back lean and right/left side lean; remember that one or both can be zero. So, not every tree has two leans; any one tree has one lean, two leans, or no lean, but only one of those possibilities can be made to happen by the operator.

What is your lean?

Look around you! How many of the individual items that you see right now were built and placed by your efforts alone? Pick out one item; how long would it take you to build that item from its most basic elements? Yes, you did the work to earn the money that purchased the item, but just manufacturing a few of the items around you would take all your time, leaving an insufficient amount of time remaining to earn the funds to purchase the rest of what you see around you. Much of what you view as *your* property, or the things and concepts of reality that you use and process every minute of every day were produced and left by those around you or others before you. We are literally surviving on the products of our ancestors and other people in both mind and body. If this is even partially true, where does pride in the ownership of a material object originate, or the insistence that one person can possibly be the ultimate relevance of a tradition?

Perhaps there are two levels of human consciousness, two levels of reality: me here, and everyone else there. The more time one spends in the first level without considering the impact of the second level on their existence, the higher the probability of negative results in dangerous activities. If you predominantly consider only your own welfare, your efforts at self-preservation must eventually end in failure; there is no safe ground for you to stand on; no single person has the time afforded by one lifetime to build that solid a foundation. (Except maybe one that I can think of off-hand.) My conclusion after this thought: Humans are not just a collection of individuals; we are an individual compilation of consciousness made up of many sensors we call brains. (Are you a sensor of pain or pleasure, failure or success, injury or wellbeing?) What you feel, you feel for all; what you build, you build for all; what you save from being lost, you save for the future. You are either building a place for the future to stand, or you are using up space and wasting our time.

Standing in the Lay

Slide 38: Standing in the Lay

Here I am standing on the lay with my brother-in-law; he asked me if I thought the tree would hit the electrical wires above. I took the stick I had in my hand, held it between the thumb and index finger of my right hand, and adjusted its length so I could hold my arm straight out, then bend the stick straight back with my arm still straight until the end of it touched my chin; I then tilted the stick to vertical and moved forward until I lined up the top of the stick with the top of the tree. I explained to my SP/property owner/ brother-in-law (bro) that what I had done was create similar equilateral triangles; since the length of my arm was proportional to the length from me to where I planned to face the tree, and the vertical length of the stick was proportional to the height of the tree, the top of the tree would need to land at the spot I was standing, also being the place where I wanted the center of the tree's crown to be laying when done (my *mark*). I stuck the stick in the ground and told my bro that this is where the top would be; he looked up and said, "That should miss." His stress had diminished; I could tell by the tone of his voice. That's what CSS operators do—they turn fear into confidence with logic and K&E for everyone in the cutting area. This little method takes the place of a statement like "Just trust me; I've been doing this all my life," which only increases stress for the non-operators.

(On YouTube, watch "Stick Trick: How to measure the length of a tree.")

Center of the Crown

Slide 39: Center the Crown

Still standing in my lay, I take the mid-point between the outside branches on each side of the crown and plumb it down to a point two feet left of the tree trunk. That means that while standing at the tree, looking at my mark, the tree has *two feet of right* lean; it will keep that lean to the ground—it has no choice—so I need to compensate for that by aiming my face *two feet to the left*; I aim my face opposite the side lean. There are some fair examples of this on YouTube; I hope you found the one mentioned in the last section, and were able to translate the accent; those two should go on tour! It shows what looked to be a "professional" SP/operator standing on a street and letting a tree fall right beside him; did he trust his coworker that much? Actually, that is not the right question; the question is: How did that operator get x-ray vision attached to that hard hat so he could see what the wood looked like inside that hinge? Actually, it was a very good stump that they showed at the end, but it also goes to show that the stump can't tell the whole story; you have to be there to put it all together.

Just because a hinge is properly cut and sized does not mean it is going to hold the tree as intended; wood is simply too variable a material—it contains too many unseen defects under the bark to be that predictable; a real risk existed of that tree kicking sideways and hitting his SP, standing on the street. The operator bypassed a risk for the sake of stardom, but that did not mitigate the possibility of the tree doing something unexpected and "sticking" his SP. Even if he knew it wasn't going to happen (it's a distant outlier to his perception), it didn't look good; it diminished the guys' image when I'm sure the video's purpose was to strengthen it; not even a video shows the whole truth of what happened. What he did is probably something he's been doing all his life; he may even someday be saying that to an emergency room nurse. (Sure, he gets a date with the nurse, but we all get to help pay the hospital bill if we live in Sweden.)

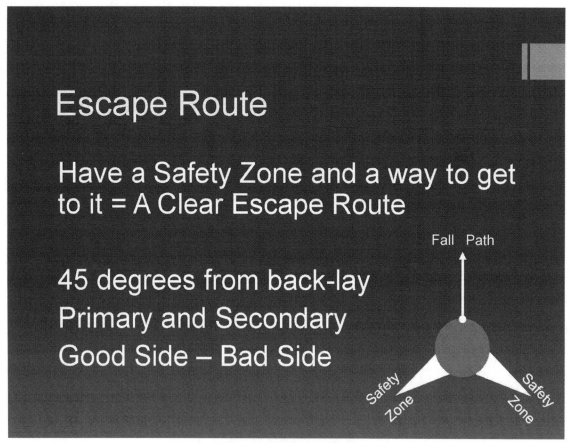

Slide 40: Escape Route

I told my bro where to stand so he could watch for vehicles coming up the road; I told Pops to watch in the other direction, even though I knew the road from that way was not a concern; I had to give him an assignment, which is always something fun to do with your father-in-law. I picked up my saw, checked to be sure I had my wedges and hammer, and went to the stump. I had my hazards done, no unmitigated risks; I had seven feet of forward lean and two feet of right lean.

This element of the size-up is called the Escape Route because the place you are going, to be safe, is not as important as actually taking the steps to get there. I read a statistical report one time that said most fatalities during tree felling happen within five feet of the stump. That's the kind of statement that begs a "Duh!", and maybe a thought like: They actually pay people to come up with this stuff. Even small children understand that large things striking your body carry larger forces at slower speeds, yet I have many times, probably more often than not, watched experienced operators not in the CSS stand right next to the stump and watch the tree all the way to the ground. What is going on in a brain that thinks that is okay? Perhaps the sight of the tree falling in the right direction stimulates a conquering feeling. There's nothing wrong with confidence, but this is like celebrating the victory before the game is over. Once you have a clear indication that the tree is falling, immediately start moving away from those large forces! Have the place where you are going predetermined because if something should go wrong, it usually happens fast; stopping to think about it is usually not an option. You may not make it to a safe spot before the tree hits the ground, but you must be on the way there to be in the CSS.

Standing at the tree's side, I look down my lay, then 180 degrees from that, behind the tree, I select two escape routes in two directions 45 degrees off that line; a route has to go somewhere to be defined; it must lead to a safety zone (SZ). The safety zone is not chosen only for the operator; in your PSS that would be akin to CYA, something most chainsaw-type people call cowardice; the SZ must be a safe place mostly for your SP. It's the place where the student and the teacher meet to discuss how the drop went, even if on occasion you are acting as the operator and the SP, like when the only other person on site is your kid with the phone in the truck two tree lengths away. Others' safety in the cutting area must be the operator's first and greatest concern. (Did you think of that when you listed the hazards in the cutting area pictures?) The SZ for a large diameter tree can be behind a larger tree, or at least twenty feet from the subject tree. The distance might be shorter for less complex or smaller diameter trees down to a point where the tree is considered brush; as long as you are not static when the tree starts to fall, you must be thinking "move." So, is there an escape route consideration when I'm cutting a 3" diameter maple? Yes, it may merely be a matter of standing up, setting the brake, and placing the bar on the tree to supply some force to help gravity; that's okay if it is a planned mitigation action that best gets the job done safely. Safety has to make sense; that's why the CSS allows you to have your PSS; you are allowed to use common sense as long as you don't break a rule or bypass a risk, so there must be some thought of an escape route and, therefore, a SZ for every tree you cut; it's size depends on your SAACRAM, and, therefore, the amount of planning involved.

The large gray circle represents the tree; the "fall path" is to the lay; the primary side/good side/light side, is the side away from the side lean; it follows then that the secondary side/bad side/heavy side is on the side of the side lean. If you think about it, these are different names with different considerations for the same decision. Which of the two escape routes are you going to use? The best choice is the side that makes you safest, the "good" side; that is away from loose or dead branches in the crown, the light side; that would be your first choice—your primary one. If for some reason that choice is not available, or it presents more added risks than the secondary side, you can choose the bad and heavy side, which becomes the good side by clearing out the path—brushing/slashing out your escape route and moving any tripping hazards. Clearing the ER also includes cutting and removing any small trees and/or brush around the subject trees, and any branches on the tree that could get in the way. Remember: reach only as high with the saw as where the anchor point of the left arm/elbow is maintained. Many times, risks presented by the size-up can only be mitigated by clearing out both escape routes to accommodate the "if/then" scenario.

I've noticed that SPs are a greater concern while cutting around the tree and opening the escape route, especially if this is the only tree you will be cutting, or it is an unusually complex drop; SPs often seem overly eager to help, and sometimes, they get too close to the running saw. Before you start cutting, have a little safety meeting with your SP and any swampers who may be there to help; tell them, "Keep an 8-10 foot radius distance from the saw. Don't touch anything I am cutting. If I have the saw in my hands, don't enter the circle unless I look at you and call you in. If I set the brake and put down the saw, you can enter the circle and move brush or help me move something without an invitation; I will be expecting you." Confidence is contagious; anyone who has anxiety in a situation is constantly looking for a leader/"good system operator" to take control; it allows their subconscious to relax!

When you "escape the stump," if you prefer to bring the saw with you, set the brake as you start walking. If you want to leave the saw, set the brake and put it down, or even drop it; unless you are on concrete, and you paid more than a hundred bucks for the saw, a "half drop" of the saw will not hurt it. If you set your saw down to pound in a wedge to bring the tree past center, set the brake or shut off the saw, and make sure you don't put it down in your escape route. While you are on your way down the escape route, walk at a steady quick pace for the first ten feet; then as you proceed, select a good footing location to pause and take a quick look back at the tree, especially if you had your eye on a particular hazard you anticipated would become kinetic during the fall, or as in my case, if you really like watching large trees crash to the ground. I actually saw this as an added risk in my PSS, so I usually try to get to the SZ as quickly as I can without running, so I can turn at twenty feet and watch the show. Of course, if some outlier risk shows up as the tree is coming down, and I see it coming toward me, I run like hell; my SP may need to grab me to stop me as I pass the SZ; when your brain learns to understand the invisible possibilities in the physics of felling a tree, you too will find yourself giving "reaction forces" more room. It's not fear, it's part of the fun; you are skilled enough to have your body in the right place at the right time to avoid an injury you would have gotten if you had not had a good PW *and* a good WP!

On trees with back lean, safety zones may be harder to find; if a tree has back lean, with no trees in the back-lay to stop it and it is not living wood, the hinge may not be trustworthy, so naturally it is a much larger risk for my SP, who may be standing at 45 degrees off the back-lay; if I haven't already sent the SP out of the cutting area, or at least a tree length away, I always have a signal for my SP where I will get eye contact and bend my up-pointed arm away from the tree on the back-lay; from that point on, it is prearranged that it is up to my SP to find a new safety zone based on the probability that the back-lay could become the lay, or leave the cutting area entirely; then I turn back to cutting and check my SP's location again before cutting the strap. If I cut the strap, the hinge goes "crack" and the tree starts falling in the opposite direction of what the PW envisioned. What do I do? I don't know; I can picture all kinds of possibilities. I'll tell you what I wouldn't do: Stick to WP #1, and head down the original escape route. I would instantly go to WP #2, which I probably mentioned to myself when making #1 because of the back lean and because I was cutting a dead tree; this is the only time you pause by the stump, just long enough for the tree to "commit" to its fall path. Most likely, the tree is going down the back lay, 180 degrees from where you expected it to go because the hinge has a long flat side in that direction also, but if the hinge completely breaks, you have no control on the tree according to physics; the tree can go "anywhere" in 360 degrees.

When this would happen to me, usually while cutting rotted trees or snags, I would look up the trunk to determine which direction the stem was moving; since I was right next to the tree, I would look up the side of the tree to determine the direction it was to go; at the same time, I'd push off the tree and go in the opposite direction, usually down the lay from the first plan. The second version of WP happens in an instant. Not even the system can work with that kind of quick thinking; it has to be a reflex. To change to an opposite plan in an instant comes from *practicing with small trees* that come back at you; as they do, imagine they are huge ones in your mind, and then dance with them, and try not to step on their toes. Remember learning in elementary school science class about Galileo's experiment with dropping large and small balls off the Leaning Tower of Pisa? Well, the same is true with a large tree and a small tree; even though they carry different force, they fall at the same velocity. If you can instantly redo the WP, and pick a new escape route with a small tree, without it touching you, believe me, you can do it with a big one. If you are very good with the system and have exceptional SAACRAM, this situation may never happen, even once in a lifetime of cutting; a tree with a heavy back lean, which is dead or rotted to an extent that cannot provide a strong hinge, would be recognized as such in the cutting plan, and other assets employed to mitigate the risk of a free-fall.

I brought this topic up so I could say this: Often operators get injured and property is damaged by events with a low probability of happening, what I call statistical outliers— events that only the most experienced mind can see coming, and only the most knowledgeable brain can prevent without involving paranoia, so even in the system, you need to be always thinking while executing the cutting plan, and be ready to CYA with your well-trained muscles, especially when cutting in complex areas such as with dead/rotted trees. That way, it will not be fear that saves you by making you scream like a kid and start running; it will be wisdom that makes you say, "You SOB," and calmly start walking down the escape route of your alternate PW.

Something that surprised me when I first started my "lecture tour" around Michigan was the existence of storm-response teams around the larger cities in the south. I had no idea there were people like that; drive them from storm to storm, feed them, give them some challenging and dangerous work to do, and they're happy with minimal monetary compensation! I can imagine a way that some smart, young, and free operators could build a good cSS using the CSS, sustain their healthy existence, and have one hell of an exciting and rewarding summer.

Maybe I should get a few retired folks together this summer and load up my old pickup. Let's see; I'll list what it should look like:

- CSS Team (good mix of three or four PSSs) working as a cSS

- Team has practiced together (trail clearing crew, invasive species eradication, local small storm damage, tree felling for friends and family, etc.)

- Sponsored by a reputable agency, organization, neighborhood, or extended family

- Goal: To cut on a first-response basis for storm-damaged areas regionally or nationally

- Could start small/local for practice, then go longer distances when needed

- Donated equipment, logo on the truck, saws, equipment, per diem

- All CSS barter items go on the truck

- Members agree not to work outside the cSS for profit when on detail

- The entire detail is under the CSS cutting area dome; perhaps more rules needed

- We take turns showing off our PSS cutting areas; can get paid to cover expenses if prearranged

We could take solicited work cutting problem trees for local contacts. We would make sure we stay completely in the system by making each property owner we cut for a CSS member so the liability is under ethical authority. We could teach about what the cSS is to everyone we cut for; we would V&D the rules and the No-Go option for everyone involved. We could build a good K&E base by volunteering at the county conservation department, for trail groups, land preserves, or the like; they always need operators. We could use this opportunity to get good practice time together, build up the cSS, and maybe even outfit it by bartering with those we cut for. After a summer or two of removing hazard trees for folks, we might be able to go "on tour" with this cSS, but even if we didn't, it still sounds like it would be a lot of fun.

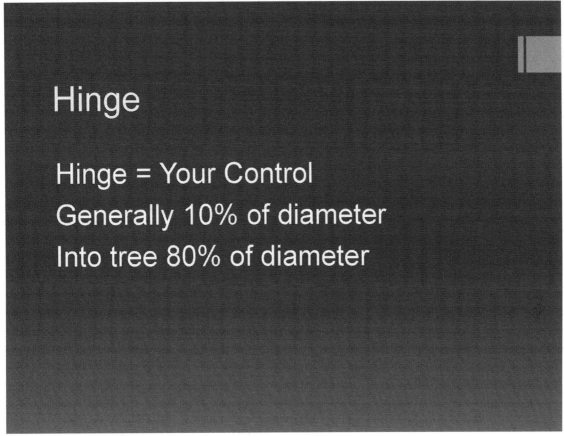

Slide 41: Hinge

I'm still in the size-up; in practice, everything up to this point—hazards, lean, and escape route—are all done in my mind; I don't need a saw to see or do any of it. It can be processed in my brain on any tree at any time. I can train my PSS in this if there is a tree present, any tree, and it's the same mental process as when I'm actually felling a tree. Things change drastically on the next element, however; whether you have a saw in your hand or not, you cannot see the hinge directly when you are doing Rule 4.

The cutting plan is all about the hinge, and how the operator plans to get maximum performance from it; the operator needs to get it aimed in the proper direction and have adequate physical properties for the plan to be effective. The hinge is your only control for how the tree will fall on the intended lay. Like turning the steering wheel on your truck to point in a particular direction and then locking it in place, where it is aimed is where it must go when the brake is released, unless some other force factor intervenes; like if the condition, shape, and/or size of the hinge changes the physics of how it will break during the fall—how much strength it has to hold the tree on the chosen fall path. If the cutting plan involves a single back-cut, as with a forward lean, the dimension and makeup of the hinge will decide when the tree will start to fall as it is being formed by the advancing chain; it will bend and start to fracture when the force vector of gravity, pointing down on the plumb line from the center of the tree's gravity, is far enough from the hinge's center to impart a rotational force on the hinge, which increases the horizontal force vector pointing at the hinge's center from the direction of the fall path.

The tree's mass, combined with gravity, bends the hinge to cause the weakest resistive force in the wood, the radial fracture, to yield.

If there is enough side lean, the hinge can also start fracturing from one end, sending the tree falling in the direction of the side lean. The resultant wood on the stump will appear as "spikey" fibers protruding from the holding wood of the hinge after a *live* tree is down; if the wood in the hinge is dead, the fibers will break under a tensile/compression fracture and appear "blocked off" or crushed; if the wood in the hinge is rotted, the holding wood has such a minor amount of potential energy left that it can be considered to have the holding strength of air in its ability to resist force. You get it; don't assume you have any control of the hinge when cutting a rotted tree (the kind we cut the most these days). It takes a close examination of the stem at the location of the hinge and a trained eye to have any indication of what the hinge is composed of; it's a very good practice to look at the finished product of every hinge, especially if you intend to be cutting more trees that look similar to the one you just cut.

Your brain must have an indication of what the end result looks like before it can make an accurate prediction at the start; you can understand how this is nearly impossible for an untrained eye to accomplish since the material you are depending on to perform in a certain way is inside the tree and, therefore, invisible to mere mortals. You need to "train your brain"; when you are looking at your stump, think back at what you saw during the size-up: What did you notice as an indication of rot, decay, or defect (evidence of higher risk) in the tree that turned out to be a fact? There might be similar issues on the next tree, and you just became an experienced operator, with a trained eye, if everything else about your stump happened exactly as planned; your thought and regimented processes locked down a lot of variables; you can actually use the constants—what the wood and everything else must repeat (approaching the truth) because it has no choice—as a means to mentally see into the wood; it's like *super-vision*: the ability to see hidden risks, statistical outliers that the normal, common sense person simply cannot see; when you have this ability, you will be safe, you will be more productive, you will be a good teacher, and you will have a lot more fun!

On a 10" diameter tree, the hinge is 8" long and 1" thick; the hinge is, in essence and in reality, a 1" x 8" board that the operator has "carved" with the saw; a board with predictable fracture parameters, based on the length of its long edge vs. the length of its short edge as a proportion or percentage of the total area of the tree's cross-section. The hinge has this shape because it is the optimum geometry to provide the best resistive forces; it's the same reason the rafters in your barn are placed with the short edge up; the down force vector of gravity from the weight of the roof encounters more wood T&C, and less in the weak radial direction. The wood is trying not to break; that's its job. The forces take the path of least resistance; that's their job. Gravity is trying to pull the tree to the ground on the shortest path; that's its job. Perfectly shaping and placing the hinge so the tree hits the mark is your job! The choices made while doing the job are the same variations we started with at the start of the book: what your brain considers to be perfect versus the defects, condition, species, lean, dimensions, location of the wood, and the ability of the operator and the saw to work together to produce a safe product. You see why it is complete idiocy to *start with* "Let's get 'er done"? That's why I say to operators who insult me as a CSS teacher by proudly refusing to be my student, "Good luck!" Luck is literally the only thing they have that they can count on; I refuse to stand there and watch it; all they see of me is my back moving away, and I'm fine with that—no guilt!

Lots of videos are on YouTube about the hinge; the "How to Fell a Tree With a Chainsaw" by Husqvarna is my favorite because the operator examines the stump when he's done; that fits into the CSS better. I also really like the one by Stihl because the operator is working with a safety person, but I definitely see both these operators as good teachers, and I know I would find it enjoyable to work with them to benefit my PSS; to glean information from their SAACRAM, or perhaps identify something I might teach them to make them even safer operators, like a reciprocation. Watching these guys, though, I think I would probably wait to discuss my contributions to their PSS, until we are alone; I may find out that I am not as good an operator as I think I am. I can, however, tell by an edited video that we agree on the rules, so I would say that these gentlemen would be instantly recognized as members of the CSS, but I would still keep watching for the slightest breach of the rules; expert operators/teachers get tired and sloppy at times too. The most novice operator in a cSS could save the most advanced teacher in it from injury by the smallest verbalized observation; see why there is no rank in the CSS? You don't have the option to be too embarrassed to say something; you must protect your PSS.

These videos use the OBS as a cutting plan; it's the same method I use most of the time when a tree diameter can accommodate a face, a strap, and the width of my bar. Why wouldn't I? It gives me the most control of when and how the tree falls. The most prevalent problem I've found with people accepting this method is the bore cut because the kickback quadrant of the saw is used to cut wood near the tree's surface, and there is an increased chance of cutting into the hinge in the process. Many operators experience the dreaded kickback when they first attempt to "plunge" the bar into the wood; their brain does its subconscious job, and it scares them, so they decide to stick with the same way they've always done it, the conventional face with a full back-cut. That's not logical thinking; limitations should always be extended; by controlling the situation, you can control the apprehension. I encourage all my students to find a stump and practice the bore cut until you master it without the saw kicking or "chattering" too much during the turn and plunge; you don't need to make a face in a stump, unless you want to practice that at the same time.

A couple of hints on how to get this done easily are: Start with how you hold the saw—place the rear handle against your hip with the flat of the bar pointing at the sky and level on the right side of the tree; imagine a drop of water or a marble on it, and move the bar to a position where the marble stays on the bar. Place the initiation quadrant at the apex of the face while standing farther behind the tree, with the bar kind of pointing down the lay. Draw the saw back about halfway to the back of the tree by moving your arms and body along the back-lay. At *full rev*, cut into the tree until the rivets for the nose sprocket disappear into the wood, creating a pocket that the bar's tip is in with no wood on the kick-back arc. Keeping the chain at *full speed*, think of cutting with the *initiation quadrant*, or as said in one video, with a "pulling chain," and rotate the saw around the right side of the tree to place the entire bar into the pocket with wood above the kick-back quadrant. I'll get into the "bore cut" more later; I mention it here because the thought process of thinking you are cutting with the pulling chain is actually how to prevent cutting into the hinge—something to avoid at all times.

As you are operating a saw, you are going in and out of the system; this is common for many system operators. Your thumb somehow slides to the top of the bar, or while you are moving with a running saw, you forget just that one time to set the chain break; during those lapses in your PSS, you are out of the CSS. Savvy system members see these small inconsistencies because they have learned how to catch them every time, back when they saw themselves doing the same thing. The time you are out of the system is a great concern for another in the system who witnesses it; it's like a little spurt of stress chemicals in the brain. Some in the system will teach at this time; some will remain silent until later when they find you alone, and some will take your action as a lesson and say nothing. When a system member has the integrity to say something to help you, *thank them*; make a big deal out of it in your head because it is! They just responded to a possible injury to you, before it happened!

This next slide is my stump! The length of the hinge is about 80 percent of the tree's total diameter, and its width is about 10 percent of the tree's diameter. Why do I use the word "about"? The system does not demand that you hit "perfect" every time you cut; that is physically and mentally impossible. It must, however, demand that you "aim for perfect" every time you make a cut; to aim for anything less would be the same as working your SAACRAM in reverse; you would be teaching the student in you (your PSS) that the logical mitigation you have chosen to repeat as a "habit" to regiment is, indeed, not the best mitigation; that is illogical and anti-productive. It's not just the relevant knowledge and similar experience that gets the tree safely to the ground; it's also the mental talent and physical ability (hand/eye coordination) that each individual operator is able to attain. As long as you try your best to stay in the system, the system provides a buffer, a range of actions that approach perfect, and still get the job done safely; that's why you

Slide 42: My Stump

always need to look at the stump when you are done; it can be as short an examination as a glance, or it can be an hour lecture, but you must at least look at it with an unbiased evaluation of the information it contains; otherwise, your PSS will never get better, so you will not be able to teach your student.

The face is placed with two cuts preferably at a comfortable standing position. First is the slant cut, top cut, or vertical cut. Place your left shoulder on the tree, left leg back, saw held with rear handle on the right thigh, thumb on the trigger, left hand on the curve in the front handle, looking down the "gunning sight" on the saw at a point two feet left of the mark in the lay, in this case because I had two feet of right lean. Cut down until the bar is committed in the cut, about half the bar. Now watch the cut's depth until it reaches a point just less than halfway between the lay line and the diameter line at right-angle to the lay. Then level the bar, level as in 90 degrees to the longitudinal fibers in the tree. Pull the saw out of the slant cut, and look into that kerf to find the bottom of the cut. Place the bar at the start of the "horizontal cut" (in open face this may be slanting more downward to increase the opening of the face) while aiming the kick-back arc of the bar at the line on the bottom of the first cut's kerf so the second cut meets the first all the way across the kerf's bottom. Watch for either the chain to enter the kerf, or for the chain to meet the first cut's plane; if the cut is low, you'll see the chain coming out of the kerf's far end, like water out of a hose. Then come back to the first cut and cut down until the notch falls out.

If you miss—the two cuts don't meet—you need to clean it up all the way across the stump. In my stump, I could not see the kerf's bottom, and I cut too deep—too far in—with my second. My second cut was low and past the first cut's plane. I had to take another slice off the first cut's plane; I had a "Dutchman," an over-cut. This over-cut has to be cleaned up; those two cuts must meet at the face's apex. If they don't meet, you are cutting into the hinge, which starts fracturing the fibers in the hinge as soon as that small kerf closes. The closure is only the chain's width, but it closes quickly, and it takes away control and adjusts the hinge's aim, making it higher risk. So, that I did not make the two cuts meet is not the problem; the cutting plan is compromised only when I refuse to take the time to clean up my mess! It becomes a PSS issue; nobody is going to make you clean up after yourself except you! Since I aimed for perfect, and obviously missed, I know what action I need to take to hit perfectly on the next tree; I need to spend more time determining where the bottom of the kerf is that I am aiming at; I need to pay more attention to when the bar is level, or when it is 90 degrees to the stem, and where the arc of the bar is aimed before committing to the kerf. (Maybe I should make a high stump on the next tree and spend some time practicing the two face cuts until I can make them meet on the first try.)

In my cutting plan, I ascertained that the bar may not reach all the way across the stump in my bore cut, so I cut away part of the tree's side. If you look closely, you can see the curved marks the bar's tip made in the stump where the plunge was made. The 6" wedge and the 20" bar are for perspective. (Perspective in any high-risk activity is very important.) The notch should be 70–90 degrees, and it looks like it may be around 70; with this kind of fall, the minimum 70 allowed the hinge to break before it hit the seven-foot berm on the lay. (AC)

This situation reminds me of a discrepancy I have seen in definitions in some PSSs. In the CSS, we have a name for the wood we take out of the front of the tree to avoid splintering; we call it the face. So, is a "notch" the hole you cut out of the wood or the piece of wood you take out? Is the "face" something you do to the tree, or is it a shape cut into a tree in the direction of where you want it to fall? Since we have a name for the part cut into the tree, we call it the face, and it is very important since it establishes the front edge of the hinge at its apex, the line where the two cuts meet. We call the part that falls out the "notch"; it obviously has the same dimensions as the hole it left behind; it takes out the wood that will splinter; chainsaws and splintered wood do not mix. The notch falls out when you cut the face; it's lying on the ground when you're done. The problem is: both words are verbs/nouns, so they tend to make communication difficult due to definitions of terms. If you point at a tree in the place where I just made two cuts into the trunk and ask, "What's that?" I'll say, "That's the face." If you point to the thing that fell out of the tree, I'll say, "That's the notch." You can use these same definitions, or you may have different meanings and words where you cut. Use whatever words you want to communicate; just make sure all who hear your words define them the same as you do—that's called training! Verbalization is defined in another person's brain by demonstration, like an intersection of your PSSs that is honored each time you communicate; that's the CSS. You talk the language that best aids communication between the operator and SP (the CSS), your "brain and body" (the PSS), and the "saw and the wood." (Actions speak louder than words.)

You can see the "strap" on the back of the tree; it looks like a step up in the stump just to the left of the wedge; the shape of the stump dictated its location and shape. What I wanted to happen in my cutting plan is that the "basal area" of the "holding wood" is sufficient to hold up the tree until I release it. I usually like the thickest part of the strap to be, like the hinge, 10 percent of the width. In this case, was it big enough? All I can say is that it held the tree up while I chased Grandpa back down the road after he had come up next to the tree to get a better look at the action; then I checked with the bro, yelled, "Here it goes!" and cut the strap. The tree was still under my control until I was ready to release it; that presents a much less stressful event for my brain—much smoother chemicals flowing around in there. It also makes me look like I know what I'm doing because I do!

How do I feel about the story this stump is telling everyone who comes by and knows what they are looking at? I'm not exactly proud of what it is saying, but it is the truth; I have to deal with it, and try to improve. I do feel good about my PSS, though; it was a complex drop because of the high-risk hazards and the heavy forward lean, but the system turned out to offer a big enough range of acceptable talent and ability to accommodate my lack thereof to execute the plan perfectly; the tree ended up exactly on the mark with the top branches a foot from my mark. I decreased the stress in the cutting area; I kept all the rules; I used my SAACRAM, combined with the rules to figure out a good plan that worked! I'm not exactly proud of the stump, but I would be glad to talk about what it says with a good teacher or student, like my bro, for example.

If you noticed all the details of that stump before I mentioned them, and you were shaking your head, and thinking all kinds of negative things about my proficiency as a chainsaw operator or teacher, I would need to cut with you for a while to see how well *you* keep the rules, to listen to your verbalization, to watch your demonstration, to compare your PSS to mine, and then to participate in the critique of *your* stump.

I've had the opportunity to talk to several business owners in the recent past. I've discovered a negative trend with severe consequences for their business plans. You would think that trend would be high medical insurance, high taxes, or slow sales. Not so. The biggest problem for these employers is finding qualified people who are willing to work. I should point out, also, that these businesses all had one thing in common: They involved manual labor. I saw this coming years ago while working with field crews made up of young people, like youth corps groups and summer hires. I think what society is seeing today is the result of so many screens in our lives; it came too fast to adjust to the mind-bending power these machines have over us. Just like the introduction of the chainsaw caused us humans to personalize the saw's power, so the power of video games and movies have diminished innovative thought in our brains; we think what we perceive to be the best for us based on the external power source, rather than the power in our minds. They say young people expect to get paid for just showing up, let alone working well and safe. "You're dead" is removed by hitting a button, usually on a phone! If you are a young person who wants to learn the CSS, you may be a rare exception; you will be a valuable asset to some wise business owner, especially if he has dead trees on his property.

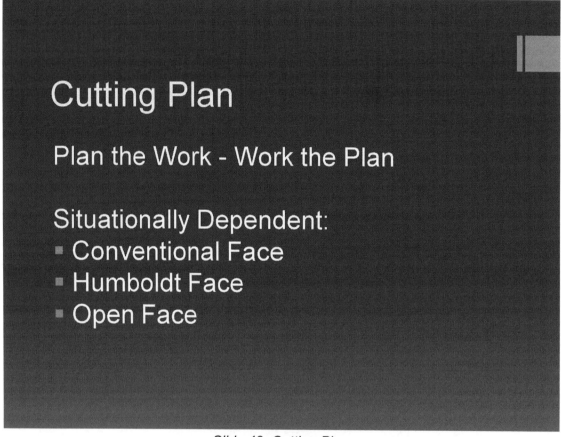

Slide 43: Cutting Plan

This slide lists three types of faces you can use when cutting. I used the conventional face exclusively for a dozen years before being taught the open face. The main problem I had with the conventional was that I never learned an adequate procedure for making the slant and horizontal cuts of the face meet. Sure, they occasionally met well, but I couldn't trust the method to produce good results because there was no visible target to aim the bar's arc at on the second cut; the intersection of the two cuts is a blind spot on the tree's other side.

Once I learned the open face, which provides the option to look down the kerf of the first cut and see the target-line at the bottom of it, I stayed with it because it was much easier to accomplish a good result—two or sometimes three cuts, and the cuts would meet to form a nice apex. The open face was more productive, built confidence, was better for aiming the tree, and allowed the hinge to hold the tree to the stump throughout the drop. Of course, the hinge holding all the way to the ground introduced another difficulty: If control is assumed, it must also be taken. If the aim of the face is not precise, there is a greater possibility of the tree missing the "hole," and getting hung up on another tree. I had to stop reading the subject tree's lean from the bottom of the stem, and walk away from the stump *on the lay* and at *90 degrees to the lay* to read the lean, especially with trees in dense stands. I learned after doing that very deliberately two or three times that I could return to the tree and look straight up to let my brain remember what a tree looks like with that particular amount of forward/back and side lean. After practice, I could remain at the tree and just look up; the lean in both directions was apparent, and I could aim the face properly with the gunning sight and the placement of the first cut. As long as the two cuts met, physics, geometry, and wood physiology took over, without me ever looking at a diagram or a screen. It became a rare occasion when I had such a tight hole that I had to walk out and take a closer look at the side lean, but when I did, the similar pictures in my K&E were very quickly scanned by my brain, and the most pertinent ones chosen, much faster than it could even be done with a computer. The app for that is the PSS.

As the slide indicates, the type of face you use is situationally dependent. If you are a beginner, just learn the open face; that is all you will ever need. If you have always used the conventional face, try the open face; you'll find it much superior for aiming and seeing what you're aiming at; if you give it a chance, you'll never go back; I'm just an average operator, and I use the open face all the time, after having used the conventional face professionally for more than ten years. (Try it; you'll like it.)

Storm Damage: Things I wrote down after talking to storm-response operators:

- Create a group write-up of Job Hazard Analysis for each type of storm damage.
- Have continuous communication within the team, and with the supervisor.
- Do not be distracted; think about your safety system.
- Prepackage equipment for each work group with extras (sharp stretched chains, winches, ropes, throw line).
- Use a size-up technique on each segment of the process.

- Do not go immediately to the most difficult cut; start small and slow.
- Use other tools whenever possible (winch, ropes/cables, heavy equipment, other cutting tools).
- Understand your system when you are working with others and using heavy equipment; be in communication (at least hand signals).
- Relieve stress in the wood, whenever possible, first with other tools; then cut.
- Prioritize objectives: roads first, emergencies, high impact areas.
- Work in teams of operator, safety person, and overseer/expediter; then rotate.
- Consider your wellbeing first; don't become part of the incident.
- Do not work in emergency mode unless a life can be saved only by doing so.
- Work methodically; pace yourself for the duration; analyze before acting.
- Use the entire team to analyze complexity.
- Understand that large trees or clumps of trees are like "pick-up-sticks" under stress.
- Work, when possible, from high to low, slow to fast, simple to complex, and remove potential energy above your head first.
- Watch your kerf; a small cut can release great stress.
- Allow only one saw to be cutting on a single tree or bundle of trees.
- Do not let heavy equipment move a tree while it is being cut, and do not apply pressure/unusual bind; train any swampers with safety sessions.
- Assume any power cable is charged until somehow proven otherwise.

This is another slide that was in the pre-existing chainsaw safety presentation when I took on the lecture circuit; it is a good summation of what is covered pertaining to the cutting plan. This is the kind of information that is valuable to go over with your student after they have read the entire book. It lets you know how much they have gleaned from the information: their knowledge level. I offer this statement to my students: *"The only time the apex of the face is perpendicular to the fall path to the lay is when the tree has no side lean."* If they understand the concept and the definition of the words in this context, they understand a lot!

Tree Complexity = Cut Complexity: The forthcoming rant is an attempt to reach those who can't imagine how the CSS could possibly be more productive than the "Get 'er done" system they're using now—those who may own or work for a tree-trimming service with an old scarred-up boss giving the orders. They say stuff like, "Oh, sure, this may be a safer way to do it, but I make a living with this saw; my way is faster; sometimes you need to sacrifice a little safety for production in order to make it in this business."

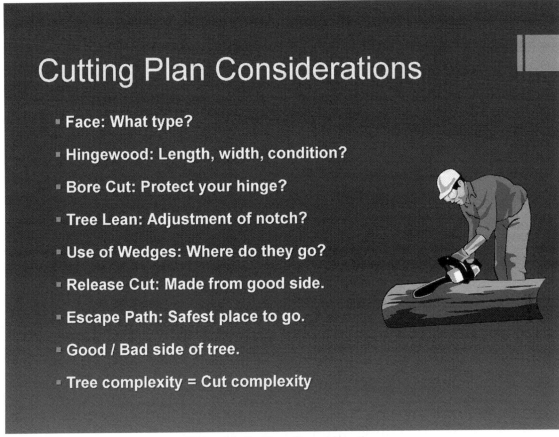

Slide 44: Cutting Considerations

If that is you, consider what complexity is in your arena of operation: complexity for your business would definitely include a lawyer standing in front of a witness box that you occupy; complexity for your livelihood would definitely be a stack of medical bills on your desk that the insurance company won't pay because you accepted liability on the fast track to fortune. That LLC on the side of your truck only goes so far; what it really is saying is that we will let the lawyers decide who is to blame, and not try to cover every detail on paper. You need a more inclusive definition of complexity that only *you* can ponder!

The CSS will be the best and cheapest new equipment for your business you will ever find; it will produce the best possible outcome for you in a risk/reward analysis. Get this: If I am cutting a stand of 4–6-inch aspens, all leaning toward an opening, it takes only a few seconds to run through Rule 4 for each tree because the complexity is low; it was met with a faster thought process; lots of work gets done in a short amount of time because the risk was not there. If, on the other hand, I'm cutting a large tree in the city, with infrastructure all around, Rule 4 *should* take a *long* time. The operator and the boss should be walking around that tree for a while looking at it from all angles; that's what the rule is for.

Rule 4 forces you to take more time now so you don't lose more time later, and all business people will tell you, "Time is money." If, from the start, the complexity of the entire workday is considered and logically controlled with Rules 1, 2 and 3, it indicates a faithful anticipation of complexity because of the business's dangerous nature. That is the kind of evidence your lawyer will enjoy bringing into court; that is the kind of liability your LLC *will* limit; stay in the CSS and your LLC insurance company will be very happy and much richer. Hold on a second; the benefit of using the CSS doesn't end there! An injury isn't just a permanent change to your company's business plan; an injury to yourself or one of your employees is a mental leap to a higher stress level for your employees and your future customers. Losing a business is never only about insurance premiums; it's also about your workers' attitudes and the reviews in your customers' minds. Even someone who has never run a chainsaw knows what a safe operator looks like; they will see your adherence to the CSS as integrity, honor, reliability, and K&E at work, because that is what it is; they will gladly pay their bills and write good opinions of your work. Your employees will see your PSS actions as concern for their welfare over concern for the "almighty dollar"; you will earn their respect because that is what the system does. If the tree's complexity is properly respected, the complexity of all the work you do will come into perspective; in the end, you will save time and money with your own deliberation; there will be no need for lawyers or doctors.

If you own or are employed by a tree-trimming service, learn and use the CSS to the best of your ability in all the work you do. Use it as a template to develop other job-specific systems like bucket work and chipping. Follow it every day in everything you do and you will have a more successful, more productive, safer, and more enjoyable occupation. Based on all I've seen in my fifty-plus years' involvement in dangerous occupations and pastimes, I guarantee it!

The WMDH when applied to trees demands your best SAACRAM, or you are working outside the system; you are putting your own interests first. This principle also means there can be no alcohol, drugs, or phones in the cutting area; these are all too personal; they are indications of a poor PSS being added to the CSS, no matter how good you are at cutting or carving stumps. The only place a phone would ethically be allowed is if its use was to mitigate a risk through communications within the cutting area or with other CAs; in other words, it's part of the plan of work.

This is a slide I cut and pasted in; I was going to take it out of the PowerPoint on several occasions because I hated it. Then one day I asked myself, "Why do I hate it?" Let me count the ways: it says "Standard" when I call this the conventional face; it says 45 degrees when there are no 45-degree angles in that triangle; it highlights the "air" in the face instead of the wood that makes up the face; it shows an old stump with a total hack job done on it, with the actual face closed; it actually shows two faces cut one above the other, and

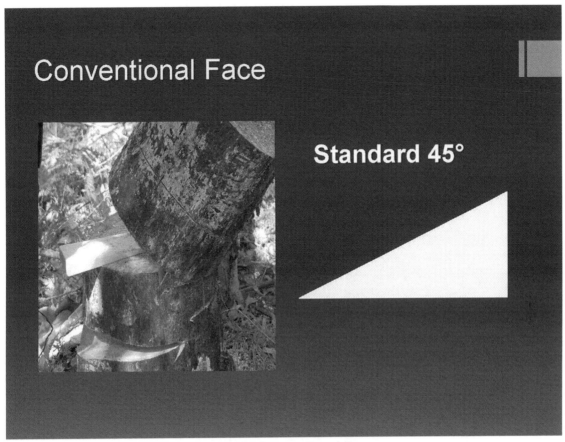

Slide 45: Conventional Face

even though both show good "stump shot"—the elevation of the back-cut above the apex of the face—neither leave sufficient hinge width.

So why is this slide still here if it is so screwed up? I learned from it! While teaching, I learned! That bad feeling I had inside me every time this slide flipped up in my lectures finally surfaced in this old brain as understanding. *Don't take the slide out,* I thought. *It's a perfect example of using AC to show there can only be a 45-degree angle in a right-isosceles triangle.* It's a basic definition in trigonometry; the rest of us on earth are not going to change that for the sake of the guy who made this slide, and we should not allow it to change our minds either; just because something is labeled 45 degrees doesn't mean it is. "Done wrong" has a very important function; its severity helps define the vastness of the spectrum of possibilities between it and "done right."

You need to realize that in this "cut and paste" world we live in, just because something is written down or even shown in a picture does not mean it is total truth; it's a good exercise for your situational awareness, even if the picture is of a bunch of stuff done wrong; you can learn from it if you logically recognize how far from the truth it is, or what small bit of truth it contains. It's like a gut feeling you get when you look at something with contemplation—when the numbers, facts, and statistics you find being formulated in your thought processes just don't line up with what is in front of you; you get that thought, *What the hell is this?* or *This is some kind of trick?* It looks suspicious, but when we go out in the woods with the chainsaw, some leave that very valuable safety device in the barn.

We aim for perfect, but there might be only one perfect in many possible variables, so our brains try to categorize by similarity (can't see the trees for the forest), and deal with the variables in groups; it's the path of least resistance for the brain; a brain that works like this, added to the WMDH, and applied to some random tree equals injury. There will only be one person at the base of that tree when the face is being cut—no groups, just you and your SAACRAM working through a plan one fact at a time. When you've dropped that big old dead tree, you have cut a tree, and pasted a "How I did it" on your stump; it's the same story told over and over for years, but it won't be a message just any Joe Shmoe can interpret correctly; it will require a trained brain to read the truth into it. The picture will be clear; the numbers will add up; the acronyms will take on meaning.

When you add your PSS to a cSS, you may assimilate into the cSS by adding rules, as long as you uphold the CSS rules, and the cSS rules don't negate a PSS rule; if they do, you may have a cSS without being in the CSS. If they do go against the CSS rules, your role in the new cSS is as a teacher. You may need to negotiate a new rule or declare a No-Go to protect your PSS. Much of Rule 4 is open to individual interpretation, which is verbalized, but Rules 1, 2, and 3 have less wiggle room. What you're learning or teaching must be supervised through the rules. Do not cut with a friend or relative until they agree to accept the CSS rules, or you must do all the cutting yourself with them as your SP in your new cSS. If the people you are working with are not trying their best to keep the rules, they are out of the CSS, which takes you out. Your PSS may be the only qualified operator in the cSS when you cut with and for new acquaintances. The best SP is one you have trained or practiced with because your cSS has grown into the CSS, but if that is not possible, use the person who asked you to cut for them as your SP. Verbalize everything you are thinking to them, and get them into the cSS you just created by getting their attention—eye and ear attention at a minimum. Have a "tailgate" safety meeting to discuss things you see as risks, and talk about the five rules. Do a size-up of each tree or project; you will be teaching a new SP, and creating a new cSS; the next time you arrive at this location to be greeted by a person wearing chaps and a hard hat, you just may find yourself working body and mind in the CSS with your new dedicated member; the "c" then gets capitalized!

The CSS's ability to keep you safe and productive always comes down to its simplest component: two individual "personal safety systems" in the cutting area. The interaction of one PSS to the other must be based on ethical authority; they must understand personal expectations and communication in the cutting area, and legal expectations and communication in the CSS at the same time; create a "CSS cutting area." Sound complicated? It's not. If you develop your chainsaw cognizance at all times, learn and practice the rules, and remember the system's foundational principles as you build your PSS, it's all already in your head, waiting to be understood. Practicing it makes sense out of it; doing it correctly makes it an easily recallable *good* memory where everyone walks away unscathed.

(Note: author vs. authority vs. authentic = CSS operator with a PSS)

Slide 46: Humbolt 45

This slide is obviously from the same source as the last one, but I kept one so I had to keep both since the Humbolt face is the same as the conventional face except the slant cut is made from the bottom. It is used mostly on very large trees because gravity pulls the large notch out to the ground as soon as the two cuts meet. It is also used on high value trees to eliminate cutting up into the marketable lumber. It has a stump shot as you can see; however, if you imagine a vertical line at the face's apex, and another at the end of the back-cut, they look to be well short of 10 percent of the diameter apart, and that is the width of the hinge. It's insufficient in this case; that is really not an issue here, though; these are all practice cuts on stumps. Half the danger of the operation, the tree, is literally removed from the picture. You probably noticed that this slide is from the same source as the last one before I told you. Maybe you also noticed that the triangle showing the supposed 45 degrees had the same problem as the last slide.

The information that allowed you to notice the similarity of errors results from another very important "grouping" function in the brain; it's actually beneficial for survival to lump all negative results into one group after the knowledge of what was done incorrectly is gleaned from the situation; you need to be able to forgive yourself when you make a mistake in order to be in a state of wellbeing. The brain must have an understanding of what is unsafe, collect all the usable information from that experience, and move back to neutral and beyond that to safe. So don't beat yourself up when everything goes wrong and your stump looks like crap; maybe just give a mental pull or two on the rope of the ass-kicking machine and start speaking in positive terms again to yourself and your SP. Maybe talk about all the *facts* in the drop and the truth in the stump; cut a slice off the top of it, and Frisbee that sucker into the woods. Take with you "just the facts" to the next tree. Trust me; your brain will remember the misses all by itself, so you don't need to keep rehashing it by talking to yourself or others in negative terms. What you need to do is get more training, and do more practicing on simple levels like these stumps; the things you do well need reinforcement to stay that way; the bad memories get more negative all by themselves; they must be analyzed, rationalized, categorized, and neutralized before they are sanitized and memorized or they will decay into apprehension. This is the behind-the-scenes (or should I say "inside the skull") work of the CSS, the subconscious instincts used as tools to benefit our wellbeing with the saw and the wood. That's the way my average brain works, so that's the way your average brain works; the two large groups of memories are actually stored using different chemical reactions in the synapses of different parts of the brain; one is made "better" by remembering; the other is made better by forgetting.

The Humbolt and conventional faces both have a "stump shot" to stop the tree from sliding back on the stump if the tree should hit a resistive force after or near the time that the hinge breaks. When does the hinge break? If the opening on the face is 35 degrees (close enough for government work), it is fully closed when the tree falls through 35 degrees from vertical; from that point on, the tree can become like a giant pool cue if it hits another tree at the same instant the hinge breaks and slides down, forcing the bole toward the stump. The reason the Forest Service started promoting the open face in training is because several operators were killed in just such scenarios where the butt end of the tree slid down the stump toward the operator. One truth about the physics of how a tree falls when cut with a chainsaw was used to mitigate the risk; opening the angle between the two cuts in the face, and thereby allowing the hinge to hold the tree to the stump while it was falling saved operators' lives. It turned out to be a big deal. Who knew? (A whole bunch of people knew back in the early 1970s.)

A browser or YouTube search will turn up more information than you can handle on "chainsaw notches." While you're going through it, remember what else these slides taught you about sorting the behavioral safety that keeps the rules from the misbehavior that breaks them; clear pictures of accomplishing the actual rules make sense in your PSS (your SAACRAM); find them and concentrate on them. The bad pictures will display themselves to you with no effort on your part; look them over and then put them in that big "not CSS" trash bag.

V&D is another way of saying communication and expectations (C&E), making sure your SP freely accepts your direction to stand in a SZ. The C&E are between the operator, the SP, and the tree. Take the subject tree and put it in the middle of a flat field, on a beautiful day in the middle of nowhere; I would have no problem simply pointing at a place on the lawn, twenty feet away, and at a 45-degree angle off my back-lay on the tree's good side and saying, "Stand there," and start on the cutting plan I just shared. The SP fully understands what you just shared in your cutting plan; the tree will do the one expected thing it must do based on physics, and you have the ability to make the plan happen within the CSS. Drop the easy one and learn more about complexity on the next one. The complexity will be defined by the K&E and the C&E of all three. The amount of safety in all three defines the system, provided each is committed to the BCS for the other two, and the tree is already committed to the laws of physics.

This next slide is another one I really don't like much, but as with everything else in this world, it contains usable information. Notice how the slide calls this single action a "notch" and a "face." That does not work in my brain; I need to give one name to one thing whenever possible because I see it as added risk if I am attempting to communicate with you and we don't have common definitions of the terms we are using. How can I say something you will understand if my own brain doesn't understand it? This is why you must always be ready to instantly change from teacher to student, because understanding can come as quickly as a falling branch. This part of felling or cutting a face can be called anything in my PSS. I can call it the Paul Bunyan cut if I want, as long as I am sure that my SP or my student understands and shares the definition of what a Paul Bunyan is. I like what the slide is teaching; it shows the open face's shape; how the back-cut on the stump in the upper-right picture does not require a stump-shot.

If you don't understand what I'm talking about when I say, "The back-cut on an open face can be at the apex of the face or a little above since the hinge holds the tree to the stump, which performs the function of the stump-shot," you need to increase your knowledge, with research or consultation, and then bring your experience up to the level of your knowledge through practice. Then make sure your SP/student understands the words coming out of your mouth—the terms that define a mitigation and actually avoid the risk in the action because each word has one meaning you both share. My advice is:

Slide 47: Notches

Practice the open face when felling; you'll be glad you did; bring the notch home for firewood. (If it's a perfect 90, make a knick-knack stand for the wall.)

In the slide's image, the operator has placed the face on the trunk's bottom, probably because the tree is marketable, so he is trying to leave as little of that wood as possible on the stump. This is perfectly acceptable in the system; the different body positions required in doing the cut are simply done while bending over, or if your body is as old as mine, from a kneeling position so the lower vertebra can be held straighter. The added risk of bending over is that the operator presents a larger target of vulnerable, unprotected body parts; the vertebrae in the back are pointed up at any falling branches. In the kneeling position, this may be diminished, but escaping the stump or moving away from a risk from the kneeling position takes more time since the operator first needs to stand.

If the tree being cut will not be merchantable, or will only be used for firewood, I always cut the face from a comfortable standing position, with my left shoulder as an anchor point on the tree, my left foot back, right foot forward, and the underside of the rear handle resting on my right thigh or knee. I aim (gun) the saw at the lay, adjust for side lean, and start the first cut of the face. I keep my attention on the mark until the bar is around halfway into the wood; then I take my attention off the lay and place it on the slant cut; once that bar is well into its kerf, the kerf's plane cannot be changed because of the bar, so forget it and concentrate on the length of the slant cut and continue cutting down into the tree until the kerf's bottom is slightly less than halfway between the lay line on the front of the tree, and the diameter line of the tree 90 degrees from it. I pull the saw out, slide my left hand to the bottom of the saw handle, right up against the cowling, and make the second cut up to meet the end of the first cut's kerf while looking into the first cut at the bottom of the kerf. (I know; I kind of went through this before; if you actually understood it this time, either you've been doing some studying, or you're like me; you need to hear something explained over and over to understand the same picture you get in practice in a split second; that's why it is very important that you watch the videos or find a teacher to demonstrate this stuff to you. A picture is worth more than a thousand words.)

Do you see the gray circle in the face cut into the stump? That is a single growth ring on slanted surfaces; it was probably caused by a disease, or even a fast-moving fire the previous summer. If you look at the face after the notch falls out, check for a Dutchman, and check the wood's condition in the face; the area on the apex is your hinge's outside edge. If the wood inside the circle on that picture was found to be rotted, its strength properties would be diminished; depending on the lean of the tree, this situation may require a change in your cutting plan. Maybe make the hinge a little thicker so you have more holding wood on each side of the rotted wood; explain to your SP why and how you intend to change the plan so you don't need to explain it later when you're both looking at the stump; by explaining the change to your SP, you'll hear the plan again.

(Search for "open face chainsaw" at YouTube and take a look at some of those videos. One shows a firefighter in a yellow shirt; he demonstrates the OBS doing the bore cut from the left side of the tree.)

Since the open face holds the hinge to the ground, the tree must be aimed to adjust for any side lean, and hit the intended mark. One reason the conventional face became so popular after the advent of the chainsaw was that a tree could be felled with little attention to the lean; the tree could be aimed in the lay's general direction, and the hinge would break as the tree fell, allowing the subject tree to roll off any tree it struck. Some operators who were really in a hurry would even cut the hinge as the tree started down—something that would be impossible to do fast enough with an ax or a crosscut saw. As you can imagine, hang-ups were common occurrences, especially when cutting in a stand of trees; trees would fly around loose from the stump with no control for the operator except fast feet and luck.

In order to aim the tree, you need to have a line on the saw that is 90 degrees from the bar (the gunning sight). Most saws already have these somewhere on the cowling or on top of the front handle. If your saw does not have this feature, I would first check the saw's

Slide 48: Aim Notch Using Sight Lines on Saw

age and make sure it is not missing any other standard safety features found on modern saws; if it's old, don't use it; get a new one! If it's just fine and doesn't have a visible line when using the open face cutting plan, you can put a line on yourself.

Place the saw on a table with a wall next to it; measure *exactly* three inches from the bar's tip to the wall; then measure exactly three inches from the bar to the wall near the bucking spikes so the bar's plane is parallel to the wall; take a carpenter's square and place it on the wall and over the top of the cowling; then etch a line in the plastic. If you want, paint the inside of the line to make it more visible; you will have a line on the saw that can be used as a sight down the lay or at your mark; you will have a "gunning sight."

If you are cutting with a conventional face, as in the upper left picture, a gunning sight can be used to aim the tree. Start the cut on the near side around one-third the diameter into the tree; then swing the cut into the tree until the gunning site is pointed at the lay. That's the easy part; next make the slant cut, and make the two cuts meet; if they don't meet, you most likely just changed where the tree is aimed. It's not easy to make them meet, and you need to clean them up; make sure each time you take another full slice on one of the two cuts that the aim is still good. Good luck on that; I could never do it consistently!

The upper right picture shows the gunning sights placed on top of a modern Husqvarna saw to be used for cutting an open face; on the slant/first cut of the face, the saw is nearly upright; this mark will be easily visible for accurate aiming.

I always ask my class to identify in the bottom two pictures what the operator on the left is doing that indicates he is in the system, and in the right picture, what he is doing that indicates he isn't. Obviously, it is the same operator, so is he in the CSS on one cut and not in the next? That would qualify as a stupid question! You can't be in the system and then out of it, and then back in it; this sequence of events would put you out! The answer to this dichotomy is that in the left picture, the operator is actually cutting the first cut of the open face; he has good anchor points at his right elbow, and on the tree with his left arm, he has all his PPE on, he has his thumb wrapped on the bar, and he has a stable stance. The only thing I see wrong with the picture is that this is obviously a training session because the edge of a student can be seen in the picture. I have no problem with students watching the face being cut on a healthy tree, but if it were me teaching, I would have that student stand a little farther away (8-10 feet).

In the lower right picture, the instructor looks to be demonstrating how to hold the saw to sight the mark when using the conventional face with the saw shut off. His face shield is up, which is not a problem if he also has safety glasses on; glasses come in handy for more things than eye protection; they give the option of lifting the shield to get a better look at something small. His bare thumb is up on the bar, which is pretty close to his left leg; it also appears that the person standing beside him is in his kickback arc. Again, this is no doubt a training session, but the point is: Are you starting to get a feeling for what kinds of things the CSS operator and SP look for? That you are an operator who sees these small things, and mitigates them as they are recognized, allows me as an observer to *trust* that you also have the big things under control; the opposite, however, is *not* true; if you miss many small things, I need to lie to myself to *assume* you have the big things mastered.

A first look at the bottom two pictures may indicate two operators—one who is doing it right, one who is not—but when a good SAACRAM figures out the story, what the truth is about the situation, the pictures take on new meaning; this gathering of information and definitions is the teacher also being a student by allowing the situation and all involved to teach continually; to be a teacher and a student at the same time—the *only* way your PSS will get educated.

I'm still on the fifth element of Rule 4: cutting plan. I haven't even scratched the surface of how many different ways there are to fell a large diameter complex tree. Just like everything else in life that comes with many variables involving more than one person, especially in dangerous activities, the participants like to start with some basic ground

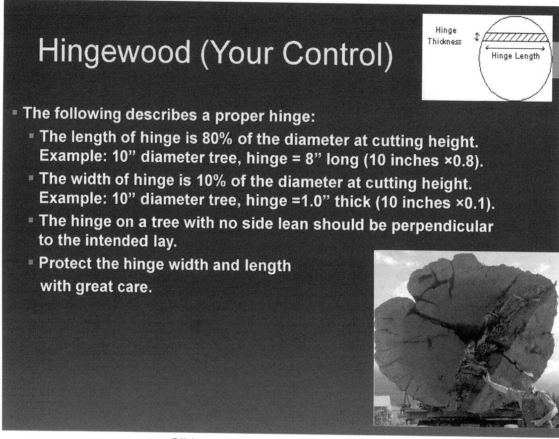

Slide 49: Hingewood (Your Control)

rules. To define a zero, or a norm, define what the final product will be; the hinge is that goal, that target, and your only control.

The strap on the back of the tree is referred to as the "holding wood" by many operators; it is cut to "release" the tree to fall with the "release cut." The hinge size to shoot for on a round, living, defect-free, homogeneous, straight-up tree with a 10" diameter would be 8" long and 1" thick. On a 24" diameter tree, move the decimal over one time for 1/10 or 10 percent for 2.4"; the length of the hinge ideally would be 8 x 2.4 or 16 + 3.2 or 19.2, so I would look for around 19"; a 2.5" thick hinge 19" long would be my target on a "nice" 24" tree. If the tree was a hardwood, however, with a heavy forward lean, I would prefer that the hinge be slightly thinner, say 2", since my main concern would be a barber chair; I would state that in my cutting plan either to my SP, my student, or myself. I would say something like, "This diameter calls for a 2.5" hinge, but because of the heavy forward lean, I'm going to thin that up to 2'." The hinge might also be adjusted from the basic parallel lined 10 and 80 percent for other reasons; the side lean is severe, which will require more holding power in the wood opposite the side lean. I can make the hinge a little thicker on the upside as long as the hinge's total basal area remains the same, and the alteration is a logical mitigation for an observed risk. Remember, the hinge can only hold so much side lean though; it is intended to work like turning the page of a book; if one pulls on a corner of the page, it can get torn out.

As on a previous slide, if I find rotted wood where only dead wood was expected or dead wood where green wood was expected, when the notch falls out, I can leave the hinge thicker for its full length since the total holding force is less. It won't sound like an excuse when you read the stump since you stated that in your PW or when you changed your PW during your WP. The hinge must go all the way across the stump to ensure the tree will fall on the intended path; this could, however, be altered if the wood in the hinge contained any defects or dead wood. The calculations for the 80 percent are cumbersome for me, but the hinge length is not hard to hit, and it really doesn't need to be calculated if the previously mentioned method of cutting the first cut of the face is employed; cut down into the trunk until the bottom of the cut is just shy of halfway between the fall line on the tree's front and the diameter measurement line at 90 degrees to the fall line. This 80 percent distance may also be made shorter in small diameter trees where the OBS cutting plan is used and concern exists whether the tree's diameter can accommodate the face, the bar, and a strap. It's also possible with the OBS in this situation that the operator could simply establish the hinge, check the area, and then cut straight out to back without leaving a strap if the tree has a definite forward lean and the CA is known to be clear of risks.

Trees that have a back lean and are too small in diameter to accommodate the face, the bar, and a strap will set back on the bar. These trees can be cut using the "quarter cut": a shallow face is aimed and cut; the first back-cut is made like the first cut of the bore cut process with the operator behind the tree and the bar pointing pretty much at the lay; the initiation quadrant is leveled and brought back from the face's apex to allow for the hinge width; a pocket is cut straight into the tree to a point just past the stem's center; a wedge is set in that kerf and driven in firm; the operator then moves to the tree's left side and cuts in from its back just above the wedge and with a slight overlap of the cuts; then the operator cuts in to establish the hinge's left side; the wedge is driven to bring the tree past center. (Note that the wood between the cuts breaks with pure radial fracture. Many operators use a push pole for these types of drops. I don't have a problem with that on small trees if the risks are discussed and understood by those cutting and pushing; it's almost like a separate or add-on rule.)

Trees whose diameter is larger than the bar, but not more than twice the bar, can also be cut using the OBS using "double cuts." The slant cut and the under-cut or horizontal cut are both made from the right side of the tree as with a smaller diameter tree, except that great care must be taken to make the two cuts meet; the bar is then placed in the kerf of each of these cuts, and continued to complete the apex on the left side of the tree; the back-cut is made first from the right side with the bore cut, the same as with a smaller diameter tree. Establish the hinge width; then cut back to establish the strap, possibly letting just the tip of the bar protrude through the bark on the opposite side as an indication of the cut location. Move to the tree's other side; then either continue the back-cut where the saw tip came through, or repeat the bore cut with the bar pointing toward the back lay. Cut toward the face to establish the hinge on the left side; cut back to establish the strap on the left side, *making sure the cuts overlap* and that the wood between the overlap is not too thick; otherwise, fracturing it with the wedges will be difficult. If the tree has back lean, set wedges and drive them tight; cut the strap when all is clear, and drive the wedges to bring the tree past center. Driving in many wedges spread around the bole in small increments works better than one beaten to a pulp.

An alternate method for such a tree is to cut the first bore from the tree's right side, as with the first method. Establish the hinge on the right side; then "walk" the saw around the stem, adding wedges as you go to establish the hinge on the tree's left side; in this instance, the holding wood, the last wood cut after rechecking the cutting area, is on the left side. It is difficult to make this cut without cutting into the hinge, so the operator must be mindful of where the bar's tip will reach inside the cut; these cuts should not be attempted by operators with low K&E and those who have never had a teacher V&D them.

No matter how big or small the tree, no matter how simple or complex the tree, the CSS operator must first be loyal to the system. The system will do what it is designed to do; it will show you a No-Go with risks you are unable to mitigate; respect the progress in your PSS enough to ask for a V&D, or start small and work your way up, start simple and work your way to complex; extend your limitations in controlled increments within the system.

The main objective in all the different ways of cutting all the different trees is that we agree on a standard 10 percent and 80 percent hinge size; we have a target to aim for: a proper hinge for the tree being cut, and control that is protected and maintained until the wedge is driven. The potential energy in the tree becomes kinetic energy, steered by the hinge and placed by the PSS as stated by the CSS.

Some operators will never become system members. They will not dress properly. They have their own tried and true methods, and they find solace in them. They have built a system of their own. However, there is a major problem with the system they have constructed: it cannot be taught; it cannot be emulated without causing stress. No matter what talents, abilities, or history were involved in forming their method, they are 100 percent certain to be different from the experiences students will garner because they are different people from different times and places. The main problem here for the CSS is that these operators *do* teach their methods to beginner operators! Whenever they run the saw without chaps on, or no hard hat, or so haphazardly that it is apparent there can be no relevant thought involved in the actions, anyone watching them, including system members, is being taught by demonstration how to perform the tasks incorrectly, at a higher than needed risk level. Since safety is based on the statistically safest methods, any other methods must be less safe, and, thus, present a higher risk. Any system member would always choose the low-risk action when given a choice.

A CSS member cannot let an operator outside the system teach them, nor can they stand by and let them demonstrate practices that undermine the system; if they do, they are in effect pulled out of the system by the non-system operator. What system members need to do is stop the action by consciously illuminating the higher risks to the non-system operator. How do you do that without handcuffing the non-system operator? You don't give their system any power—that includes the power in the saw; you don't let them run the saw. You can't be their safety person; you can't pile brush for them; you can't even stand quietly and watch them. If you are a CSS member for the right reasons, one of those reasons is to be a good example; another is to teach when you see something happening outside the rules. This is why you can't just stand there and watch; you must insist they at least attempt to follow the simple safety rules. Remove yourself from the situation, or place the power in the hands of a system member, yourself perhaps. I have taken to blaming it on the system: "Look, Dad, I joined this new system for running the saw, and it says all operators need to wear chaps; you don't want me lying to you, and I can't lie to myself; please wear the chaps and the hard hat I bought you, or I can't ethically stand here and watch you run the saw."

ITAP stands for: Initiation – Turn – Angle – Plunge

I delivered a lecture once at MIOSHA, a government agency of safety experts. When I mentioned using the bore cut in the "open face bore cut with a strap" cutting plan, one of the experts said, "We don't allow the use of a plunge cut with a chainsaw." I think my response was, "What we have here is a failure to communicate." When I mention the bore cut, I am talking about a process of several steps, one of which includes plunging the saw's bar into the wood. The possibility of a kickback if a "pure" plunge cut is attempted is very close to 100 percent, so the process of how to begin the plunge cut is very necessary to avoid a kickback. If the only thing above the tooth on the end or above the bar as it makes contact with solid wood is air, the wood will win the force battle, and all the following teeth will proceed out of the wood, very quickly; they have to—they don't have a choice. The result is what we like to call a kickback. (I *can* sometimes be a jerk when my PSS is challenged by an assumption of superior K. I don't care if the E is in an expert or not; there *must* be a logical definition of the terms that agree, one that reconciles with my PSS, and, therefore, the CSS; otherwise, I can't teach it, and if I can't *ethically* teach it, I can't *legally* teach it. In this situation, I didn't need V&D, only V because the gentleman had enough E to gracefully adjust his K.)

The problem here was "definition of terms," which could lead to someone being injured; if I had told the gentleman to just trust me, and insinuated that it's safe to use the bore cut without explaining what it *means* to me, he would have an entirely different picture in his mind of what a bore cut is; it would be a dangerous process in his brain that

The BORE CUT (ITAP)

- Once you have established the face at 80 percent of the diameter, the bore cut is made.
- The bore cut comes in flush or a little above the apex of the face, pulled back & leveled
- Cut with the Initiation quadrant of the bar; saw at full RPM past the rivets; turn to aim the bar into the tree, holding an open angle to the apex; plunge through the diameter of the tree.
- The cut is moved slowly toward the apex to establish the hinge width.
- Once the hinge is established, cut toward the back of the tree and leave sufficient holding wood in the strap.

Slide 50: The Bore Cut (ITAP)

is much different than the one I have in mine. The product my words are describing is designed to mitigate the inherent danger in his.

It's like the notch and face dilemma; sometimes the risk and the mitigation have very similar names and actions that can be referred to interchangeably, defining terms in chainsaw operation many times must include demonstration along with an explanation of what each word means; thus the reason we in the CSS should agree on what *we* are calling it, and then stick to it. We alone, as the chainsaw operators and people of safety, can stop well-intended information—words—from turning into bad news—injuries, blood, and bills!

I had to figure out a way to teach the difference between a bore cut and a plunge cut in my seminars. One night, I was just on the verge of sleep, when the phrase "I tap the tree" popped into my brain; I jumped out of bed, went to my desk, and wrote it down. The next day, I looked at the note I had left for my PSS; it said "ITAP." I said to myself, "Let's see; I hold the saw left side up, with my left hand slid down the front handle, and my right thumb on the trigger. I anchor the back of the rear handle on my hip. I place the tip of the bar at the apex of the face, raise it up just a little, and then pull it a little over halfway to the back of the tree parallel to the lay line. I level the saw and ITAP: 'I' is for initiation of the cut and the chain at full rev, to form the pocket; with the saw anchored, and straight in front of me, so I stay as far out of the kickback arc as possible; at full rev, I 'T' for turn; I walk the saw around the tree cutting with the initiation quadrant until the bar is pointed across the tree; I look down at the face's apex to be sure the 'A' angle formed by the apex and the top of the bar is an opening angle, and that the chain is far enough away from the apex to allow for the desired hinge width; if all looks good, I P' plunge the bar through the tree at full rev, pushing with my arms and hip; it's a process that includes a plunge cut. Even a student giving it half-effort (oxymoron) can remember this!"

I watched the YouTube video mentioned a couple of slides back that depicts the yellow-shirted firefighter demonstrating the OBS. I liked that guy right off! He had on the uniform of a firefighter, and at the same time, he had on the uniform of a CSS member, but he was representing himself as a teacher: two levels of legal authority demonstrating under ethical authority—a teacher. I think he would make the perfect subject for a CSS poster if there were such a thing. He had my full respect before a single word came out of his mouth. That does not mean I did not listen and watch very carefully throughout his presentation. His V&D was video-recorded with that particular tree felling, but I would bet what he did was identical to his everyday method of teaching any Class A faller in his agency. I had no problem being his student as I watched; I was looking for knowledge to corroborate my PSS because what I was looking at and the words coming out of his mouth screamed CSS.

If, instead of that being in a video, I were actually there on a typical work day twenty years ago, and the gentleman was doing a V&D of this new thing called an OBS, I would have had a few minor questions to ask him: "If you are cutting the bore cut from the tree's left side because your escape route is on the left side, and at the same time your plan includes holding wood in the back, why not do the bore cut from the right side where you cut the face from and where your initiation quadrant is cutting away from the hinge, and then stand on the primary escape route side before you cut the strap? What is that cut called, a bore cut or a plunge cut? You seem to use the terms interchangeably. Why would I allow my back-cut to be below the face's apex if I didn't have to? You say to cut the strap below the wedge; is it all right to cut the strap above the wedge where one can more easily see the depth of the cut?" After that, I would have told him that I really liked the way he made the little pocket in the wood as the first step of the bore cut, how he so carefully shaped the hinge, how he uses anchor points to firm his grip on the saw, and how he immediately started down the escape route as soon as the tree started falling; hell, I could praise this guy all day; he's a good saw operator. I would have loved to have been standing there with him critiquing his stump, and to have asked him if he would act as my SP on the next tree, and to let me know what I can improve on in my PSS; not to make me a great operator, nor to build his ego, but to have something valuable to teach my son when he asks to learn how to run a chainsaw! He makes me want to be an ethics teacher too, not for money, but for that respect shared between CSS operators, while being productive, having fun, meeting the challenge, and going home safe. I would have probably offered to meet that guy down at Bill's Bar, and buy him a beer or two.

I was at a fire in New Mexico back in the late '90s with a type 2 fire crew. As was the case many times, the crew was just sitting around on a small hill up the line from a two-person contracted saw crew. We watched as the operator misread the lean of a 150-foot Douglas fir, and ended up dropping it across the fire-line where the entire crew could see it. The operator must have been embarrassed with his error because he quickly began simultaneously limbing and bucking the tree so our crew could move it off the line. He had on the mandatory Nomax fire shirt and pants, along with his fire shelter, which was held by shoulder straps much like those on a backpack. I noticed the gentleman having trouble with his shoulder strap sliding down his shoulder; he would periodically, while the saw was under power, reach his left hand over to his right shoulder to pull the strap back up. Several of the chainsaw operators on the crew saw this, and we began talking about what would happen to him if the saw happened to kick back. I cringed when I saw him—while in a bucking cut, with the saw running at full rev, and the bar's tip buried in branches on the other side of the tree—lean far over the line of the cut to retrieve the strap that had somehow slipped down to his right elbow. I could not sit there any longer and let my fellow saw team operators watch this blatant disrespect for safety go on. I got to my feet and marched down the hill, wondering what to say to shake this guy back into reality.

He shut the saw off as soon as he saw me coming; he must have thought I was the division supervisor coming to chew him out. "How you doing?" I asked. "I was sitting up on the hill there with the crew, and I had this vision with you in it. In the vision, just about the time you bent over your bar to retrieve your strap, the tip on the bar struck a branch on the other side of that log, kicked back out of the kerf, and at full speed hit you on the side of your neck. It cut your head clean off, and your head went rolling down that hill with twenty people watching. Now I know that would definitely have changed your day, but it would have also changed the entire lives of all those kids up there on that hill."

By the look on these guys' faces, I started to get more nervous than I wanted to be, so I turned and started walking away with the safety man screaming all kinds of expletives at me, surrounded with words like "rookie," and something about my nose and their business. I went back to the crew, sat down, and hoped I would never see those guys again. That hope vanished that evening in the chow hall when that operator sat down at the table across from me and said in a deep voice, "Remember me? I came here to thank you." I exhaled. "My safety man got a little insulted there today," he continued, "and said some stuff he shouldn't have. I apologize for him. I got a little hot about it myself; I realized what had happened after I cooled off, and it scared the hell out of me. You made a scene of it so I would recognize what I was doing, and the way you did it profited you nothing. I got in a great big hurry, and what I was doing with that saw combined with that crepitus piece of equipment they gave me to wear was not right; one small wrong movement could have ended just as you saw it in your vision."

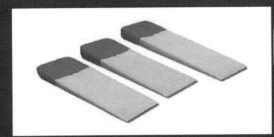

WEDGES

- Now wedges are installed, to encourage the tree to fall in the intended direction.
- Pound the wedge into the cut.
- Wedges should be installed on the heavy side of the tree.
- Once the wedge is installed, the release cut can be made; be sure to cut it all.

Slide 51: Wedges

One of the main reasons for using the OBS is that it allows the operator to set a wedge in the back-cut kerf in a back-lean tree without the tree "sitting back" on the bar. This is of particular importance when cutting a back leaner with insufficient diameter to accommodate the hinge, the bar, and a wedge; if you cut too far in, the tree sits back on the bar; if you don't cut far enough, there is no room for a wedge and the bar in the kerf to finish the fall; if you leave the hinge too thick to stop the tree from sitting back, the wedge hits the chain and stops it from turning when you go back to cutting. This can be a stressful cat and mouse game, especially if you have an audience watching your performance. The OBS and wedges were made for each other! That's why, if you are a CSS operator, you will be compelled by the SAACRAAM in your PSS to use the least risk method to fell a tree;

if the state-of-the-art safest and most user-friendly method is the OSB, *you must carry wedges*; you are out of the system if you are asked to cut a back leaner and you have zero wedges. It really doesn't matter if you cut the tree or not; once the wedge becomes a safety device, you are demonstrating a need for knowledge if you don't carry them. The procedure needed to grow your E level up to the level of your K is to go down to a hardware store where they sell chainsaws and buy at least one wedge for the pocket in your chaps. The next time your aunt or uncle offers you some money for doing a cutting job for them, don't reject the gratuity because they are family; say, "Well, you could buy me a couple of more wedges." To be fully prepared for all contingencies, you need at least three—two in the chap pocket for felling, and one in your back pants pocket for bucking.

The bigger the trees you cut, the longer the wedge. Pound them in tight when you set them; listen to the sound as you pound; the sound will go up in tone as the wedge goes in; when the sound levels off, it is set. Watch that you don't pound them in too tight when cutting dead or rotted trees; wedges can fracture wood in tension and break your holding wood in the hinge or the strap. A wedge close to the hinge will add more lift, but it will also put more tensile forces on the hinge's fibers. If you really need to be pounding hard on wedges, you may need to put more thought into your cutting plan, but make sure your SP is watching overhead for any branches that may be broken loose by the vibrations you are putting into the wood with all that kinetic energy.

If one wedge doesn't lift the tree to bring it past center, two can be stacked; they should be set in a "V" shape when pounded in one at a time. If you stack them directly on top of each other, pounding them in one at a time, the one you're not pounding can come shooting out with great velocity. They can also be thrown through the air when used to hold a kerf open during bucking when the log falls open and the wedge drops onto a moving chain. They're not big, but they can hurt, and what's worse, cast shadows on your SAACRAM. (Embarrassing yourself = personal experience.)

The brain processes information to find logical explanations for what is perceived in the environment; some memory processes are electric; others are chemical. The chemical processes work with significant events, ones that attempt to gather mostly electrically stored information in the neurons. The brain does a search for information when it has a picture of what kind of information it is looking for. This is why humans use pictures, acronyms, stories, similes, metaphors, jokes, etc.—to collect electronic signals created by the same chemical reactions, but in smaller amounts that were originally attached to the picture used to collect the data.

Your PSS works in the same way. Through practice, we get a picture of our muscles performing a task. We attach information to that task chemically in our brain by telling our brain that this is a significant event; remember it for my PSS; add it to the picture in my frame. When you add your PSS to a CSS, you are refining the picture you placed in your memory with how others do the same action to promote optimum safety. Teaching and learning are what we call this sharing of information; it creates a V&D picture that gets attached to the statistically proven best possible outcome that we help each other attain. This sharing of information is safer than the sum of the two when both our pictures are formed from the same facts, the same actions that promote a safe outcome statistically. If the system is used properly, you will come out safer when all your information is materialized in your stump. The resulting product (multiplication) of your combined actions (PSS and CSS) is the new picture of safe results to place in our brains, chemically and electrically reinforced. "Success 'breeds' success!"

"A miss is as good as a mile," unless you are aiming at the bullseye, and hit the second ring. If the miss is a chainsaw bar going past my shoulder, I'll take the mile as a perfect hit.

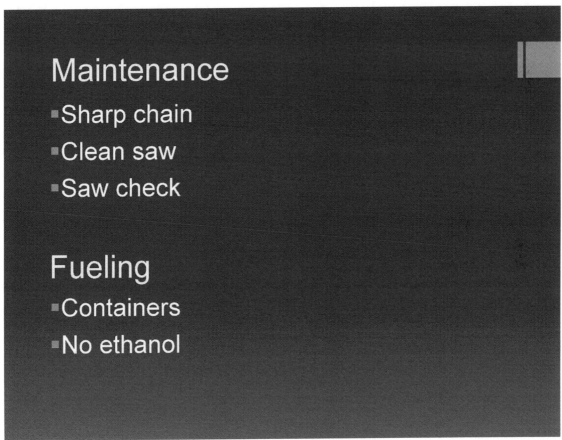

Slide 52: Maintenance/Fueling

I don't cover much on maintenance in my lecture because I have only average K&E when it comes to taking a saw apart and putting it back together, so it would be presumptuous of me to begin this slide assuming the role as your teacher. I know the basics, enough to keep the saw running safely; I figured out the fastest way to replace a thrown chain or to change a sparkplug, gas filter, or starter rope, but I worked for the government, so we brought the saw to a maintenance person to have it repaired. There are much better teachers of saw maintenance on the internet; the videos sponsored by major saw manufacturers are the ones I would stick to. If you are like me, though, the ability to fix a problem encountered while cutting is really all that's needed; you don't want to have a problem with the saw that you can't fix on the first cut because it will severely limit your WP.

The most important maintenance talent to have as it pertains to the saw's safe operation is the ability to correctly sharpen a chain. A CSS operator is always cognizant of where the chain is in relation to wood in the cut, and everything close to the chain, like the ground for instance; a very short encounter of a speeding chain and mineral soil can dull a chain instantly, and a dull saw is not only ergonomically difficult to run, but also higher risk to run. Try to "feel" the teeth cutting the wood; a sharp tooth will cut into the longitudinal fibers like your finger grasping a bunch of straws out of a box; the rivets on the teeth create a pivot point, and the beveled edge of the cutting edge actually allows it to "go up into the wood and take a bite" as it cuts into the fibers; that's what makes most chains "cross-cut" chains. A tooth on one side of the chain goes up and cuts one side of a "chip," and the next tooth on the other side of the chain goes up and cuts the other side of the chip. A sharp saw will produce long chips; a dull one will produce sawdust. The thickness of the chip is the elevation difference between the raker/depth gauge, and the cutting edge of the top plate on each tooth. Let the chain cut; a properly sharpened saw will "pull" itself through the wood; don't hold it back, and don't push it through; depending on the power in the saw, the sharpness of the teeth, and the amount of potential energy in the wood, there is an optimum speed and downward force on the chain at which the saw will make the most productive cut; if you are a beginner, or you are using a saw for the first time, get used to the power before you attempt to fell a tree with it; practice with the saw to find that perfect cut speed just before the saw starts to "bog down"; then "feel" for the best combination of forces during the cut with the trigger pulled to full rev; a big person with a small saw can actually stop the chain by pushing down on it too hard, or using the dogs for leverage. Look for that place with the perfect blend of forces where the optimum amount of cutting is being done when the chain is in contact with the wood.

A lot of students ask questions about how often to sharpen a saw; I tell them to go by the feel of the saw and the condition of the chips. A few strokes of a file can do wonders; the rakers determine a chip's thickness and should be shaped down with a flat file as the cutting edge on the top plate moves down the plate with repeated sharpening; this not only determines the chip's thickness, but how long the chip is since it is the depth gauge that acts to turn the tooth out of the cut; watch your chips. Your cross-cut chain is also doing some "rip" cutting when the slant cut on a face is being done; the chips in this case will be smaller since a directional element of the cut is with the grain; it acts as a good indicator that your chain needs a "touch-up" if the slant cut is proceeding slowly. The angle on the tooth's cutting edge can cause a tooth to take too big a bite, depending on the wood's density, such as whether it is softwood or hardwood, heartwood or sapwood; if you don't know what these different types of wood are, find out so you have an intelligent response ready when a beginner complains because "The saw won't cut."

I was sitting on top of a hill in Utah once with some other chainsaw operators, and we had just finished doing some work around the LZ; one benefit to firefighting for the feds is you sometimes get to work in a helicopter. We were there waiting for the rest of the crew to be shuttled up; a lot of fire-fighting involves PW. An operator was sharpening his saw when the guy next to me mentioned that he wasn't doing it right. I told him I have a problem with sharpening; I file the crap out of it and it still doesn't cut right. "I'll tell you two things to do to fix that problem," he said. He took a stick, cleared a drawing surface on the ground in front of him and wrote: #1. Then he said as he drew, "This is the top of the top plate; this is the cutting edge; this is the file up against the cutting edge as you are slowly guiding it forward with careful pressure; focus on the gap between the file and the cutting edge as if it were a miniature version of the kerf between your bar and wood; keep those two exactly parallel from one end to the other as you push the file through the tooth." He put his foot forward, erased the picture, and wrote: #2. "This is the side of a tooth; this is the top plate, cutting edge, gullet, and raker; most people push the file down into the gullet, but if you look at the difference in height between the raker and the cutting edge, you are looking at the chip's thickness and the place where the cutting is taking place; so the place where you should be doing the sharpening is up underneath the top plate's leading edge; the pressure on the file is more in the 'up' direction than down into the gullet. If you do these two things simultaneously, you will never again have problems with sharpening." I tried it, and it worked; it became a very valuable part of my PSS; a sharp saw is a safer saw!

I bought a small backpack at a rummage sale in which I carry extra parts for the saw: a pre-stretched and sharpened chain; an extra sparkplug; extra wedges; an extra pair of gloves, safety glasses, and earplugs; some files; a scrench; and a small screwdriver. Use your imagination to outfit the bag with the items that pertain to your kind of cutting. I always keep a scrench in my chap pocket with my two felling wedges, but as you saw in some of the slides, some operators put these items and others in a tool belt—a very professional look.

I mention "clean saw" because in my mind I may have a different picture of what this means than you do. It is important that a saw be cleaned as soon after cutting as possible, especially when cutting softwoods because of the gums and pitches in them; if left to sit on the saw for six months, these resins can harden to a point where it might take a chisel to remove them; they can even completely stop the sprocket from turning. What's more important to me, though, is "the rest of the story" about a clean saw. The saw is the other half of the definition of the operator; the saw can be "lame"—some parts broken, standard/modern safety features missing, some not working right or badly worn, dirt, sawdust, and grease everywhere. That inefficiency becomes a deficiency in the picture the operator portrays; proper respect for the power translates into proper respect for the image and, therefore, for the system. It can easily be dismissed as "all I can afford," but a picture of poverty does not mix well with a wealth of knowledge. Your perspective and priorities are only known by you; only you as the operator, or the safety person with the cash, can alter the saw's behavior to match the PSS's quality; one is a reflection of the other. The saw carries the operator as much as the operator carries the saw, as if they were one entity. I'm less inclined to follow a teacher into the woods who is stumbling along; in my PSS, I'm obligated to talk about how they are carrying the saw. If you have an old, dirty saw, please buy a new, clean one; if it is just dirty, please clean it up before you show the CSS your PSS. Thanks!

The saw check is something I like to do so there are no surprises when I start cutting. If I'm getting the saw from a cache at work, or borrowing it from someone else, I do it immediately, the first time I pick it up; if it's a saw I use and maintain myself, I usually do it on the first start at the project site. I look the entire saw over to make sure: it has all the modern safety devices; the sharpness of the chain and condition of the bar are adequate; the trigger and interlock work properly (the trigger will not go down until the interlock is depressed); and the chain brake "clicks" when the brake is set and released. If I have gloves on, I may even pull up on the chain to see if one drive link can nearly clear the bar; make sure it has fresh fuel and bar oil. If I am on site and/ or dressed to cut, I start the saw: I set the brake; hold the front handle at the first curve; pull the choke out; grab the starter rope handle; step over the rear handle and grab it with my legs; give short, quick pulls until it fires; reach down and push the choke in; and pull again. When the saw starts at half to one-third rev, depending on the make of the saw, let it "high idle" for a few seconds as you look to see if the chain is jumping. Hit the trigger, and the saw will idle down. Listen to it idle; then work the chain up to full speed by depressing the trigger a little, then a lot. When at full rev, let go of the trigger and think, "one thousand one," "one thousand two." You want the chain to come to a full stop somewhere between two and four seconds, not one, and not six. Set the brake, place the chain on wood, and try to pull the chain on the bar; if it moves, run the saw at full rev and hit the brake to make sure it will stop the chain. (This is hard on the brake band, but on a saw I have never used, I need to know that the brake works.) Let the saw idle, and listen to it while held at different angles; it should keep running, and the sound of the engine should not change to lower revolutions. Turn the saw with the base toward you, and check to be sure a chain catch is attached to the saw.

I have fuel containers on the slide because more than once I've seen a well-dressed operator with a fine saw blow his image out of the water when the gasoline comes out of the back of the truck in a Pepsi bottle. Nothing spells obvious danger and carelessness (a.k.a. poor behavioral safety) more than a blatant disregard for an explosive liquid. At least have your gas and even your oil in an approved container, preferably red; the ones that pre-mixed gas is shipped in would be better than a milk jug. Don't forget to move the saw away from where you fueled it up to start it; it shows others that you don't miss much. Pay very close attention to the gasoline's proximity to fine fuels and the saw's muffler, or some other heat source, especially when working in hot, dry, grassy fuels; if you start a wildfire, the operator can be held liable for the suppression costs!

I've had many small engine mechanics tell me not to run ethanol in my various small engines; since these people were successful at doing something I could not do—taking the engine apart, repairing it, and making it run again—I listen when they teach about small engines. Even though ethanol's effects are long term, so I may never know what the benefit is to the engine, I still pay the extra cost for premium, no-ethanol gas for all my small engines from my weed eater to my motorcycle because I respect the "engine teachers." The engine that was fixed tells the story of the mechanic's success or failure; it is an individual manifestation of that person's unique knowledge and experience expressed in the product.

I told you there were five rules. Just like a running engine tells a story about a mechanic's ability to produce a running product, the fifth rule tells an action story about the operator—the PSS as the product of the CSS; like the notch is to the face, the stump is to the tree; they both tell the same story from opposite sides of the bar, like entangled particles, until the trained eye of a CSS operator happens by and reads the story, knowing that "Stumps don't lie."

I'll give you a mental picture to paint in your logical mind: Look in your mind's eye at the cellular structure of wood; imagine a large bundle of straws held together (longitudinal cells); the straws are many different lengths and pointed on the ends with a rubber adhesive holding them together. When you try to bend the bundle, the straws in the center resist more than the ones on the edge; they slide together, stretch, and shrink as the bundle is bent back and forth, like a tree in the wind. The bundle is very strong if you stand it on end and push down on the top (compressive strength); each small segment of the straws at the bottom of the bundle are supporting the entire weight; the bundle is also very strong when you pull on each end of it (tensile strength), but the bundle is very easy to pull apart with a force applied 90 degrees to the length of the straws (radial strength), like splitting firewood. The failure of the strengths is called fracture; stresses applied to the wood increase in the wood until a limit is reached where the wood splits; the action can be slow or very rapid; it can even be caused when a human comes along with a speeding sharp chain and cuts away the wood that was stopping the fracture from happening. Bam! You should have seen it coming by looking at the tree and the forces being applied to it and the defects in the wood, whether the wood is alive, dead, or rotted; then you would have known where to stand when you made the cut! You would have found a way to release the force slowly or in a controlled manner because of your great perceptive abilities. You would have seen the stump before the first cut was made.

Slide 53: Stumps Don't Lie

RULE #5 – STUMPS DON'T LIE

S URVEYING AND CUTTING OPEN PROPERTY lines for the Forest Service, by definition, always placed private property on one side of the line, and government property on the other. Most of the time, the trees on the private side had in some way been harvested; more often than not, the private cutting extended onto property that you co-own if you are a US citizen. Since I was surveying the line, I was the first to recognize these "encroachments." I would spend some time looking at the stumps in the cutting; as a "forest protection officer," I would examine the stumps for my incident report: how many, what species, what size, what condition, how far over the line. The operator who produced the stumps on the government side of the line was, in my mind, a thief, so the stumps were scrutinized with a biased eye as I looked for additional evidence that the operator intentionally encroached to strengthen my resolve to catch the guy and ticket him.

I could tell the operators' K&E level by the consistency in the stumps around the cutting area; I could even tell how many operators had done the cutting, and what evidence they used as to the location of a property corner where the owner's rights ended according to the legal authority. I also listened to my ethical, co-owner authority to interpret the information in the saw marks and the shape of the stump to tell me if I was dealing with the kind of person who would ignore the legal authority of property boundaries just like they had safety to suit their purpose, or if they had the rights of other taxpayers in mind; was it an honest mistake, or blatant greed? If a person was cutting trees with the WMDH without knowing how it is done safely for the sake of others in the cutting area, it can logically be concluded that the same person would have no regard for his obligation to locate a properly surveyed property line, just because the adjoining property owner cannot be looked in the eye. I was determining how much respect and honor to attribute to the operator's character and intentions by the information in the stumps; my attribution would then determine whether I should honor him with a citation.

I added this method of forensic investigation to my PSS to strengthen my SAACRAM to build strong PW; the PW is communicated in the cutting plan to predict the stump and to identify the product before the process begins; the WP is the application of the authority to produce a safe and predictable product. The rules are the legal and physical authority in the saw and the tree; the SAACRAM is the ethical authority in the operator and the brain; the resulting product of this conglomerate of variables can only rightfully be appraised within the CSS; the system created the stump as much as the saw and the tree. In order to learn and improve as an operator or SP, the stump must be read with the realization that it had no choice of what it would end up looking like; the operator with the aid of the SP did that when they decided to carve a stump from a tree; the entire difference between the plan and the product is a true and accurate representation of the quality of the operator's PSS, combined with the safety person's PSS, when viewed through the eyes of the CSS.

When the cutting is done, there are three left in the cutting area: the operator, the SP, and the stump; the two CSS members go home healthy; the stump stays there, ready to tell its story; it is physically there for many years in some cases, forever imprinted as a picture only in the minds of the operator and SP—that is until the next CSS member happens by and glances at it; in an instant, the information in the picture the stump displays is verbalized and compared to the observer's PSS. The stump *cannot* lie; it has no free will; it is what it is. Your legal work on this earth will never be placed under more deliberate scrutiny than when a CSS member stares at your stump long after you have left the scene. (I sometimes find myself looking at an old gray stump, shaking my head, and saying a little prayer that wherever the operator is today, they are still healthy enough to learn how to operate a chainsaw. That's one of the reasons I'm typing at my desk right now; I know the CSS is the answer, but it needs your PSS to make it happen.)

The three questions in the above slide can all be answered "No." So does no, no, and no indicate a bad or negative product? No! This stump was purposely cut this way; it's called a "swing cut." It was used back in the days when saws were large lengths of sheet steel with teeth cut in them and a handle bolted to each end. Trees grow straight up even when on slopes; those trees are best dropped on the contour of the slope if they have to be moved uphill, but how do you face the tree to fall on the contour with the hill in the way? One operator can't pull the saw because the hill is right there, and the other operator would need to be up in the air; operators of the day came up with this cut to "swing" the tree onto the contour with the face pointed downhill; you get the picture; the horizontal cut of the face is sloped up so when the face closes, the entire weight of the tree is on a very small surface (look at the shiny spot on the far side of the horizontal cut in the face; that's highly compressed longitudinal fibers). The hinge directly behind that surface is completely severed so as the tree falls, it "pops" up; the hinge on the low side, in the direction of the swing, is left thick; the result is that the tree will pivot on the thick part of the hinge, and like a barrel on concrete, roll; the angular momentum or the roll being held at the hinge causes the tree to "follow the circle" around to the contour: a *curved fall path*.

The issue here is: We don't use those old saws anymore outside of wilderness areas, so you would think there would be no reason to use this kind of cut—not so fast; I had a very experienced operator tell me once that he always uses this cut on large diameter trees. I couldn't believe my ears; I asked him, "Why wouldn't you just aim your face where you wanted the tree to end up? Why would you purposely cut a more difficult face and higher risk face? How can you know what the part of the hinge that holds the tree looks like? Do you understand that if the hinge breaks mid-fall, the tree can roll off the side or back of the stump with added forces?" "Yes," he said. "I just do it to show off!" (Then he downed another shot of whiskey!)

If I saw that stump in the slide out in the woods and was told that it was intentionally cut that way, truthfully, I would think to myself: "F___ing show off!" If I had met that operator in the woods instead of at the bar, he would not be a guy I would even bother to try teaching, except maybe to tell him why he should never touch a chainsaw again, for the sake of the safety of anyone watching him show off his "great talents." If he was standing at the stump with me, and *refused to change his behavior*, I could not be his SP on the next tree, or even use him as my SP so I could demonstrate the OBS. Is this because I dislike him as a person? No, it's because I can't ethically respect his PSS, and I would be introducing more risk into the cutting area if I allowed him to be my extra set of eyes— the ones watching for the "safety of others." It would have a negative effect on my PSS to take part in producing a stump like that. If he said he was a professional cSS member, had on the most expensive PPE on the market, owned the newest and biggest saw, followed all the rules to the smallest detail, and appeared to be the most savvy operator around, his stump would never get past the Rule 4 cutting plan if I was his SP; it introduces unneeded risks for which there is no mitigation except the self-control not to use a chainsaw to show off; he would have to demonstrate a willingness to change his habits, or this would be a definite *No-Go*!

I use my wife as a SP quite often, but she hasn't quite gotten to the level of knowing the rules yet; I just asked her if she knows what Rule 5 is, and she said, "Don't get killed!" I told her she was close; sometimes I look at a stump and wonder if the operator survived the ordeal in one piece. After I told her the rule was "Stumps don't lie," she responded, "So the only one who knows the truth is the one who got killed." Kids say the darnedest things, don't they? This little exchange actually hit on the "stump" version of Rule 5—the negative side—the place my dear wife tends to reside more than not, the worst-case scenario side. If any behavioral safety included in the plan of work is gone with the tree, if all the rules are ignored during the process, she's right—the truth in the information the product holds is lost forever; anyone looking at it will think, *"What was this guy doing?"* You will never hear "The stump looks perfect. He was really a smart operator; he went by all the rules. What happened?" You would need to see the operator produce more product with an understanding of the plan of work, and the cutting plan for the subject stump in order to have an ear to hear the truth, because the source of the truth, the proof, is no longer with us. The CSS puts the teacher and the student at the stump together, thinking the same way, dressed the same way, and speaking the same language. The stump cannot change to fit the plan; it has no choice; it is a record of all the choices that were already made. Only together can you and I—operator and safety person—glean the real truth of success: determining the equality of the PW and the WP, and doing it while having fun!

The Rules
The Frame of Your Safety System

- Always use Personal Protective Equipment
- 3 Starting Methods (knee brace)
- Handling = Two Hands, Thumb Wrap, Stance
  Chain Brake Use, Kickback Arc, Ergonomics
- Hazards, Lean, Escape Route, Hinge, CP
- Read your stump = Learn, Teach

Slide 54: The Rules

THE RULES – YOUR SAFETY SYSTEM'S FRAMEWORK

AT THE CONCLUSION OF MY lectures, I offer a pdf file of these slides to the class. By that point, I know which students will be sure to get one, and which were there just to attend another mandatory training. I put this slide together a few years ago for the naysayers, and suggested to them that if they took anything away with them from their six-hour investment, it should be a copy of this slide; in fact, they should have it laminated and nailed to the wall where they keep their saw.

You didn't get your personal safety system when you bought this book; you've been building it since you were born in your subconscious brain; it became wiser as your senses became keener in your conscious brain. Everything you have learned in your life, from your parents, peers, schoolteachers, friends, mentors, and enemies has been for the purpose of obtaining the best-case scenario (BCS) for your survival—to keep you happy, content, stress-free, fed, healthy, secure, and safe. You did the best you could with what you were given. Then you decided to mix into the equation the world's most dangerous, strangest tool, and your PSS took on an entirely different character; the subconscious once again took control of your senses.

The reason I told the non-believers to make a shrine of the rules was because it's scientifically proven that the subconscious mind can use the information without the conscious mind's consent the next time they have a close call, but only if the information is recallable. A moment of fear, apprehension that the current level of their PSS cannot consciously handle, and boom! There's the picture, the acronym, the stump—suddenly available with all its information, conscious information; then the voice, reassuring you that this is not a No-Go. My PSS can handle this tree with this saw to produce that product safely. I know this is all true for an average person because I am an average person, and this is what happened to me. Out of the back of my head comes this often rude voice. I hear that voice right after the saw suddenly kicks out of my hand and I am barely able to catch it before it just misses my shoulder, or when a tree does something really weird, seemingly defying the law of gravity, or another operator I knew I shouldn't trust proves me right. Here comes the voice's response to each of those situations: "Wrap your thumb around the front handle, Dummy." "You didn't see that coming; maybe your SAACRAM needs more practice." "Are you going to just sit here and watch that guy get hurt?" Over the years, I slowly *taught myself* to trust and follow that voice—to accept the quiet, logical reasoning in the established and practiced rules, to learn how to best employ my unique K&E to reach the BCS for all involved; there must be an *all* for perspective—it requires at least two people: perhaps a teacher and a student to increase the perception.

The reason I wanted to leave these thoughts with you, my student, is because as a human, you can teach your neuroplastic brain with that very same brain; you can bypass the error part of trial and error, by teaching yourself as if you were teaching a loved one because, in effect, you are. The system stores the logical information learned in your trial (your practice)—the building of your PSS—and recalls it instinctively when surrounded by like-minded, subconscious voices because the system will help all to agree on the product, each of us passing on to one another the best way to reach our objective productively and safely by the words we speak, the way we move, and the way we listen. It may even be that we enjoy having each other there, especially when we recognize our common goal, and respect each other's contributions as together we take on danger and produce a systematic product from a random tree.

If I say that the two types of authority are legal and personal, it is logical that the legal kind deals with laws and regulations, or in other words, liability and compensation. A monetary exchange quantifies and authenticates the process of sorting out the results of injury or damage. This cannot be true in the personal type since it deals with ethical aspects of human behavior like respect and responsibility, which are, as the commercial says, "priceless." With a small stretch of the imagination, it is also possible to associate legal authority with a conscious state, and personal or ethical authority with a conscience state; remission in one costs time and money; remission in the other causes guilt and remorse.

This is why a CSS teacher cannot charge their student a fee—it's personal; we don't charge money for interpersonal relationships because, by definition, the benefits should go both ways. We do, however, barter in these relationships; you teach me what you know, and I assure you that I will be ready to reciprocate with valuable advice of my own, as my barter; if I see your PSS is operating outside the rules, I teach; if your PSS amazes me, I give respect and learn. Does this mean you can't ethically make money teaching the CSS? No, if you think about it, it means that you cannot make a monetary profit from it when in the teacher/student authority; you can only cover your expenses. How I determine what is a reimbursable expense will define which authority I use to determine the value of my contribution to the CSS, which will thereby define my PSS, and the level of personal commitment fellow members can expect from that PSS. (Of course, if your teaching coincides with actual cutting applications that benefit your student, or you prearrange to charge a fee for teaching the system to many students simultaneously, I see how you could justify making a profit beyond expenses; you need to sort that out for yourself through V&D with those willing to pay you.)

Slide 55: Discussion Points

DISCUSSION

HERE IS WHERE I USUALLY ran out of time in my lectures. (A nice thing I learned about writing a book—it's like a time warp; I'm done deciding how much of my time to put into this; the rest is all yours, at the same time in a different time.) Time allotted for the lecture usually ran out because the next place the class and I were headed was to a tree were I would demonstrate the OBS. Since so many of my classes were held at county road commission garages, I saw this method of felling a very valuable tool for these operators, and I never found any who disagreed. Many of these operators had much more experience cutting complex, high-risk trees than I did; they were constantly cutting trees, by definition, along the sides of roads, around infrastructure, with people watching. I told many of them I was not trying to show them how to be a better operator; my real intent was to leave in their memory a picture of the use of a very applicable method while in the system, and that it could be done safely, efficiently, and productively, with a team effort, and nobody had to give anything up to get it done.

Another reason I liked to put on the PPE, start the saw correctly, verbalize, and demonstrate the rules was that many of these students were well into the mandatory safety rules at work because they had to be to keep their jobs; however, many of them admitted in class that they did not use the same safety measures while cutting at home, away from the job. The thought process involved in deciphering this dichotomy brought me back to the reason I first thought of a chainsaw safety system twenty-five years ago. "What is it about me that is willing to jump through the hoops for my boss so he can see the best me at work so I can get promoted so I can better support my family so I can go to my happy home and cut firewood so I can disregard the same rules that keep me safe at work so I can cut my leg so I can let my children see me injured so I lose my ability to support my family because I can no longer go to work?" That illogical thought process is not what I call "crazy"—it's what I call "insane." The difference between those two was always very apparent to me as a psych-tech; I could see the logic in the plans of the crazy ones; their logic was a lot like mine. The insane ones were simply lying to themselves—something no one else could possibly keep up with!

If the system is an accumulation of all the truths in your life, and you willfully or carelessly dismiss it even on a minor occasion, you run the risk of destroying the whole thing; one small lie can obscure a very large truth. The lie doesn't jerk you away from the truth; it merely deflects your path ever-so-slightly, like a Dutchman cut into your apex, so that by the time you see the tree in the lay, it's over there instead of here on the mark; this is why risks need to be appropriately mitigated before proceeding. You can be a good CSS operator and still be a little crazy; it might even be a prerequisite to picking up the saw to begin with, but you are also the kind of person who wants to practice the best way to accomplish the task or you wouldn't have gotten to the end of this book. It's just that the people watching are unable to process your truth as quickly as you do while you are trying to have some fun with a dangerous activity; the only indicator they have that you are in control of your actions is their ability to evaluate your behavior, or what is accepted by all involved as proper behavior; there can be no lies told if the behavior is written down before the action and read by all. The CSS will not recognize an operator in the cutting area if their PSS is insane; however, there will be a bald head with bare legs, a crappy old saw, pinches, pushes, pulls, hang-ups, cuts, bruises, and bad stumps; the lies will become apparent by their disparity from the plan. That operator will become the worst kind of risk—a deceptive, hidden, outlier risk, not allowed to cut in the CSS; to let them would be a lie; it would be insane!

The chemical reactions that occur in the brain that make us feel apprehension, stress, trepidation, and anxiety, happen instinctually; they are not dependent upon what we look like, look at, or look past; they memorize a reaction to a risk; they change behavior without conscious thought; that's why they are called autonomic reflexes. Whether we behave in the way the chemistry dictates we will behave is a choice to the human brain. (Weird, eh?) When someone sneaks up to you in the dark and yells "Boo!" you don't think, *Stimulate adrenaline production in the muscle of my arm so I can swing it around and strike the attacker*; that is all pre-programmed in your brain to happen automatically by what your DNA and your memories have built in your brain. The good news is that, as a human being, you can add to what your brain does automatically by reprogramming it to respond in a different way when the stimulus of the chemical reaction appears; after a few iterations of this controlled response, you might just jump, or maybe scream like a little kid, because your brain has learned that the "Boo!" is coming from your wife, who thinks scaring you in the dark is funny; as soon as the lights go out, and you haven't accounted for her exact location, your brain learns to expect it, and brings up the pre-programmed and appropriate response; no wild arm through the air toward a frisky lady.

Your PSS is your "practice" in the sense of a "livelihood"; it is self-preservation in action. It is never static when you are conscious; when you accept the risks associated with operating a chainsaw, whether by desire, or by necessity, your brain collects all the information it has from the stories and personal experiences it has remembered, and from autonomic preparation for the reflex and the chemicals. The PSS is the agreement you make with yourself, your behavior manipulation, your practiced response, and your confidence in the mitigation. When in the cutting area, under the dome of danger for which the CSS was created, for which your SAACRAM was nurtured, your PSS becomes the CSS. You are teaching your PSS methodology to other PSSs, but you appear to others to be the CSS by how well you keep the rules, and by your product. What about outside the CA? Does your PSS go away? As far as the chainsaw is concerned, I suppose it does, but if you are a chainsaw mechanic or tree climber, you probably dream CAs.

There are other applications for your PSS; it just takes time to learn them, define the terms, and work out the rules that best mitigate the expected risks; the SAACRAM doesn't change much. I don't know anything about your PSS until I see you in action in a CA. Only you know your PSS; I only know the part we agreed to share in the first four rules—our prearranged contract so we both understand where we stand as teacher and student at the appearance of a common or an outlier risk. What's an unforeseen risk for me may be an expected one for you; I need to know if I am responsible for your safety, or if you are ensuring mine. I need to know you are a CSS member by the look in your eye, what you say and don't say, what risk you can mitigate, and what is a No-Go for you; we must go through this systematically to identify the least risk PW. We choose our joint reaction to the action; we display our individual perception and perspective to produce a good stump, and leave the CA smiling.

Anybody can come into my cutting area and tell me I'm crazy and try to teach me a safer way to drop the tree as long as they have on chaps and a hard hat, and stick to the rules. I'll verbalize Rule 4 and listen to what they teach, but when I decide to pick up the saw and I say, "Let's clear the cutting area," it's going to be directed either to that person willing to act as my SP and watch out for "crazy," or my brother-in-law, who is most likely the SP I brought with me. If anybody tries to control the CSS with a PSS by ignoring a rule, that is crazy to me; I'd tell my brother-in-law with the legal authority to "Get this clown out of here, at least two tree-lengths, and bring him back for the limbing." I know how my bro defines "crazy"; he's been trying to find it in me for around forty-five years, and he has been successful many times, just not while we were sharing a CA to fell a complex tree; I would need him watching the CSS.

This is my critique of my stump from the ASS (Author Safety System): I always thought the CSS was part of my PSS; after many months writing this book, I think I understand it better now. The CSS is the chainsaw; my PSS is my brain, like a behavior emanating an energy in both directions, like the two become one in the CA. My story has accumulated enough K, and my E enough practice, for me to know that I know what a damn good CSS operator looks like. I'll bet you next week's pay I can limb and buck a complex tree, and you will not once find my thumb up on the bar. This book is my attempt to get you here at this stump, able to understand my words; if you are here with me, you have avoided injury to yourself and others; you have brought respect for ethical authority into this CA, at this stump.

Maybe one day I will hear your critique of my stump in one of yours along a walking trail. I'll see some of my PSS and the basic CSS part of yours in a glance. Go; have your discussion between the operator in you and the safety person in you—both halves of the same brain; practice together; respect each other; see the good CSS member in you. When you pick up the CSS saw, you can turn the safety person part over to a SP for a while. (Hey, maybe that stands for "special person" too—someone you trust to watch your back, the only place your eyes can't look and still keep the CA safe, while you carve the stump or clean up a mess.) The operator will attempt a feat that many would call crazy— entering a giant mess of trees, mixed with power lines and parts of mobile homes, and use the world's most dangerous hand-tool to open up a path for the two guys with the ambulance and other first responders (or would that make them the second responders? I can only think of one way it wouldn't!)

Be smart. Be good. Behave!

Part Two Notes:

A Final Note, a.k.a., My Stump

Call me crazy if you want! I've always occupied my thoughts with intricate emotional details that placed me all over the spectrum of how much to get involved, not just with other people, but with everything; I always have to "look deeper into it" to a fault. I don't understand myself; why do I always try to make a perfect stump? I seldom am successful; when I do somehow make a pretty good one, I give the credit to the CSS. As it turned out, I didn't really see myself as the operator in this CA I call a "book"; the operator or writer in this case was really each and every operator in the past who was inquisitive enough to sit and listen to me talk for five or six hours without throwing something at me. When they did need to leave early because they worked at a different garage for the CRC, or were tight on time, they always did so as perfect ladies and gentlemen with an appropriate mix of apology and regret for "missing the best part." If ten years from now this book is still in print, and you are a long-time CSS operator, you will be the author; you will be the teacher. I hope you have fun; how much you enjoy cutting and helping new operators learn will be a gauge for you of how good your SAACRAM is, how well you keep the rules, and how well you learn to talk in a slow, calm, and logical voice. "Nothing but the facts" from the operator.

I also taught groups of students of more diverse demographics: from age seven to seventy-seven, from farmers to politicians, from beginners to experts, from operators to safety persons, from swampers to observers; all will make their own stumps in a different part of the never-ending forests. I have had so many different versions of my lecture I could not possibly write them all, especially when I can't see my student(s); they are in a different space and time. It wasn't until I was well into the writing before I realized that the exact words didn't really matter, the product I based my plan of work on is the CSS, not your PSS. The PSS is all you! Do you see how it works? The readers who understand what is written here will get a benefit from any words they read; the ones who don't understand it will not be hurt by trying to accomplish it; they can only come out to the positive, and at the very least take away nothing. But based on the diversity of those already in the system, a perfect nothing is an almost impossible mark to hit. If all you change after reading this book is that you start using your chaps and a hard hat every time you cut, the CSS will grow, and your PSS will follow. This book, as it turns out, is the entirety of the legal authority of the CSS; how much you comply with the rules depends on your individual SAACRAM, your PSS; whatever your interpretation of the words herein.

The possible variations are innumerable, but the system makes the probabilities manageable because being able to read a CSS stump cannot change the tree that was dropped; it can, however, make the next stump contain different information—closer to perfect perhaps—one mark at a time, and teachable, whether your PSS is the teacher, the student, or both! My intent is that this action will bring you to a new level of understanding; that it will train and educate your perception and perspective by convincing you to always practice your SAACRAM on all levels of complexity, until your attitude builds an efficient P for your PSS, which blends nicely into whatever cSS you find yourself in; that you will without bias decide at any moment where you stand as T/S in the CSS; that your K&E will always be able to find a SP with adequate C&E to keep you safe, no matter the size of your CA. If you fully understood all that, maybe you'll stay in contact as I cover my ASS, and we read our next stump together.

Acronym Table

Acronym	Meaning
CSS	Chainsaw Safety System
PSS	Personal Safety System
cSS	Corporate Safety System
BS	Behavioral Safety
SP	Safety Person (Special Person)
WMDH	World's Most Dangerous Hand-tool
	Weapon of Mass Destruction Here
K&E	Knowledge and Experience
CA	Cutting Area
V&D	Verbalize and Demonstrate
SAACRAM	SA - Situational Awareness,
	AC - Analysis of Complexity,
	RAM - Risk Analysis and Mitigation
PW	Plan the Work
WP	Work the Plan
T/S	Teacher/Student
SZ	Safety Zone
C&E	Communication and Expectation
OBS	Open face, Bore cut with a Strap
ITAP	Initiation, Turn, Angle, Plunge

Made in the USA
Monee, IL
20 April 2021